THE PEOPLE OF WALES

BBC RADIO WALES: A MILLENNIUM HISTORY

THE PEOPLE OF WALES

edited by

GARETH ELWYN JONES

and

DAI SMITH

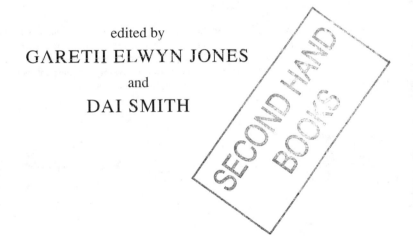

GOMER

First Impression—1999
Second Impression—2000

ISBN 1 85902 743 1

Printed in Wales at
Gomer Press, Llandysul, Ceredigion

ACKNOWLEDGEMENTS

The editors wish to thank the Open University in Wales for permission to reproduce the maps on pages 25, 30 and 50, and the University of Wales Press for permission to reproduce the map on page 208.

We are greatly indebted to Mairwen Jones and other staff at Gomer Press for the care which they have taken in seeing this book into print, and to Annette Musker for her preparation of the index.

We owe a particular debt to Kath Jones for her meticulous administration of this project since its inception.

CONTENTS

POPULATION TRENDS

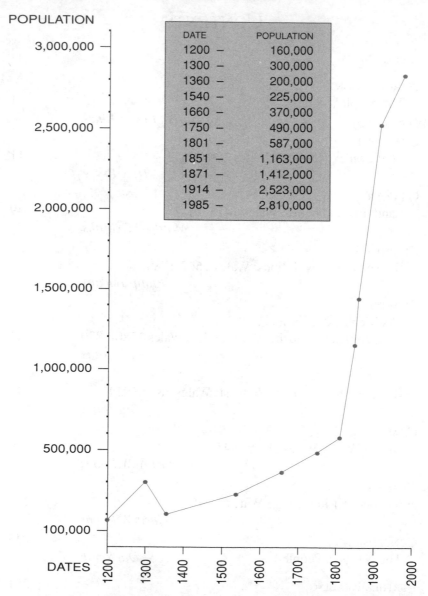

POPULATION

DATE	POPULATION
1200 –	160,000
1300 –	300,000
1360 –	200,000
1540 –	225,000
1660 –	370,000
1750 –	490,000
1801 –	587,000
1851 –	1,163,000
1871 –	1,412,000
1914 –	2,523,000
1985 –	2,810,000

DATES

(Before the first official census of 1801 it is possible to provide only informed estimates. Even the statistics provided in the early censuses need to be treated with caution.)

LIST OF MAPS

INTRODUCTION

THE PEOPLE'S NATION

GARETH ELWYN JONES

In the last century we have been driven to an obsession with power. Peoples have seemed to be defined not so much by cultures and a shared history as by the power of states and the claims of ideologies. In this, the bloodiest epoch in human history, we have been forced to grapple with the ideologies which have articulated themselves through the institutions of the state and the violence of war. Communism and Fascism have systematically subordinated peoples, cultures and the complexities of shared histories to the brutal simplicity of their own ideological certainties. In the almost binary opposition which has defined the twentieth century, representative democracy has offered an alternative vision of state organization, emphasising individual rights and market freedoms. With the demise of Communism and Fascism, in Europe at least, our perspectives have shifted to a preoccupation with the competing claims of religious fundamentalism on the one hand and market capitalism on the other, both operating within and beyond the nation state, with their emphases on universal religious imperatives or the supranational claims of international companies and stockmarkets. Appropriately, perhaps, the fashionable intellectual fad has become a nihilistic postmodernism.

In such contexts, the fate of Wales and the Welsh might seem insignificant. From time out of mind, the people of Wales have been a people without a state. Their identity for centuries could not be sustained through, but was often preserved in spite of, policies of the 'England/Great Britain' state. Yet the existence of small nations, indeed their recent re-emergence, particularly in eastern Europe, testifies to other pre-eminent themes in human history, the centrality of individual actions in the context of community loyalties which, however anonymously, have been indispensable to any larger picture.

The survival of Welsh identities, and the possibility of national rebirth, now look less like a peripheral curiosity and much more like characteristic features of the longer-run development of nations' identities within Europe.

The end of this millennium coincides with the establishment of the most far-reaching degree of institutional independence in Wales since the thirteenth century. The inauguration of the National Assembly also serves, paradoxically, as a reminder that, within the wide timescale of this book, our modern concern with the politics and power of the state is misplaced. While certainly not attempting to minimise the significance of the creation of European nation states in the fifteenth and sixteenth centuries, or the importance of the realignments of the nineteenth, the framework of the chapters which follow indicates many different contexts in which Wales and Welshness have survived political and military monoliths. Arguably, the survival of Wales in the heyday of imperialistic Great Britain in the nineteenth century is best evidence of resilience. The often quoted, notorious entry in the *Encyclopaedia Britannica* of Victorian times, 'For Wales see England', is indication enough of a contemptuous dismissal to the dustbin of history; the 1999 *Encyclopaedia Britannica* attends to matters Welsh in dozens of articles, on everything from the Rebecca Riots to Ivor Allchurch, as well as in a lengthy, detailed history. Dafydd Iwan's chorus, *'Er gwaethaf pawb a phopeth, 'Dyn ni yma o hyd'* (in spite of everybody and everything we are still here) has its truth for a wider time-scale than this century, and for more small nations than Wales.

The Welsh have no vested interest in that obsession with state sovereignty and integrity which has dominated the lives of so many recent generations. The specifics of the history of Wales have compelled its people to conceive of nationhood in quite different terms which must embrace complex identities, varied communities, cultural and linguistic tolerance and an appreciation of the extent to which identities are reshaped. This is a richer and more inclusive concept of what might constitute a nation in the Europe of the twenty-first century. Not ever having had an empire, Wales will never have to come to terms with having to find a role in a world of very different economic realities and power blocs where imperial grandeur is best recalled in immaculately organized state ceremonial. Nothing emerged more clearly from the debates over the History National Curriculum for schools than the desperate yearning among certain sections of the 'Great Britain/England' establishment and intelligentsia for national heroes to act as icons of former greatness and a prized social hierarchy. Welsh national heroes are of a very different order.

For once, then, the people of Wales may be swimming with the historical tide. In the new European Community the role of small nations and powerful regions combines in an internationally respectable case for the kind of devolution which is now to be enjoyed by Scotland and Wales. Because such political and economic developments have taken place at breakneck speed in the last few decades, it is essential that the people of Wales know something of their roots. This knowledge alone can help to give meaning and perspective to present-day debates, which are no longer mere abstract formulations but focus on realities of democracy and government.

Of course, for much of the last millennium the people of Wales have operated within political and social hierarchies substantially determined by a greater eastern neighbour. No history can ignore this. Nor can there be any unique template of Welshness. Its people have made a very different community at various periods. When Hywel Dda died c. AD 950 one of his chief legacies was a system of law which was a major defining element in Welsh nationality; that corpus of law, ever more limited in its purchase, effectively disappeared with the Acts of Union of 1536-43. The system of government which operated in Wales for the first three centuries of the millennium provided varying degrees of unity under often warring princes and Norman lords, but by the mid-thirteenth century there was a native prince of Wales whose hegemony extended widely, even if he owed allegiance to the English king. Any dreams of an independent Welsh state disappeared with the conquest of Wales in 1282-3, to be conjured up forlornly once again with Owain Glyn Dŵr's exploits in the first decade of the fifteenth century. Residual poetic visions of Welsh independence, which came, ironically, to be centred on Henry Tudor, 'the son of prophecy', were dealt a final blow, at least legislatively, by the Acts of Union, when Wales was subsumed into the wider state of 'England and Wales'. This imperialism was cemented by statutory endorsement of English as the common language of administration and law.

The Welsh language, one of the oldest in Europe, and at the time of
the union, in its contradistinction to its increasingly powerful and
imperious neighbour, one of the major identifying features of Welsh
community, seemed sentenced to death. But, under the impetus of
religious revolution, the Welsh were eventually to define themselves
again. At the expense of forsaking traditional aspects of their
character exemplified in, say, music, and much popular culture and
custom, a majority, at least, of the Welsh embraced first the Welsh
Bible, then Dissent, especially Methodism, and its puritanical
concomitants in the eighteenth century. In this new Wales the Welsh
language survived because it was the language of religion and, linked
to this, a rudimentary education. The distinctiveness of Wales was
reinforced in the eighteenth century by the combination of an appeal
to the past, conflating genuine insights into language and culture with
the spurious but romantically effective inventions of Iolo Morganwg
(Edward Williams). Furthermore, Romanticism promoted a
fashionable appreciation of the beauty of the topography and
landscape of Wales in which, from that time, its inhabitants might
take pride.

Many of these aspects of Welsh life in the eighteenth century were
to become props of Welshness in face of the dynamic events of the
nineteenth. As in the thirteenth century, and again in the sixteenth, it
seems in retrospect little short of miraculous that Wales should
survive. The country had no national institutions and no legislative
independence. It was faced with unparalleled population growth and
redistribution along with a sustained influx of in-migrants. But, despite
the difficulties of assimilating the realities of both rural and industrial
communities out of many contradictions and distortions, images were
fostered of a people embracing religious enthusiasm, respectability, the
centrality of family and community, a love of poetry and song – a
talented, cultured working class of coal miners and slate quarry
workers, along with the more traditional rural *gwerin*.

In the first half of the twentieth century the Welsh had to cope with
the Depression, seen sometimes as the equivalent of the great famine
in Ireland in its effects on the nation's psyche. Since the end of the
second World War there has been a different order of influences,
which again would seem to threaten any concept of Welshness. Those
residual illusions which the Welsh have of themselves as significantly

more religious and respectable are now rooted only in history. There has been heart-searching in recent decades about the fate of the Welsh language, now the language of fewer than 20 per cent of the people. It has withstood conquest and legislation, and even the massive in-migration of the late nineteenth century. But, despite an unprecedented degree of official support since the end of the second World War, Welsh has steadily contracted as a community language and hopes for its permanence reside now in the schools. It is ironic, too, that at the end of the millennium there are overtones of the beginning; Wales is now, once more, being defined increasingly by its independent institutions, to be capped by the National Assembly.

The story which unfolds here, then, is of the different kinds of Wales which myriad generations lived and projected. That in itself is testimony, paradoxically, to a kind of continuity, the sense of which will doubtless be reinforced in reading the following pages. It is inevitable that each generation concentrates on present difficulties, whether individual, local or national, but the justification for this book is that these problems need to be seen in perspective. In one sense, the main concerns of the people of Wales are the timeless concerns of peoples everywhere: individual and family welfare, the hope of prosperity through one's own labour and fortunate circumstances, an aspiration to identity within families and local communities, and an attempt to satisfy spiritual and cultural yearnings. But beyond this, throughout the last millennium, there have been aspirations towards some kind of expression of national spirit and will, from the Wales of the princes and Owain Glyn Dŵr to that of Gwynfor Evans and Gareth Edwards. The strength and mode of expression of such manifestations have varied enormously but all have both had their day and left their legacy. The position in which Wales finds itself now is, of course, unique but the concerns of the present have some parallel in the past, not only for citizens but for the country.

For example, Wales has always been a multi-cultural society, a blend of native Welsh, English, Normans, Flemings and Irish centuries before the economic changes of the nineteenth century enriched the population mix so substantially in south-east Wales. In other ways, too, Wales has never been one neatly-packaged parcel. It has always had its regions, more marked in the Gwynedd or Deheubarth of the Middle Ages than in the east-west or north-south divides which so exercise present-day commentators. For centuries the major trading centres lay outside Wales – in Bristol for the southern seaboard, in Shrewsbury and Oswestry for the wool producers.

If it can be argued that in 1267 there was an embryonic state under a prince of Wales, Wales was soon to become a wholly-conquered country, having been invaded both by Norman lords and now, more devastatingly, by the English king in 1282-3. As the conquered, the Welsh suffered both economically and legislatively. They were a second class people. But the degree to which the Welsh have always been able to assimilate their conquerors is remarkable. Indeed it was not until the eighteenth century that the landed leaders of society were finally to be alienated from the mass of the population. Certainly, movement of population in and out of Wales was of a different order in the second half of the nineteenth century, in the Depression, and in the post-second World War period. About a fifth of present-day inhabitants of Wales were not born in the country, and it is still the leaders or managers who come in greatest numbers. But neither the racial mix nor the imbalance of economic influence which it might represent is unprecedented.

There has been continuity, too, in the domination of a voracious neighbour. For much of the millennium, integration with England has posed the most potent of threats to the survival of Wales. Devoid of any of the trappings of statehood since the thirteenth century, and in the face of a substantial body of official British/English imperialist opinion in the nineteenth century which believed those of different culture and language to be of second class status across the world, let alone across Offa's Dyke, continuity of national identity must count as a remarkable achievement. The country which had its own codified laws at the beginning of the millennium had no legal independence after the Acts of Union so that for 350 years afterwards no legislation applied solely to Wales. Yet, at the height of British imperial grandeur, the Westminster Parliament began to condone a creeping and accelerating recognition of Wales in a series of devolutionary measures. Ironically, given earlier attitudes towards the Welsh language in schools, the best example is the recognition of distinct needs in Welsh education. A charter for the University of Wales in 1893 followed only four years after the Welsh Intermediate Education

Act which provided for state secondary schooling in Wales where none existed in England. A Welsh Department of the Board of Education was set up in 1907. Various departmental committees of inquiry continued to recognize Wales throughout the inter-war years and, immediately after the second World War, Wales was granted a separate advisory council for education, alongside those for England and Scotland. More dramatic devolution followed in 1964 with the creation of the Welsh Office and, in 1970, the delegation to it of responsibility for all primary and secondary education.

By that time, of course, other significant activities had been devolved to a variety of unelected Welsh bodies. With the growth of 'quangos' in the 1980s, Wales enjoys an alphabet soup of delegation, from ACCAC (*Awdurdod Cymwysterau, Cwricwlwm ac Asesu Cymru*, the Qualifications, Curriculum and Assessment Authority for Wales) to the WTB (Wales Tourist Board). As we enter a new phase with the democratically elected National Assembly the people of Wales will assume a political and institutional identity in very different circumstances from those of one thousand years ago, once again, perhaps, in tune with the political and cultural European world.

There is also an opportunity for Wales to forge an identity which befits a mature society, far removed from the stereotypes which still provide the worn material for lazy caricatures. The Wales of vibrant heavy industry, based on iron and especially coal, has gone, and taken with it some of the potency of the valleys culture which so often seemed to convey the essence of Wales on the screen. The image of respectable religiosity, firm as its foundations were across much of Wales in the nineteenth century, has been substantially subsumed in the mass culture which embraces the whole of the developed world. The evolution of radical politics into British New Labour has undermined both the the image and the reality of the kind of Labour politics which have dominated Wales since the second World War.

Any new identity will have to derive strength and moral authority, as always, not from caricatures but from the reality and paradox underlying past characterizations. These did not take root accidentally. In a very different context we shall see that the Welsh of Gerald of Wales's day esteemed freedom. They were a cultured people in the arts of music and verse, and were particularly hospitable. Yet they persevered with the capture of slaves in war. In the eighteenth century they made much of the notion of a moral economy to try to right some of the worst communal injustices which confronted a society in transformation. In the twentieth, this defence of freedom and commitment to social justice manifested itself in such diverse causes as the manufacture of the welfare state by Lloyd George and Aneurin Bevan, and the sacrifice of Welsh lives in the Spanish Civil War. Again, on the darker side, Welsh people have in this century been capable of perpetrating their own brand of racial and social intolerance.

In its search for the real experience of the majority, Wales is now in another mainstream. Just as the quest for the heroes of a glorious British past seems increasingly anachronistic in our realigned world, so has a historical discipline devoted to kings and queens and politicians been substantially modified in recent decades, both in academic circles and in schools. Whole sections of the population have been rescued from anonymity. Working class groups, women, and ethnic minorities provide obvious examples. Inevitably, Welsh historiography has reflected such changed perceptions. For too long, the history of the nation seemed to end with the death of the last native prince of Wales and with him, those aspirations to statehood and independence which seemed, in the nineteenth and early twentieth centuries, indispensable to national identity.

But the history of the Welsh is, perforce, substantially about people without the kind of power wielded by elites of wealth and status. It is about people least likely to leave written record of their experiences, still less to leave likenesses. These were the people whose economic circumstances meant that the majority left no wills and no trace of the substance of their lives. Mass literacy has been a recent phenomenon; the unlettered and those without property have usually been without memorial. Only very recently, in any case, has it become fashionable to treasure and catalogue the letters of the ordinary along with those of the good and the great, so it is inevitable that we know infinitely more about rulers than the ruled. Their houses, with such exceptions as might be dotted around the Museum of Welsh Life at St. Fagans, have succumbed, while the luxurious gentry mansion at the core of that Museum has, like many of its ilk, survived the centuries unscathed.

Yet these lives, fragmented by powerful forces in their own time and fragmentary in the archives that survive, were the lives of the people whose existence has truly given Wales its distinctiveness over the centuries, the people who spoke the language, worked the land, endured the conditions of factory and mine to make their employers, and their country, wealthy. They are the people who, in that new language which became the tongue of the majority of the Welsh, created new and vibrant common cultures which even allowed them to endure deprivation during the Depression on an almost unendurable scale. They are the ones who have had to come to terms with another, more recent, economic and technological revolution. They are also the people who have sustained, at different periods, a cultural, religious and sporting life of distinctiveness and distinction. Deep and subtle research into their lives has made this book about the mass of the people of Wales possible.

CHAPTER 1

MEDIEVAL EXPERIENCES: WALES 1000-1415

HUW PRYCE

At the close of the twentieth century the advent of a new millennium looms large on our mental horizons. Whether the first millennium of Christ's birth made a comparable impact on Welsh people is, by contrast, very uncertain. True, educated clerics, as the chronological specialists of the age, must have known that the year AD 1000 would shortly arrive; moreover, it is likely that some of them will have read in the Book of Revelation (20: 2–10) that Satan would be freed a thousand years after Christ, thereby triggering the events leading to the Last Judgement. But whether they took this prophecy literally is open to doubt: a strong body of theological opinion going back to St Augustine held that the precise day and hour of the Last Judgement could not—indeed, should not—be predicted. The terse Welsh annals for this period, which probably originated in the church of St David's, treat the years around 1000 no differently from previous decades: warfare, killing, mutilation and the succession of rulers continue to provide the annalist's staple diet, without the addition of millenarian seasoning. In any case, the vast majority of people in Wales were experts in neither chronology nor the Bible: their sense of time was probably structured far more by the recurrence of the seasons and of saints' festivals than by the passage of calendar years; and even if people realized that the millennium was imminent, they were not necessarily gripped by apocalyptic fears that they were about to reach the end of human history. Nor, with the benefit of hindsight, is there a strong case for seeing the years around 1000 as a significant turning point in the history of Wales. Admittedly, the lack of surviving source materials makes it difficult to say how far Welsh society changed between, say, 950 and 1050; however, there is nothing to suggest that

that century saw any radical changes, still less that changes clustered around the turn of the millennium.

Because the sources are so few, it is possible to describe Wales in 1000 only in the most general of terms. Settlement and economic activity were entirely rural; as was common in early medieval western Europe, the key to power lay essentially in the control of land and the people who worked it. Political authority was fragmented between a number of different kingdoms, dominated by a land-owning élite of warrior aristocrats and kings, as well as by the churches which they and their ancestors had endowed—Christianity had been well established in Wales for five centuries or so. The violence perpetrated by Welsh leaders and their warbands was compounded by frequent Viking raids from Ireland; indeed, in 992 Maredudd ab Owain (d. 999), ruler of Deheubarth, south-west Wales (who possibly also exercised authority in Gwynedd) used Viking mercenaries to help him ravage Glamorgan, the first recorded instance of such military co-operation. Maredudd's grandfather, Hywel Dda (Hywel the Good), who died c.950, had established an hegemony over all of Wales apart from the south-east in the final years of his life, but the power of Maredudd seems to have been more limited, if only because Anglesey and other parts of Gwynedd may well have been effectively under Hiberno-Scandinavian overlordship in the later tenth and early eleventh centuries. Churches were prime targets for the sea-borne raiders, especially St David's: one of its bishops, Morgenau, was killed by Vikings in 999—as a divine punishment, so later tradition alleged, for having been the first bishop of the see to eat meat, thereby abandoning the ascetic diet established by its sixth-century founder, St David. Such attacks suggest that churches, though themselves perhaps not very imposing (they were almost certainly built of timber like all Welsh buildings at this time), possessed fine metalwork and other treasures worth taking. However, probably the most valuable commodity seized by Welsh and Viking warbands alike was human. Warfare served to replenish supplies of slaves, who formed an integral element in Welsh society, as they did amongst the Irish and Anglo-Saxons, providing a source of agricultural labour as well as of profit in the slave markets of Dublin. Nor were war and enslavement the only threats faced by Welsh men, women and children in the decades around the year 1000: natural disasters threatened them too.

According to one Welsh chronicle, 'there was a great mortality upon men because of famine' in 989, and another famine struck five years later.

At the end of the first millennium, then, the people of Wales were subjected to the warfare of competing kings, Viking raids and famine. In one sense, this sets a fitting tone for the period covered by this chapter. In the first decade of the fifteenth century, the rising of Owain Glyn Dŵr plunged Wales into widespread war and economic dislocation, and much of the intervening period was likewise marked by violence and deprivation. The Norman conquests from the late eleventh century onwards culminated in Edward I's conquest of Wales in 1282–3 and, while fourteenth-century Wales was rarely disturbed by war, the lives of its inhabitants none the less remained precarious as the result of famines caused in part by a deterioration in the climate, followed, from 1349 onwards, by the bubonic plague known as the Black Death. Yet to present medieval Wales simply in terms of suffering would be as misleading as to dress it up in the clothes of Arthurian romance. The aim of what follows is to convey something of the variety of experiences in medieval Wales as well as to pick out some of the changes in the circumstances of people's lives. The discussion will be broadly chronological, focusing on the worlds of three figures, two well known, one not: Gerald of Wales in the late twelfth century; Gwladus, a religious woman living in Llanfrothen, Merioneth, in 1292; and Owain Glyn Dŵr.

A TWELFTH-CENTURY VIEW: GERALD'S WALES

With the writings of Gerald of Wales (1146–1223) Wales and its people first come clearly into view. Gerald was the product of Norman conquest: his maternal grandfather, Gerald of Windsor, was one of the conquerors of Dyfed at the end of the eleventh century and was appointed keeper of Pembroke Castle by the English crown, while his father, William de Barri, was lord of Manorbier. Yet Gerald's maternal grandmother was a Welsh princess, Nest, daughter of Rhys ap Tewdwr, the king of Dyfed, killed in 1093. As a member of a Marcher family Gerald was a subject of the English king, and was keen to see the further expansion of Marcher power in Wales at the expense of the Welsh; yet he was also related to the native ruling house of south-west Wales (Deheubarth) whose fortunes revived in his youth, principally under the leadership of the Lord Rhys (d. 1197). His social position was highly privileged; moreover, his education and career—including two periods at the schools of Paris, a decade as a royal clerk in the service of Kings Henry II and Richard I, and an unsuccessful attempt to become archbishop of St David's (1198-1203)—set him apart still further from most of his contemporaries. Yet it was precisely this combination of circumstances which explains why Gerald wrote so prolifically and acutely about Wales, throwing invaluable light on Welsh society in his own day and thereby providing a vantage point from which to survey some of the changes experienced by the Welsh over the previous two centuries.

Two of his books are particularly important, for they were the first to be written specifically about Wales: the *Journey through Wales* (1191) and the *Description of Wales* (1194). They still provide an excellent introduction to medieval Wales. The *Journey* recounts the mission in 1188 of Archbishop Baldwin of Canterbury, accompanied by Gerald, to recruit troops from Wales for the Third Crusade, called to recover Jerusalem from the Islamic forces of Saladin. However, the journey provided a framework for an account of the places travelled through, together with their history and folklore: the book thus gives us an invaluable portrait of Wales. It is complemented by the *Description*, which offers a more analytical and abstract view, beginning with the geography of Wales before going on to describe, first, the good and, second, the bad characteristics of the Welsh, and ending with advice on how the king of England could conquer the country and how the Welsh might resist.

Fundamental to both accounts was the assumption that Wales was a separate territory, distinct from England. This distinctiveness was already well established by the end of the tenth century. True, the Welsh of Gerald's day were still proud of their descent from the Britons, and lip-service was paid to long-cherished hopes that one day they would recover the hold over the island of Britain which their post-Roman ancestors had lost as the result of the Anglo-Saxon settlements from the fifth century onwards. But, by the twelfth century, this British allegiance served above all to furnish the Welsh with an illustrious pedigree, thereby reinforcing a national identity focused firmly on

Wales rather than on Britain. At the same time, Gerald makes it clear that Wales consisted of a conglomeration of regions, each with clearly delineated natural boundaries, and other sources show that these provided important focuses for identity. For example, a Welsh poem of the late eleventh century recounted an imaginary tour round Wales enumerating over thirty regions; Ieuan ap Sulien of Llanbadarn Fawr, in a Latin poem about his father, Sulien (d. 1091), an eminent scholar who was twice bishop of St Davids, praised his homeland of Ceredigion as 'once extremely rich, spiteful to its enemies, kind to travellers, excelling all Britons in hospitality'; in the mid-twelfth century Llywelyn Fardd extolled the splendours of Meirionnydd in his poem on St Cadfan and his church at Tywyn. Such loyalties could have a political complexion too. Native chronicles refer to the decisive role played by groups of regional notables in the bloody struggles for power of the day: thus it was 'through the treachery of the evil-spirited rulers and chief men of Ystrad Tywi' that Bleddyn ap Cynfyn, king of Powys and Gwynedd, was killed in 1075.

The Wales depicted in Gerald's *Journey* contained not only a patchwork of regions but also a mixture of peoples: when the crusade was preached at Llandaff, for instance, 'the English stood on one side and the Welsh on the other'; we also learn how rams' horns were used to foresee future events by the Flemings of Dyfed, settled in the region by King Henry I (1100–35). For Gerald, as for many other sources, both Welsh and Anglo-Norman, the most important social differences in Wales were ethnic. This in itself was nothing new. The fifth and sixth centuries had seen substantial Irish conquests and settlements, above all in Dyfed: the earliest bilingual notices in Wales were memorial stones written in both Latin and Irish. Anglo-Saxons had briefly established a defended settlement or *burh* at Rhuddlan in the early tenth century, and Vikings had settled in Anglesey in about the same period. Nevertheless, until the late eleventh century such incoming groups had made little permanent impact: Irish did not displace Welsh in the way that it replaced Pictish in Scotland; by the mid-eleventh century Rhuddlan was held by Gruffudd ap Llywelyn (d. 1063/4), whose devastating raids put paid to Anglo-Saxon settlements along the eastern border. The onset of Norman conquest and settlement in the 1070s marked a significant change. From then on Wales truly became what it has remained ever since: a land of several peoples and identities. Lords and knights from northern France, mainly Normans but also some Bretons, carved out lordships in the southern lowlands and along the Anglo-Welsh border, and English peasants were brought in to work the land—customary acres of Devon were used in Gower and elsewhere along the southern coast, for example. Gerald was very much a product of this multicultural world, and his own mixed parentage no doubt helped to sharpen his consciousness of ethnic differences.

Gerald also throws much light on the landscape, describing the rivers which often formed boundaries between the districts of Wales and revealing that much of the country was densely wooded. Thus Cantref Mawr in Carmarthenshire was 'a safe refuge for the inhabitants of south Wales, because of its impenetrable forests', and the Welsh sought to take advantage of this terrain by attacking their enemies in woods; it was not for nothing that Henry II ordered trees to be cut down in Dyffryn Ceiriog during his ill-fated campaign against Owain Gwynedd and other Welsh princes in the summer of 1165. The Welsh laws highlight the economic importance of woods as places for hunting and keeping pigs as well as sources of fuel and of timber for building houses or making a wide range of domestic utensils, including buckets and elm-bark rope. Welsh timber was prized by the Anglo-Normans too: in the early twelfth century Abbot Faritius of Abingdon used beams and rafters from the Welsh border in rebuilding his abbey. The conquerors also introduced forests in the legal sense of specially designated hunting reserves, on the pattern of royal forests in England. The largest of these in Wales was the Great Forest of Brecknock, established by the Norman lord, Bernard of Neufmarché (d. *c*.1125). Above all, though, Wales was seen as a land of mountains. On the whole Gerald, in common with other medieval writers, viewed these with awe rather than with the admiration typical of travellers from the later eighteenth century onwards. True, he devoted a short chapter of the *Journey* to Snowdonia, observing that its mountains 'seem to rear their lofty summits right up to the clouds', and a little earlier Hywel ab Owain Gwynedd (d. 1170) sang the praises of the coast and mountains of north Wales. However, such praises of nature are rare amongst the surviving Welsh poetry of the twelfth and thirteenth centuries, which tended to find beauty in the domesticated contexts of princely courts, while what moved Gerald most was the taming of the landscape by human hands. Thus Dyfed was both the 'most beautiful' district of Wales and 'the most productive', and it was not merely family pride which prompted him to lavish his most ecstatic praise on his birthplace of Manorbier, with its castle, 'excellent fish-pond', 'most attractive orchard' and watermill.

Nor was the landscape of Wales perceived simply in physical terms; it was also a key to the past, evoking a wealth of traditions about legendary heroes and saints. According to *Branwen*, one of the tales of the *Mabinogion*, the name of Talybolion, a commote on Anglesey, derived from the 'payment of young horses' (*tâl* + *ebolion*) made there by Bendigeidfran, king of Britain, as compensation for insulting Matholwch, king of Ireland. Pen-y-fan, the peak of the Brecon Beacons, was known as Arthur's Fort, after King Arthur, while Carmarthen was named after the prophet Merlin, who was discovered there as an infant according to Geoffrey of Monmouth in his *History of the Kings of Britain* (*c*.1138). Welsh saints' Lives of the later eleventh and twelfth centuries reveal how natural features were linked to traditions about the saints. Thus, to take a well-known example, the church of Llanddewibrefi sat on the top of a mound which, so it was believed, had risen under the feet of St David as he crushed the Pelagian heresy with his persuasive preaching; likewise, Lifris assured the readers of his Life of St Cadog that a ditch which had swallowed up a band of robbers who had had the temerity to attack St Cadog's monastery of Llancarfan was still visible, while the spring at Holywell marked the spot where St Winefride had been decapitated by her thwarted lover.

What of the people? The *Description of Wales* sets out to depict the distinctive qualities of the Welsh, and offers a compelling portrait of a society very different from that of the Anglo-French world of its intended readership. What struck Gerald most about Welsh society was its militarist ethos. 'The Welsh are light and agile. They are fierce rather than strong, and totally dedicated to the practice of arms. Not only the leaders but the entire nation are trained in war. Sound the trumpet for battle and the peasant will rush from his plough to pick up his weapons as quickly as the courtier from the court'. . . They are passionately devoted to their freedom and to the defence of their country . . . They esteem it a disgrace to die in bed, but an honour to be killed in battle.' This emphasis on warfare as a way of life is convincing, at least if restricted to the adult male free population— and an adult in this context could mean someone in his early teens: the Lord Rhys participated in his first campaign aged fourteen, and Llywelyn ap Iorwerth (Llywelyn the Great) of Gwynedd may have been even younger. It was their reputation as warriors which made the Welsh such attractive recruits for the crusade in 1188, and Welsh troops were used as mercenaries by Anglo-Norman lords and kings from at least the reign of King Stephen (1135–54); indeed, service as mercenaries in royal armies in Wales, England and, by Henry II's reign, France represented valuable employment for Welsh men. Opportunities for fighting were plentiful: Anglo-Norman conquerors compounded the political fragmentation and violence of a land already well accustomed to war, in which members of native dynasties along with their retinues fought out succession disputes amongst each other and raids were made on neighbouring Welsh kingdoms.

Because they valued military pursuits above all else, the Welsh in Gerald's eyes had a relaxed attitude to labour and were content to lead frugal lives. They 'plough the soil once in March and April for oats, a second time in summer, and they turn it a third time while the grain is being threshed. In this way the whole population lives almost entirely on oats and the produce of their herds, milk, cheese and butter. They eat plenty of meat, but little bread. They pay no attention to commerce, shipping or industry, and their only preoccupation is military training.' Gerald also claimed that the Welsh 'do not live in towns, villages or castles, but lead a solitary existence, deep in the woods', where 'they content themselves with wattled huts on the edges of the forest, put up with little labour or expense, but strong enough to last a year or two. They do not have orchards or gardens . . . Most of their land is used for pasture. They cultivate very little of it, growing a few flowers and sowing a plot here and there.'

How should we assess this picture of Welsh society? Its key characteristic in Gerald's eyes was freedom. Warfare was not restricted to an élite of knights, as in Anglo-Norman society, but involved all free men, from princes to peasants. Elsewhere Gerald stressed that the Welsh were not burdened by dues and taxes, and noted their boldness of speech, even before their princes. The implication, then, was that Welsh society was less stratified and oppressive than that of England or northern France. This was fair, but Gerald's concern to highlight the common characteristics of the Welsh led him to understate distinctions of gender and class. To begin with, when he wrote of the Welsh 'people' (*gens*) or 'nation' (*populus*), Gerald normally ignored the female half of the population, of which he had an extremely low opinion: 'It is not to be wondered at if a woman bears malice', he once observed, 'for this comes to her naturally.' Nevertheless, Gerald was too acute an observer completely to ignore the place of women in society. Not surprisingly, he usually portrays them in a domestic role—for example, we hear that travellers arriving in Welsh homes were entertained until evening by young girls playing the harp—although he also gives an account of the Amazonian Gwenllian, wife of Gruffudd ap Rhys, killed leading troops on behalf of her husband against the Normans of Kidwelly in 1136. On the whole, however, women were simply taken for granted as housekeepers and child-bearers, or else castigated as sources of temptation for the clergy, who were supposed to be celibate.

Gerald throws more light on class divisions amongst the Welsh. Thus we hear that whereas the more powerful rode on horseback to battle, the common people went on foot; when presented with a loaf of bread, the Welsh would break off a piece and give it to the poor. We get another glimpse of such divisions a century earlier, when Rhygyfarch ap Sulien complained that the Norman invasion of Dyfed in 1093 had subverted the social order: 'each man ploughs the earth, for with curved foot the nobleman as well as the poor man turns over the soil'. Nevertheless, Welsh society was freer in Gerald's day than it had been in Rhygyfarch's. For one thing, slavery was probably dying out, whereas in the late eleventh century slaves formed up to 17 per cent of the population in some eastern areas of Wales, to judge by the evidence of 'Domesday Book' (1086). The raids on rival kingdoms by Welsh rulers often amounted essentially to slave hunts: thus in 1136 Owain and Cadwaladr, sons of Gruffudd ap Cynan of Gwynedd, returned from a raid on Ceredigion 'after obtaining an exceeding great number of captives', and in the 1150s the archbishop of Canterbury complained to the pope that the people of Gwynedd engaged in a slave trade across the sea, presumably with the Hiberno-Scandinavians of Dublin. Yet, while the number of slaves was probably in decline by the end of the twelfth century, about a third of the population was unfree, comprising bond men and women tied to the land on princely estates.

The majority of the Welsh population in Gerald's day were of free status, however. The crucial determinant of status was not wealth but pedigree. According to Gerald, 'The Welsh value distinguished birth and noble descent more than anything else in the world. They would rather marry into a noble family than a rich one. Even the common people know their family-tree by heart . . .' Likewise, the Welsh lawbooks stipulate that an 'innate nobleman is a person whose complete stock is in Wales, both from mother and from father'. For the Welsh, nobility and freedom were two sides of the same coin. Yet some Welsh were more noble than others. Broadly speaking, free society was divided between members of ruling dynasties, leading noble families comprising *uchelwyr* (literally, 'high men'), from whom princes' military retinues were recruited, and ordinary peasant farmers. Up to and including Gerald's day, the grip of rulers over their free subjects was relatively light. True, Gerald exaggerated when he claimed that the Welsh were subject to no dues: the laws suggest that the free owed some renders. Moreover, there are signs that some rulers were trying to curb the nobility's independence. Thus the poet Cynddelw gave voice to the grievances of the leading kindreds of Powys in the later twelfth century, complaining that their traditional privileges were endangered by novel princely policies. Yet the autonomy of the *uchelwyr* in particular was great. With their land vested in the kindred rather than held from the prince, living apart in scattered homesteads, highly proficient in arms, proud of their pedigrees and ready to avenge any injuries against themselves or their kin, Welsh freemen could not easily be subjected to princely authority against their will.

Gerald's account of Welsh settlement and economy also requires qualification. Where you lived depended on who you were. By Gerald's day, and probably since the early Middle Ages, bond townships formed nucleated settlements, in contrast to the dispersed settlement pattern of the free population. Moreover, by the late eleventh and twelfth centuries, at the latest, some churches had become centres of population; indeed, it has been suggested that a number of villages in Glamorgan and Pembrokeshire originated in this way in the pre-Norman period, rather than being planted by the Anglo-Normans—although the latter, as well as Flemings in parts of Pembrokeshire, certainly established some villages. Until the late eleventh century, settlements round major churches, such as Llancarfan in Glamorgan, were probably the largest concentrations of population in Wales. Towns, however, were brought to Wales by the Normans: in the late eleventh and twelfth centuries these were small, established next to castles, for example, at Cardiff, Carmarthen and, briefly, Rhuddlan. Nevertheless, urbanization had a greater impact on the Welsh by 1200 than Gerald implied. Not all Welsh people shunned town life. One of the tales of the *Mabinogion* depicts Manawydan and his companions going to Hereford to earn their living as craftsmen, while the English chronicler Richard of Devizes, writing in the 1190s, voiced the opinion that the border towns of Worcester, Chester and Hereford should be avoided 'because of the Welsh, who are prodigal of the lives of others'. In addition, some Anglo-Norman towns fell into Welsh hands as a result of Welsh successes against the Marchers in the middle decades of the twelfth century: Caerleon became the centre of the Welsh lords of Gwynllwg, Cardigan was developed as a centre of power by the Lord Rhys, who held a festival of music and poetry there in 1176 often regarded as the first eisteddfod. In Gwynedd, too, there are hints of urban development, with two burgesses at Nefyn by the end of the century. It may be significant, however, that these bore the Norman names of Robert and Stephen, and it seems that many of the burgesses in Cardigan and Llandovery under the Lord Rhys were outsiders who had stayed on after Marcher power had collapsed. Yet if the number of Welsh people living in towns in Wales before the thirteenth century is in doubt, and if Welsh towns were small by comparison with what the well-travelled Gerald would have considered true urban centres (such as London or Paris), the establishment of towns marked an important development in the economic and social life of Wales whose impact on the Welsh would increase markedly later in the Middle Ages.

Some of the most interesting observations made by Gerald concern culture, both in the broad sense of everyday habits and customs and in the narrower sense of creative expression. Thus we learn that both men and women 'cut their hair short and shape it round their ears and eyes'; they also 'take great care of their teeth, more than I have seen in any country. They are constantly cleaning them with green hazel-shoots and then rubbing them with woollen cloths until they shine like ivory.' Travellers were welcomed into homes and no one needed to beg. At meals the Welsh sat down in threes, eating off a shared dish; their clothing was simple, consisting of a thin cloak and a tunic; at night they slept in communal beds filled with rushes. This spartan life was enlivened, however, by various forms of entertainment. Music was highly valued. Gerald tells us that the Welsh played three kinds of musical instrument—the harp, the pipe, and the *crwth* or crowd, a stringed instrument played with a bow—and he commented on their skill in part-singing. Above all, Welsh culture was a culture of words: of verbal wit and repartee, of public speaking, of prophecy and especially of poetry. Poets, Gerald noted, were numerous in Wales. As well as composing poetry they preserved genealogies and prophecies, some in writing, but mostly in the memory. By the twelfth century, Welsh poetry had a long history, going back to the sixth-century compositions of Aneirin and Taliesin in the Brittonic kingdoms of northern Britain, and the court poets or *Gogynfeirdd*, whose work survives from the twelfth and thirteenth centuries, clearly saw themselves as the heirs of this tradition of early poetry. At the same time, poets fulfilled a contemporary role: guardians of traditional lore, eulogists of princes (most of the surviving court poetry consists of poems in praise or memory of native rulers), Welsh poets both before and after Gerald's day were the remembrancers and propagandists of the native elite. For this they were well rewarded. Thus Berddig, court poet to Gruffudd ap Llywelyn (d. 1063/4), held three vills in Gwent from the king free of tax, while Meilyr Brydydd (who flourished in the early twelfth century) and his descendants, the leading bardic family of the princes of Gwynedd, held lands in Anglesey on similarly favourable terms. Some poets fought alongside their princes—in 1158 the poet Gwrgant ap Rhys was killed together with his lord, Morgan ab Owain, in Gwent—and no poem in praise of a prince was complete without emphasizing his ferocity and bravery in battle.

If violence permeated Welsh culture in Gerald's day, so too did Christianity. The two were not mutually exclusive. The preaching tour in 1188 was designed to recruit warriors for a holy war, and some Welsh saints commemorated in the twelfth century had militant reputations: St Cadfan was a patron of warriors; St Cadog was depicted by his biographer, Lifris, as condemning those who thwarted him to sticky ends—two disobedient disciples ended up being drowned in the Bristol Channel; while a miracle story in the Life of St Winefride tells how God willed, through the saint's intercession, that a servant, seeking refuge in a church, who had been thrashed by her mistress should head-butt the latter, permanently deforming her face! At the same time, the Church helped to defuse violence, particularly by providing sanctuary—although Gerald complained that this privilege was sometimes abused by those fleeing to churches to recoup their strength before sallying forth to inflict further mayhem.

Christianity had been well established in Wales since the fifth or sixth centuries, and played an integral part in people's lives throughout the medieval period. The organization of the Church, it is true, changed in significant respects during the century before Gerald wrote in the 1190s, partly as the result of Norman conquest and settlement. Before the late eleventh century, ecclesiastical organization consisted of communities of clergy, some headed by abbots, others by bishops; however, none of these communities appears to have been monastic in the strict sense of following a specific religious rule, nor did bishops rule over clearly defined areas. By the middle of the twelfth century the picture was very different. Four territorial dioceses had been established, with clearly defined boundaries, under the bishops of Llandaff, St Davids, Bangor and St Asaph; within these dioceses further subdivisions were created, namely archdeaconries (Gerald was archdeacon of Brecon in the diocese of St Davids) and rural deaneries, and parishes had begun to be created. Some of the most important early Welsh churches were appropriated by the Normans and their lands given to monasteries in England; St Peter's, Gloucester took over St Cadog's church of Llancarfan and St Padarn's church of Llanbadarn Fawr, Tewkesbury received the church of St Illtud at Llantwit Major. New forms of religious life were introduced: priories and cells of Benedictine monasteries in England and France were established in the shadow of castles at, for example, Chepstow, Monmouth, Brecon and Carmarthen; and, from the 1130s, monasteries belonging to the new reformed religious orders of the Continent, notably the Cistercians (named after their mother-house at Cîteaux in Burgundy), were founded in Wales, including Tintern in 1131, Margam in 1147 and

Strata Florida in 1164. Moreover, these orders attracted patronage from Welsh rulers as well as Anglo-Norman lords: the Cistercians began to make substantial inroads in native Wales from the later twelfth century thanks, in particular, to the support of the Lord Rhys.

How much difference these changes made to most Welsh people's experience of the Church and religion is hard to assess. The recruitment of Welsh monks and lay brothers to the Cistercian monastery of Whitland and its daughter-houses in Wales from the mid-twelfth century onwards offered new opportunities to lead a religious life which had not been available before. The creation of parishes may have led to a rise in taxation, since parishioners were expected to pay tithes—that is, a tenth of their crops and other produce—although too little is known of the ways in which pre-Norman churches were supported for us to know how far this marked an increased burden. The presence of religious orders whose headquarters were in France created new links with the Continent, while the formation of a diocesan structure, subject in turn to the archbishop of Canterbury, embedded the Welsh Church more firmly in the wider ecclesiastical framework of Europe under the papacy. Wales was thus pulled closer to the Continent while, conversely, ecclesiastical (and political) connections with Ireland diminished in importance after the late eleventh century. Rhygyfarch (d. 1099) drew on Irish saints' Lives when he wrote his Life of St David; by the mid-twelfth century versions of that Life were copied at the abbey of Jumièges in Normandy.

Nor were ties with the Continent restricted to churchmen or the lay elite. Rome was the most popular pilgrimage destination for the Welsh in the late twelfth century, according to Gerald; we also know of Welsh pilgrims to the shrine of St Thomas Becket at Canterbury. Pilgrimage, like service in English armies, offered a chance to see the wider world, quite apart from holding out the hope of remission of sins or cures from various afflictions—one mute Welsh pilgrim to Canterbury regained his power of speech, both in English and, more fluently, in Welsh. But pilgrims also travelled to sites in Wales, reflecting the continuing veneration of its native saints. A splendidly carved Romanesque shrine was erected in Pennant Melangell church in the twelfth century, probably financed by pilgrims' offerings. Indeed, it is likely that for most people the cults of saints—centred on

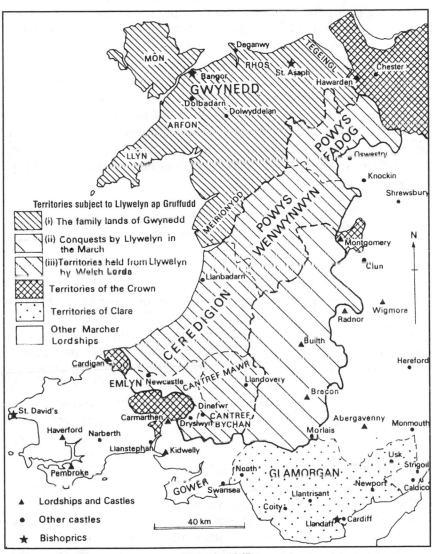

Wales in 1267.

their burial places together with holy wells and other places and objects associated with them—formed the most important focus of religious devotion. Gerald observed how in Wales, as in Ireland, gospel books and croziers (staffs) believed to have been possessed by saints were held in special esteem by the people. Nor was holiness only to be found amongst the saints of the distant past, for Gerald observed that 'Nowhere can you see hermits and anchorites more abstinent and more spiritually committed than in Wales.' It is likely, then, that native forms of devotion, deeply rooted in the pre-Norman period, co-existed with the new forms of ecclesiastical organization and religious provision which emerged from the late eleventh century onwards.

IN THE AFTERMATH OF CONQUEST: GWLADUS OF LLANFROTHEN

Within a century of the appearance of Gerald's *Journey* and *Description* the conquest of Wales was completed by Edward I. The defeat of Llywelyn ap Gruffudd and the fall of Gwynedd in 1282–3 ended an era of native rule originating in the fifth century. Llywelyn, like his grandfather, Llywelyn ap Iorwerth (d. 1240), before him, had attempted to establish a hegemony over the other Welsh princes and lords; his recognition as Prince of Wales by the English crown in 1267 seemed to signal the creation of a Welsh state, which, though ultimately subject to English royal authority and excluding the lordships of the March, possessed a unity and autonomy unprecedented in the history of Wales. Yet, while Llywelyn ap Gruffudd's principality probably had greater institutional depth than the essentially personal overlordships established by pre-Norman kings such as Hywel Dda (d. *c*.950) and Gruffudd ap Llywelyn (d. 1063/4), it was excessively dependent on the limited resources of Gwynedd, and was all too vulnerable to English offers of patronage designed to undermine the loyalties of leading families, not to mention Edward I's military might. True, the political effects of the Edwardian Conquest should not be exaggerated: political fragmentation was perpetuated with the creation of additional Marcher lordships in the north-east alongside the Principality of North Wales in the heartland of the former principality of Gwynedd in the north-west (and the Principality of South Wales in Cardiganshire and Carmarthenshire was established to absorb lands formerly held by the rulers of Deheubarth); there was some continuity of institutions, law and above all personnel, especially at a local level; and the revolt of Owain Glyn Dŵr graphically reveals that the idea of an independent principality of Wales had been far from extinguished. Yet the Conquest marked an important turning-point, none the less: from the late thirteenth century onwards the state—in the form of the English crown and Marcher lords—had a greater impact than ever before on peoples' lives in Wales.

Nothing rendered state power more visible than the castles built by Edward I in the Principality of North Wales: Caernarfon, Conwy, Beaumaris and Harlech. However, it was parchment rather than stone which made the consequences of conquest so pervasive. In order to maximize the profits from his Welsh lands Edward I introduced bureaucratic modes of governance on a scale not seen under the native princes: surveys (technically known as extents) were made, such as that of Anglesey in 1284, listing dues and renders owed from tenants on crown lands, fines were recorded in court rolls and taxes in lay subsidy rolls. As a result of these new forms of documentation (which were also deployed by Marcher lords), more Welsh people become visible to the historian than ever before. One such individual is Gwladus, a resident of the township of Llanfrothen in the north-western corner of Merioneth. She appears, along with over 2,600 others, most of whom are named, in a list of Merioneth taxpayers— brilliantly analysed by the late Keith Williams-Jones—made in the course of raising a lay subsidy in Wales of one fifteenth on moveable goods (as distinct from land) worth 15s. or more in 1292–3. Apart from her name and her township, the list tells us only two things about Gwladus: she owed 16d. in tax (implying that the value of her personal property was assessed at 20s.), and she was a *religiosa*, a woman who had taken vows of religion, perhaps an anchoress. We also know from other sources that Llanfrothen was occupied by families of free status, each probably with a small holding of land. Its religious needs were served by the parish church which gave the township its name: the church's patron, St Brothen, was an extremely obscure local saint to whom there are no other dedications in Wales. The church was re-built in stone, probably in Gwladus's lifetime, and still survives today, although the saint's holy well lying near to it no doubt also attracted much popular devotion. Despite the shortage of information about her, however, Gwladus prompts important questions about Welsh society in the aftermath of the Edwardian Conquest and the extent to which it had changed since Gerald wrote in the 1190s.

As a woman of religion, Gwladus was highly untypical of the taxpayers of Merioneth, or indeed Wales, in 1292–3. Although they must have made up about a half of the population, women account for only some 10 per cent of the individuals listed in the Merioneth lay subsidy roll; only one other is referred to by her occupation, namely an anonymous *crythores*, a crowder or *crwth*-player, living in the embryonic borough of Cynwyd in the parish of Llangar. She was somewhat wealthier than Gwladus, owing 22d. in tax. The other women in the list appear simply with their names; many are also identified as their father's daughter or husband's wife. Why some married women were included alongside their husbands is unclear, but probably well over half the women listed were householders in their own right; conversely, it is likely that most Merioneth women were omitted because they were regarded as subordinate members of their fathers' or husbands' households.

The lay subsidy roll, like Gerald of Wales's writings a century earlier, thus brings us face to face with one of the fundamental assumptions of the medieval sources: Welsh society was very much a man's world. This is equally true of the earliest surviving Welsh lawbooks, composed in their present form in the late twelfth and thirteenth centuries. These have more to say about women than any other Welsh source written before the Edwardian Conquest, including a section specifically on the 'laws of women', and, though undoubtedly schematic and archaic, offer invaluable insights into how women were regarded in native Welsh society. According to the laws, women were literally worth less than men: if a woman was injured, her honour-price was only half that of her brother or, if she was married, a third of her husband's; if she was killed, her life-price was half that of her brother whether she was married or not. Her legal capacity was also restricted: one lawbook states that no woman could be accepted as a witness against a man, nor was she allowed to buy or sell unless she was *priod*, probably meaning fully married for a period of seven years or more. Essentially, a woman's status was linked to that of her male kin: either to her father or, if married, to her husband. If a man beat another man's wife, he had to pay compensation to the woman's husband, not the woman.

The lawbooks also illuminate the different life cycles of women and men. Childhood receives little attention: in the upper echelons of free society, at least, it seems to have been usual to give male children to foster-parents—Gerald of Wales complained that ties between foster-brothers were often closer than those between natural brothers. Child-care was women's work: the laws assume that a divorced wife should have the means to make potage for her children as well as the services of a nurse; Gerald complained that not only wives but also nurses were ruinously expensive for married clergy. However, childhood was soon over: a female child became an adult in the eyes of the law at the age of twelve, a boy at fourteen. From then on, the lives of women and men (at least in free society) took different paths, for whereas an adolescent male would be commended to a lord and take arms in his household troop, a girl could be betrothed, and would then be associated primarily with her husband's kin. If her husband died before her, she would receive half of his moveable goods, the other half going to their children; if they divorced—a practice taken for granted by the laws, although it was against the law of the Church—the moveables were shared.

The equal division of goods between man and wife, and the assumption that a wife could initiate a divorce, have sometimes been seen as evidence that Welsh women enjoyed greater freedom than many European women of the period. However, it is likely that divorce was a far safer option for a husband than a wife. After all, it was only moveable property that was divided. Before 1282 inheritance of land was normally restricted to men, a restriction only partially ended by the Statute of Wales (1284), which allowed women in the Principality to inherit if there were no male heirs. (Even this concession was rejected by some Marcher lords, who sought to maximize their chances of seizing land without heirs by right of escheat: in this, as in other respects, lords were keenly aware of the opportunities for profit presented by native customs.) Once divorced, a woman would presumably either have to return to her kin or else find another husband. The latter option is envisaged by the laws, but

Wales in 1284.

given their great stress on the need for brides to be virgins, it may be that a divorcee was very much second-best in the eyes of a potential husband and his kin. In addition, husbands probably had greater freedom to repudiate their wives than vice versa: it is surely significant that the laws do not trouble to specify the reasons why a husband might divorce his wife, whereas they give three, possibly exceptional, grounds for a woman divorcing her husband, namely if he was impotent, a leper or had bad breath!

The most common alternative to marriage and child-bearing in medieval Europe was the religious life. Whether Gwladus of Llanfrothen took vows of religion as a means of avoiding marriage, or as a widow, is unknown. Indeed, her precise status is unclear. There were no nunneries in Merioneth; indeed, such establishments were singularly thin on the ground in medieval Wales by comparison with England or the Continent. Certainly, the ideals of the female religious life were promoted in twelfth- and thirteenth-century Wales: early medieval female saints, notably St Winefride, St Melangell and the twenty-four daughters of Brychan, were held in high esteem. However, opportunities to put such ideals into practice were few. There were only three Welsh nunneries in 1300: Llanllyr in Ceredigion, Llanllugan in Cedewain, and Usk. In addition, some women (and men) lived as recluses, supported by the local population. Perhaps Gwladus was one of these.

On the whole, women probably had a more restricted choice of occupations than men. Virtually all the individuals whose occupations are given in the Merioneth lay subsidy roll were male: members of the clergy, of course (for the priesthood was a male monopoly), but also numerous cobblers, carpenters, weavers and smiths as well as doctors, goldsmiths and the occasional herdsman, fisherman and butcher. If they were married most women probably combined the domestic tasks of preparing meals and looking after children with agricultural labour. True, some women were musically accomplished: as we have seen, Gerald refers to young female harpists entertaining guests, and the population of Cynwyd in 1292–3 included a female *crwth*-player. How far women were involved in the verbal culture of the poets in the twelfth and thirteenth centuries is hard to say. None of the surviving poems from that period was composed by a woman (with one possible exception, attributed in a late copy to Gwenllian,

daughter of the poet Rhirid Flaidd), although the biography of
Gruffudd ap Cynan (d. 1137) tells how the young Gruffudd, on his
arrival in Gwynedd from Ireland, was greeted by a 'woman of
prophecy' called Tangwystl. Nor do we have any religious works
which can confidently be ascribed to female authors comparable, say,
to those of the twelfth-century German abbess, Hildegard of Bingen,
although Efa, daughter of Maredudd ab Owain, a descendant of the
Lord Rhys, was the recipient of a Welsh translation of the Athanasian
Creed in the late thirteenth century. If women composed literary
works, they remained purely in the oral domain and were not
considered worthy of written preservation like the works of the male
court poets—one of whom, Llygad Gŵr, author of a praise poem to
Llywelyn ap Gruffudd, may well be the man of that name listed as a
taxpayer in the township of Carrog in Edeirnion in 1292–3.

We know about Gwladus only because she was required to pay tax.
Her 16d. was a modest contribution to the total of over £556
demanded from Merioneth as a whole, but it represented a significant
payment for all that. While Llywelyn ap Gruffudd had reputedly tried
to levy a tax of 3d. on each head of cattle, as well as demanding
payments in lieu of military service even from boys too young to
fight, the lay subsidy of 1292–3 effectively marks the beginning of
secular taxation in Wales (as distinct from tithes paid to the Church or
the papal taxations on the clergy in 1254 and 1291). It was but one of
the means used by Edward I to squeeze cash from his conquered
lands: rents from the Principality of Wales more than doubled after
1284, compulsory milling payments and tolls were imposed more
widely than before, every effort was made to charge for access to
legal procedures and to levy financial penalties in the courts. Despite
massive expenditure on castles, the English crown was in profit from
the Principality by c.1300; between the Conquest and Edward I's
death in 1307 royal revenue from the region increased almost
threefold. The brunt of these new fiscal demands was borne by the
peasants of Gwynedd, for whom the Conquest meant more than
simply a change of regime. The subsidy of 1292–3 proved difficult to
collect and was probably a crucial incentive for many to support the
revolt of Madog ap Llywelyn in 1294–5.

Since they had to be paid in cash, taxes and other financial
impositions stimulated the use of coin. The Welsh of 1300 were far

more familiar with money than they had been a century earlier. True, there were regional variations: money was more common in the Marcher lordships of the south and east, and Welsh freemen in upland Glamorgan were quick to seize the opportunities of converting land into cash by leasing lands to the Cistercian abbey of Margam from the late twelfth century onwards. And even in Gwynedd, the Conquest accelerated developments already under way under the thirteenth-century princes, who began to demand dues and renders in cash rather than kind and deliberately encouraged trade at some of their coastal centres, above all at Llan-faes on Anglesey. The Welsh élite needed money to purchase essentials of aristocratic life such as wine; and from the early thirteenth century they normally paid tributes to the English crown in cash rather than cattle—many of Llywelyn ap Gruffudd's difficulties in his later years stemmed from his promise to pay 25,000 marks (over £16,000) in return for recognition as Prince of Wales in 1267. The coins used were produced in English mints (no native ruler minted coin), underlining the way in which Wales was enmeshed in a wider economy encompassing England. Yet while use of, and familiarity with, coin grew in thirteenth-century Gwynedd, its circulation remained restricted (significantly, commutation of renders into money rents was still far from complete in 1282), and the Edwardian regime's demands for taxes, rents and other payments in cash placed new burdens on the conquered population, which had few opportunities for wage labour.

The subsidy roll lists 92 taxpayers in the township of Llanfrothen in 1292–3. Estimating population numbers from sources such as tax records is fraught with perils, but if we assume an average of four per household, the figure may suggest that the township had about 350–400 persons in all, out of a total of about 10,000 for Merioneth as a whole. The population of Wales at the end of the thirteenth century, according to one very tentative estimate, was about 300,000. What is certain is that the Welsh population had grown significantly over the previous 300 years, and especially from the twelfth century onwards. Gerald of Wales observed that the Welsh had grown more numerous in his day, an observation supported by the rapidity of Cistercian recruitment and the large numbers of Welsh mercenaries in English armies; Anglo-Norman settlement further boosted the population. Underlying this growth was the expansion in agrarian exploitation, both arable and pastoral, eased by the favourable climatic conditions which extended from the end of the first millennium to the beginning of the fourteenth century. Yet if more people lived in Wales in 1300 than ever before, reaching a peak not exceeded until perhaps the mid-sixteenth century, it was still a very thinly populated country: the population of medieval Wales at its height would probably have fitted into the Cardiff of today.

Throughout the Middle Ages, most people in Wales lived in the countryside. Of no region was this truer than Merioneth, where only about 2 per cent of the population lived in towns; moreover, urban settlements in the county were tiny—even at Harlech, one of Edward I's castle boroughs, there were only twelve taxpayers in 1292–3, by comparison with 110 holders of burgages in Conwy and a total population of probably over 1,000 in the largest Welsh town, Carmarthen. In Wales as a whole, two features stand out: towns were small—few had populations of over 1,000, bearing comparison with small market towns in England rather than with major urban centres such as London or York—but they were also fairly thick on the ground, totalling some eighty to ninety by 1300. In addition, while Anglo-Norman initiative was the crucial stimulus to urban development, thirteenth-century Welsh rulers played their part too: Llan-faes on Anglesey and Nefyn and Pwllheli in Llŷn were deliberately fostered as trading centres by the princes of Gwynedd. How far towns impinged on the life of most Welsh people is hard to assess. Whereas about 10 per cent of the population of England had lived in towns since the eleventh century, in 1300 this proportion was probably matched in Wales only in those areas, such as Flintshire and the lowlands of the southern March, most exposed to English settlement and influence. On the other hand, since they were relatively numerous, towns were probably accessible to many in the countryside, providing opportunities for exchanging agricultural surpluses and craft products for coin. Furthermore, while English settlers were recruited for the new Edwardian boroughs and made up the majority of the urban population everywhere, the Welsh were not universally excluded from towns: in Merioneth, one third of the taxpayers at Bere and Harlech in 1292–3 bore Welsh names, and at Aberystwyth almost half of the burgesses were Welsh a decade or so later. The rural population of Wales, and particularly upland Wales, was, by contrast, overwhelmingly Welsh. There were regional variations, of course. Anglo-Norman conquest had brought English peasant settlement in its wake in the lowlands along the southern coast from Gwent to Pembrokeshire; Welsh peasants were moved to the inhospitable moorlands of the Hiraethog mountains after the Edwardian Conquest to make room for English settlers in the fertile lowlands of the lordship of Denbigh. Nevertheless, while the line dividing natives from settlers was by no means identical with that separating country from town, there was still considerable overlap between the two: for all that Archbishop Pecham of Canterbury had urged Edward I to civilize the Welsh by forcing them to live in towns, in the short term the Conquest served to accentuate divisions between an overwhelmingly Welsh rural Wales and an urban Wales which was predominantly English.

CRISES AND CULTURES: THE WALES OF OWAIN GLYN DŴR

In the fourteenth century the people of Wales enjoyed an unprecedented period of peace, broken only by Llywelyn Bren's revolt in Glamorgan in 1316. Nevertheless, this was also a period of crisis. The weather turned colder and wetter: Wales, like many other parts of Europe, was hit by three consecutive harvest failures in 1315–17; sand storms engulfed settlements around Kenfig in Glamorgan and in 1330 destroyed over 180 acres at Newborough in Anglesey; arable cultivation retreated from some of the upland areas colonized during the previous two centuries. Climatic deterioration was compounded by the Black Death, the bubonic plague which reached the lordship of Abergavenny by March 1349 and spread rapidly through the rest of the country, striking Wales again in 1361 and 1369. While it cannot be quantified, the plague's impact on the population was devastating. Most of the tenants at Llan-llwch near Carmarthen were killed in the first outbreak of 1349–50, as were two-thirds of those in the Caernarfonshire commote of Nantconwy and many of the lead-miners at Holywell. As elsewhere in Europe, the fall in population caused by the plague resulted in economic and social dislocation. Some settlements were abandoned and others, including the towns of Cardiff and Tenby, contracted. Nucleated bond settlements seem to have been especially vulnerable: the ensuing reduction in the numbers of villeins, together with greater social mobility, helped to dissolve long-established legal and social distinctions between bond and free. Despite attempts to recoup their losses by pressing hard on their surviving tenants, English lords in Wales failed to arrest a decline in income and abandoned direct exploitation of their estates by 1400; the abundant availability of land enabled squires and others with sufficient means to expand their estates through lease and purchase, sharpening divisions of wealth in local communities.

The longer-term impact of the Black Death is hard to disentangle from the effects of the war which erupted on 16 September 1400 with the proclamation of a new Prince of Wales: Owain Glyn Dŵr. The causes and course of Glyn Dŵr's rising need not detain us here. Suffice it to say that in the first decade or so of the fifteenth century, and especially from 1403 to 1405, Owain established authority over more of Wales than any Welsh ruler since the days of Gruffudd ap Llywelyn in the eleventh century; that he enjoyed remarkably widespread support, from some English as well as many Welsh, from peasants and labourers as well as members of his own class, both churchmen and squires; and that he ultimately failed, vanishing into obscurity and the realm of legend by 1415. As a result, the new order established by the Edwardian Conquest was severely shaken; ethnic animosities between Welsh and English gained a new lease of life; above all, the economic fabric of Wales suffered massive destruction.

At first sight, Owain was not the kind of man one would have expected to lead a frontal assault on English power in Wales. He belonged to the Welsh élite, the squirearchy represented by the upper ranks of the *uchelwyr* and numbering at most 5 per cent of the population, which had accommodated itself to the post-Conquest regime and, indeed, played a key part in maintaining it by continuing to provide the leaders of local society as it had done before 1282. This élite was ready to adopt aspects of English law and culture when this served its interests. Thus Owain Glyn Dŵr's grandfather had prevented the fragmentation of the family's estates by ensuring that they descended by English law, rather than being divided amongst all male heirs according to Welsh law, thereby ensuring that Owain enjoyed an income from his three estates of perhaps £70 a year which, while modest enough compared to knights in England, placed him amongst the wealthiest landowners of his class in Wales. Moreover, it is likely that Owain was trained in English law at the Inns of Court in London, and he certainly served in English armies, joining Richard II's expedition against Scotland in 1385 and becoming a member of the earl of Arundel's personal retinue in 1387. He must have spoken English and French as well as Welsh, and was equally at ease in English and Welsh society. Significantly, he married Elizabeth Hanmer, a member of a Marcher family from Maelor Saesneg on the north-eastern border which likewise straddled the two worlds of England and Wales. Elizabeth's father, Sir David Hanmer, enjoyed close ties with the Welsh (marrying a Welsh lady, Angharad, daughter of Llywelyn Ddu), but also held important offices in England, becoming a chief justice of the King's Bench and a member of Richard II's council.

Yet if we probe further, it becomes apparent that Owain was uniquely well qualified to articulate discontent against English rule in Wales. Despite his status as a leading member of the native elite this was recognized neither by appointment to an administrative office nor by the honour of knighthood. He was not alone. Since the Conquest, the top jobs in government had been reserved for outsiders while, in the Church, John Trefor, bishop of St Asaph—who went over to Owain's cause in 1404—was the only Welshman to be appointed to episcopal office in Wales in the late fourteenth century, Owain thus represented a native political class, which, though influential at a local level, felt increasingly excluded from the rich plums of office which it considered its due. But he represented more than frustrated ambition. After the assassination of Owain Lawgoch (a descendant of the princely house of Gwynedd) in France in 1378, Glyn Dŵr had the most compelling claim to represent the native political order extinguished in 1282, for he was descended from the dynasties of both Powys and Deheubarth. It was precisely this descent which gave him legitimacy as a national leader, and from September 1400 Owain deliberately set out to revive the political aspirations of the past by presenting himself as the successor of Llywelyn ap Gruffudd, assuming not only the latter's title of Prince of Wales but also his arms, the four lions rampant of Gwynedd.

That Owain Glyn Dŵr succeeded in igniting such a widespread

military uprising in Wales after a century of almost unbroken peace poses important questions about Welsh society in 1400. In particular, the combination of Owain's strong English connections with his fiercely anti-English political programme and rhetoric brings into sharp focus issues of national identity and cultural assimilation. There can be no doubt that the lifestyle of native lords like Owain was deeply influenced by the Anglo-French culture which had made increasing inroads into Wales since the arrival of the Normans in the late eleventh century. To describe this influence as Anglicization would be an oversimplification: it would be more accurate to talk of the modernization of what was still a distinctively Welsh way of life. This is not to deny that Wales was far more oriented towards and dependent on England in 1400 than it had been in 1000. The most fundamental form of dependence, evident since at least the twelfth century, was economic. This is highlighted by two responses to Glyn Dŵr's rising: the return to Wales of agricultural labourers from their seasonal work on English estates to join Owain's cause, and the imposition of an economic blockade designed to deprive the Welsh of access to essential food and arms, a measure deployed by Edward I over a century earlier and one which had been recommended by Gerald of Wales in his blueprint for conquest. Conversely, England supplied the biggest market for cattle, Wales's premier export from the thirteenth century.

The assimilation by the Welsh élite of new cultural norms is clearly revealed by the famous poem which Iolo Goch composed in celebration of Owain's court at Sycharth in the 1380s or early 1390s. Neither Iolo nor, one assumes, his patron saw anything incongruous in drawing on the rich resources of the native bardic tradition to praise a home which bore many of the hallmarks of English, and indeed European, aristocratic culture. Owain's Sycharth was a world away from the spartan existence depicted by Gerald in his account of the Welsh two centuries earlier: the poem takes us to a splendid timber hall, surrounded by a moat, boasting windows (some possibly of stained glass), a tiled roof and a chimney, its cupboards as well stocked as the shops of Cheapside, a hall in which 'best Shrewsbury beer' was consumed as well as 'white bread and wine', while beyond lay an orchard, vineyard, dovecot and fishpond together with parks for both rabbits and deer. Rabbits were introduced by the Normans

into England in the twelfth century, and are known in Wales from the
thirteenth; farmed in warrens, they provided a valued source of winter
meat as well as fur—in 1387-8 over 3,000 rabbits were taken on the
three Pembrokeshire islands of Skomer, Skokholm and Middleholm.
The creation of deer parks was likewise a Norman innovation in
Wales: William de Braose established 'Parc le Breos', enclosing
nearly 2,000 acres, in Gower by 1230, and Abergavenny Priory had a
600-acre deer park by the later Middle Ages.

Iolo does not detail the cooking and eating utensils used at
Sycharth when Owain was in residence, but we can be confident that
these will have included pottery bowls, jugs and pots. Pottery ceased
to be used in Wales by the end of the seventh century and was
reintroduced by the Normans at the end of the eleventh. By the
thirteenth and fourteenth centuries it was widely used in the nucleated
villages of south Wales, and a number of local potteries had
developed in the region; pottery was also imported from England and
the Continent. In Gwynedd, by contrast, the reintroduction of pottery
occurred later in the thirteenth century, and its use was more restricted
than in the areas of early Anglo-Norman settlement: no local potteries
seem to have been existed, probably indicating a lack of demand in
rural areas, and while pottery was imported from north-east Wales,
Cheshire and farther afield, notably Saintonge in south-west France, it
is suggestive that cooking pots are virtually absent from excavated
samples. This contrast serves as a warning not to assume that the
impact of Anglo-Norman material culture was uniform throughout
Wales: even in the fourteenth century, it seems that pottery was rarely
used in the rural hinterlands of the north-west, which may have
continued earlier traditions of utilizing wood, leather and metal to
produce domestic utensils; in lowland Gwent, Glamorgan and
Carmarthenshire, on the other hand, local pottery industries were
widespread.

Pottery is one index of cultural change; literature is another. As
Iolo Goch's poem shows, Owain Glyn Dŵr, in common with others
of his class, was a patron of poets. Such patronage highlights how the
upper ranks of the *uchelwyr*, though ready enough to adopt material
comforts originating in Anglo-Norman and English society, retained a
strong sense of Welsh identity. At the same time, the literature they
supported was not immune to external influences. Thus Dafydd ap

Gwilym, the most famous medieval Welsh poet, who flourished in the middle decades of the fourteenth century, was heavily indebted to French literary traditions in the imagery and themes of his poems on nature and love. This was not something entirely new. There are hints of French conventions of courtly love in some twelfth-century compositions by the court poets or *Gogynfeirdd*, while those conventions are central to prose romances written in the twelfth or earlier thirteenth centuries which have close parallels in the poems of Chrétien de Troyes, possibly reflecting the interaction of Welsh- and French-speaking storytellers in the bilingual environment of the March, especially in the south-east. By the fourteenth century several French narratives had been translated into Welsh, including a romance on the Holy Grail (*Y Seint Greal*), whose earliest surviving manuscript was written at the end of the century for Hopcyn ap Thomas of Ynysforgan near Swansea, a renowned book-lover and literary patron who was also attributed with expertise in Welsh prophecies—Owain Glyn Dŵr consulted him as to his prospects in 1403. Yet if Dafydd ap Gwilym drew on the literature of France, quite possibly including the *Roman de la Rose*, he was also deeply familiar with native poetry and lore, both the bardic tradition represented in particular by praise-poetry and the more informal and metrically less complicated tradition of popular poetry: his genius lay in fusing these different elements to create something new.

All too little is known of popular poetry, as of popular culture more generally, in medieval Wales. Like the poets of the princes before them, the poets whose works were recited in the halls of *uchelwyr* such as Owain Glyn Dŵr voiced the conservative aspirations and preoccupations of the native élite. Iolo Goch, it is true, composed a poem in praise of an agricultural labourer, but this was no call to peasant resistance but rather a reaffirmation of the social doctrine, disseminated in sermons, that each group should keep to its divinely ordained place. Much of the medieval Welsh literature which survives was intended for the amusement or edification of those of high birth; indeed, by the fourteenth century cultured *uchelwyr* were responsible for preserving that literature in manuscripts. Thus Rhydderch ab Ieuan Llwyd of Parcrhydderch in Ceredigion, a patron of Dafydd ap Gwilym, owned the important Hendregadredd manuscript of poetry, originally copied at the Cistercian abbey of Strata Florida, and used it as a family poem-book; he may well also have commissioned the literary compendium known as the White Book of Rhydderch, just as, towards the end of the fourteenth century, Hopcyn ap Thomas appears to have commissioned another such collection, the Red Book of Hergest. Even allowing for huge losses of manuscripts, it is likely that considerably more Welsh literature was written down in books by 1400 than had been in previous centuries. This does not mean, though, that oral transmission became redundant. Poets may have deliberately prevented the copying of their work in their lifetime in order to control who performed it, while some narrative tales appear to have circulated orally without being committed to writing. On the whole, however, popular literature is invisible to us since it was restricted almost entirely to the oral domain, lacking the status which would have justified the expense of recording it on parchment: fourteenth-century poets make pejorative allusions to what they regarded as an inferior class of popular entertainers called *clêr*.

Nevertheless, the points of contact between popular and élite culture may have been greater than such comments suggest. For example, the appeal of native saints cut across the boundaries between classes and between the oral and written spheres. While the Lives of Welsh saints written, in Latin, in the late eleventh and twelfth centuries were clearly the products of a literate clerical minority, they drew heavily on a wealth of folklore and traditions about place names which were widely current in society, and which continued to flourish in local communities to the end of the Middle Ages and beyond. Above all, the historical and prophetic mythology of the Welsh, which combined a vision of a once glorious British past with the promise of political deliverance in the future under a messianic leader, was extremely broad in its appeal: not only was Owain Glyn Dŵr a firm believer in this ideology but also his success in securing popular support owed much to the widespread acceptance amongst the Welsh that he was the promised redeemer.

Wales in 1415 was in many respects a very different country from what it had been in 1000. Thanks to Anglo-Norman and English conquest and settlement, the population was more ethnically mixed; indeed, the division between natives and settlers was entrenched in legal and administrative arrangements, symbolized by the existence of Welshries—generally above the 600-foot contour line—and

Englishries in the more fertile lowlands, and given a new lease of life by the racial tensions unleashed by the Glyn Dŵr rising. Though still overwhelmingly a rural society, Wales had started on its first steps towards urbanization: many of the Welsh towns of today originated in this period. There were also industrial developments: over a hundred fulling mills had been established for cloth manufacture by 1400; silver, iron and coal were mined on a small scale in a number of areas. The creation of urban settlements, and the spread of nucleated villages in the lowlands of the March, transformed the landscape, as did the erection from the twelfth century onwards of stone churches and castles. By the late thirteenth century and in the fourteenth some building programmes were on a monumental scale: not only Edward I's castles but also Bishop Henry de Gower's palace at St Davids. These enterprises cost money. Money had made little impact on Wales before the twelfth century and its use only started to become widespread in the fourteenth, with the greater commercialization of the economy and increasing demands for rents and taxes in cash—a change reflected in the poetry of Dafydd ap Gwilym with its imagery of silver florins and copper coins. In the religious sphere, the Church had been brought into much closer contact with England and the Continent than it had been in the pre-Norman period, with the establishment of dioceses and parishes and the introduction of new orders of monks, canons and friars. Though its impact varied according to both region and class, Anglo-French culture led to a diversification of cultural life which, far from obliterating the native culture, helped to reinvigorate it.

Increasing contacts with England and the Continent also made it easier for Welsh people to find education and employment outside Wales. Of course, in the pre-Norman period Welsh churchmen had left Wales for the purpose of study and teaching: Asser of St Davids ended his life as bishop of Sherborne in 909 after helping to revive learning at King Alfred's court, the scholar Sulien (d. 1091), twice bishop of St David's, spent ten years studying in the schools of Ireland. However, from the twelfth century onwards the Welsh become more visible outside their own country, in part because the sources are richer, but also because political and ecclesiastical changes brought fresh opportunities in their wake. From the reign of Stephen (1135–54) Welsh troops served in large numbers in the armies of English kings, not only in England and Wales but also, from the 1160s onwards, in France; in the fourteenth and early fifteenth centuries they played a significant part in the Hundred Years War. Most of the Welsh soldiers who served in English armies probably returned to Wales, though some may have settled permanently in England or France (a certain John the Welshman owned property in Bec in Normandy in the 1250s, though whether he had a military background is unknown). Nor was military service the only type of employment available to the Welsh outside Wales. As we have seen, they were found in large numbers in the border towns of Chester, Hereford and Worcester in the 1190s (and also at the small Gloucestershire town of Thornbury in the thirteenth and fourteenth centuries), and Welsh agricultural labourers returned from their work on English estates to join Owain Glyn Dŵr. Likewise, Welsh clerics from the twelfth century onwards went to England and the Continent in pursuit of learning and ecclesiastical careers. In 1169 Henry II ordered the expulsion of 'all the Welsh who are in the schools in England'; Gerald of Wales was studying at Paris in the same year, and other clerics from Wales attended the university which developed from the schools there by the end of the twelfth century. Some went even farther afield: a John of Wales was one of the leading experts in canon law at Bologna, the major centre of legal learning in western Europe, in the early thirteenth century. At the same time, Welsh clerics gained employment in episcopal households in England—for example, a number served archbishops of Canterbury in the 1160s–1180s. Indeed, the largest Welsh diaspora in this period was located, not surprisingly, in England. Though it remains to be investigated in detail, this diaspora was probably substantial, encompassing a variety of occupations, and reflecting the growing economic, political and ecclesiastical ties between Wales and its eastern neighbour from the late eleventh century onwards.

How did the English view Wales and the Welsh? From the ninth century to the early twelfth, ecclesiastical writers in England express no particular antagonism towards the Welsh, in contrast to earlier Anglo-Saxon authors, notably Bede (d. 735), who condemned the Britons of Wales for both their savagery and their defective Christianity. Indeed, it is likely that the Welsh were regarded positively because of the role they played in reviving the Anglo-

Saxon Church in the late ninth and tenth centuries, a period when ecclesiastical learning in Wales (and Ireland) surpassed that of England. However, this all changed from the 1120s. For William of Malmesbury and a number of other English historians and writers, the Welsh represented the opposite to culture and civilization: they were barbarians. This shift in perceptions resulted from a combination of factors. Welsh warfare, with its capture of slaves, was condemned as barbaric after the slave trade was banned in England at the end of the eleventh century; the differences in organization and ethos between the Welsh and English Churches widened; and Welsh marriage practices, which allowed divorce as well as marriage between first cousins and other close kin, came to be seen as blatantly deviant in a world of increasingly uniformist canon law. True, the consistency with which these and other aspects of alleged Welsh barbarism were condemned should not be overstated. The charges tended to be pressed most vigorously at times of Anglo-Welsh conflict: it is no coincidence that some of the most strident criticisms of the Welsh as immoral, lazy and cruel were made by Archbishop Pecham of Canterbury in the years leading up to the Edwardian conquest, or that they surfaced again in response to the rising of Owain Glyn Dŵr. Large numbers of Welsh people managed to survive life in England, which suggests at least that such stereotyping was not applied with full force to all. Yet the creation of a fundamentally negative stereotype cannot be denied: the image devised in the twelfth century of a wild Wales inhabited by a backward, deceitful and immoral people was to prove very durable.

As we have seen, Welsh concepts of national identity were also redefined in this period. How widely these concepts were shared in Welsh society is, admittedly, difficult to assess. No doubt a sense of Welsh identity overlapped and competed with other identities, such as those focused on locality, kin or occupation, and (like anti-Welsh rhetoric in England) its character and strength will have varied according to time and place. It is likely, too, that poets and other native literati had a keener interest than most in articulating a sense of national identity and in transmitting the wealth of traditional learning and lore associated with it. It is clear that throughout this period there were two key elements in Welsh identity, one focused on descent from the Britons, the other on the territory of Wales. This is pointed up by a shift from one to the other in Latin sources written in Wales. Up to the early twelfth century those sources stuck to the old British or Brittonic vocabulary: the word *Britannia* was used not only for the whole of Britain but also specifically for Wales, probably reflecting an assumption, originating in the tenth century at latest, that Wales in a sense represented the whole of the Brittonic world which had once extended over much of the west and north of the island. Likewise, the inhabitants of Wales were called Britons (*Britones* or *Britanni*). Moreover, since the early ninth century, Welsh scholars had claimed that the Britons—like the Romans and, more recently, the Franks— had originated in Troy, a myth hugely elaborated by Geoffrey of Monmouth in his *History of the Kings of Britain* of c.1138, a work warmly received in Wales, veracity of which was not seriously challenged until the sixteenth century. From the early twelfth century onwards, by contrast, there is a decisive movement in Welsh Latin texts towards a 'Welsh' vocabulary, based on the Old English word for the Welsh (*Wealas*, singular *Wealh*, meaning, in essence, 'foreigners'): Wales is referred to as *Walia*, the Welsh as *Walenses* (and variants thereof).

On the face of it, this change is puzzling: why adopt a name imposed from outside, especially when it had such pejorative connotations? Three points are worth making here. First, the change in Latin terminology was not paralleled in the vernacular: *Cymry* (literally, 'compatriots'), though originally used for the Britons of Strathclyde and Cumbria as well as Wales, was well established by 1100 as the Welsh word for both Wales and the Welsh, and has continued to be thus used ever since (albeit with a minor modification in spelling to *Cymru* in the case of the country). Moreover, the ability to speak Welsh was clearly regarded as an important badge of identity, distinguishing the Welsh of all social classes from outsiders. Second, the Welsh identity expressed by terms like *Cymry* or *Walenses* did not entail rejecting British identity: the idea that the Welsh were the descendants of the Britons and would one day recover both their sovereignty over the island of Britain and their original name as a people appears throughout this period. Third, the willingness of Welsh writers in Latin to adopt terms like *Walia* and *Walenses* probably reflects a determination to use a vocabulary which would be clearly recognizable to outsiders in England and elsewhere, unambiguously linking the Welsh to a specific territory, Wales, in a way that the British vocabulary—which could also refer to either Britain or Brittany—did not. This territorial emphasis was arguably an urgent necessity in the face of Anglo-Norman conquest and settlement far greater in scale than any Anglo-Saxon penetration of the country. It does not follow, however, that the use of this new terminology was merely defensive. On the contrary: it was deliberately deployed by the princes of Gwynedd as an expression of their political ambitions, ambitions which seemed to be fulfilled in 1267 with the English crown's recognition of Llywelyn ap Gruffudd as 'prince of Wales' (*princeps Wallie*). After the Edwardian conquest the title was bestowed by English kings on their eldest sons; but its original significance was not lost on Owain Glyn Dŵr, whose adoption of the title in 1400 left no doubts about the political legacy which he sought to revive.

There can be no doubt, then, that the people of Wales experienced a wide variety of changes in the period covered by this chapter. Nevertheless, as the continuing appeal of the British dimension to Welsh identity reminds us, the extent and pace of change should not be exaggerated. Political fragmentation was, if anything, greater in the fourteenth century than it had been at the end of the tenth, though mechanisms for extracting surplus from the mass of the governed had become more systematic and oppressive; local loyalties, whether to leading notables or Dark Age saints, still counted for much. Gender roles remained essentially unchanged: most women's lives were anchored in the spheres of child-care and the domestic economy of their husbands' households; thousands of Welsh males experienced the military life in each generation. Although trade, especially in livestock, as well as industrial production were on the increase, the economy was still overwhelmingly agrarian in 1415; moreover, from at least the twelfth century onwards, its vulnerability to natural catastrophes, not to mention the devastation of war, meant that Welsh agriculture was not always sufficient to feed the population, creating a dependence on England for imports of grain and other necessities. Basic economic structures changed little. The same was even truer of key aspects of Welsh culture and ideology. Poets and other specialists in native lore and literature, sustained by the continuing patronage of the Welsh élite, played a central role in society throughout these centuries. Open though they were to new influences mediated in large measure by conquest, the custodians and creators of this native literary culture were above all traditionalists who sought to conserve and adapt the heritage of the past in order to make it a vital part of the present. Thanks to their efforts, crucial elements of Welsh culture and identity forged in the pre-Norman period continued to resonate loudly in the Wales of Owain Glyn Dŵr.

CHAPTER 2

LAND, LIFE AND BELIEF: 1415-1642

MATTHEW GRIFFITHS

The meaning of what happened in Wales and to the Welsh in these two centuries or so has generated a certain amount of polemic, not least around the significance of the Acts of Union, which took place in the first half of the sixteenth century, and what these meant for the way in which Wales was ruled and for the status of the language. Recent history writing has concentrated on the rise of the gentry as a class, their culture, and their engagement with the Tudor and Stuart state; and the condition of the Church, before, during and after the Reformation. For some, the whole period has seemed an age in which very little happened compared with the restructuring of society that accompanied the forging, in the eighteenth and early nineteenth centuries, of the world's first industrial 'nation'; to others, the evolution of Welsh social structure and the integration of its local rulers into a British state was an essential preparation for industrialization.

The following attempt to impose structure and meaning on more than two hundred years of history inevitably has its own blind spots and biases. It is organized around two connected themes: first, the way in which society and the land were reshaped between the fifteenth and the seventeenth centuries; second, a discussion of attitudes and beliefs – especially from the point of view of the lower orders in Wales.

There is a further sub-text: the attempt to pin down the experience of living and getting a living in Wales; to attempt a look at life from the 'bottom up', rather than from the perspective of a tiny élite. This is not to ignore the gentry, the class that came into its own as governors of the people of Wales in the sixteenth century, nor to

The Shires of Wales, 1543-1974.

neglect the importance of political history, but it is a shift in perspective that tries to get us a little way forward in understanding how things changed for the vast majority of the people of Wales – those who were ruled rather than rulers. The approach, therefore, is to see if we can achieve images of the economic and social structures within which people's lives were lived out; to reconstruct the context of material life, in the shape of landscapes and settlements, as a basis for an imaginative grasp of what life for most people may have been like; and to go on from this to ask some questions about the fundamentals of social, cultural and religious attitudes. Given the lack of popular testimony, an attempt to think about the experience of daily life through recognition of its context may be the most fruitful approach.

A POLITICAL FRAMEWORK

In 1485 came the end of the Wars of the Roses that followed the Hundred Years War – the end of the squabble for kingship amongst the noble houses that had drawn on Wales for soldiery and created opportunities for well-positioned Welshmen to step into the shoes of English lords and officials. It was the year which saw the advent of a dynasty that had a Welsh ancestry and which, to Welsh poets, seemed at the time to be the fulfilment of an ancient prophecy. Tudor affection for Wales may have helped to ensure that the Welsh were not treated like the Irish; it certainly assisted the assimilation of the local gentry élite into the English ruling class. In retrospect, this Welsh élite would put together a picture of the arrival of the Tudors as providing the basis of stability, order and economic advance; it was their opportunity to reap the rewards of loyalty as they hitched their wagon to the authority and obedience of the crown.

In 1536 and 1543 the Tudor state reconstructed the government of Wales through two Acts of Union. Although Wales was to have some distinctive institutions, and a structure of government that had strong elements of continuity with the way in which the Crown had ruled the Principality of Wales in the Middle Ages, Union legislation incorporated Wales into the new English nation state, got rid of the Welsh systems of law and inheritance that had underpinned the ancient system of kindred and landownership, and made English the official language of law and government. The establishment of law courts and county institutions relied on the Welsh gentry, poor though they might seem to Tudor civil servants, as administrators; the creation of parliamentary seats extended a further opportunity to the highest ranks in local society.

The Union legislation was made necessary not simply by particularism and the need, now that the Marcher lordships were mostly in royal hands and the last overmighty subjects toppled, to overhaul the anachronistic structure of March and Principality, but by Henry VIII's 'divorce' and the break from Rome. Other dates that are important, therefore, must be 1547, with the advent of a truly Protestant king, Edward VI; 1553, which saw the beginning of Mary Tudor's attempt to restore Roman Catholicism; and the inheritance of Elizabeth I in 1558, leading to the consolidation of a Protestant Church of England. The publication of a Welsh Bible in 1588 is a further landmark, since it was this which laid the basis for the Welsh, hitherto excluded by language from the new liturgy, to become Protestant, at the same time as it created an anchor for Welsh itself as a living language.

By 1604, and the beginning of James I's reign, the Welsh political class, while it had been drawn into the factional strife of the 1580s and 1590s centring around the earls of Essex and Pembroke, both owners of great aristocratic estates and controllers of extensive patronage networks in Wales, had acquired a place within a broader gentry society, and a world view which saw its fortunes as linked to loyalty to the English crown and state. They were on the whole a royalist gentry, rulers of a countryside little touched by the Puritanism that coloured attitudes to Charles I's government elsewhere, even if they resented aspects of royal fiscal policy, and if those who lived in the Marches griped at the jurisdiction of the Council that sat in Ludlow. Associating their success with the Crown, regarding loyalty as the basis of order and hierarchy and anxious about the impact of disorder on their estates and communities, when war came in 1642 these natural rulers made Wales a strategic resource for the king – although it is doubtful whether the tenantry dragooned into royalist armies appreciated the issues that were at stake, political, social or religious. By and large they spoke a different language from their leaders.

HOW DID SOCIETY CHANGE?

The gentry élite who had yoked themselves to Tudor and Stuart rule, and who opted for Charles I in 1642, stood at the apex of a complex social hierarchy. The 'gentle' class was itself stratified, and shaded imperceptibly into the lower orders in town and countryside who made up the great majority of the population. By 1640, too, the cultural and social implications of gentle status had altered significantly and were understood quite differently from two hundred years previously. It is when we consider the forces that underlay the success of this class that we get a broader sense of how the lives of people in Wales as a whole had changed during the same period of time.

Population and resources

Arguably, the forces which made most difference to people's lives, and to the way they provided for their families, were the same ones that reshaped all the societies of western and northern Europe in the later Middle Ages and beyond – the decline and growth of population, and the impact of demand on resources that led to changes in the prices of foodstuffs and industrial products. Following depopulation caused by Malthusian imbalances between resources of food and numbers of people in the medieval economy, together with plague and war, the period from the early sixteenth century to the mid-seventeenth century was one of population growth and inflation. The implications of demographic expansion and rising prices varied from state to state and from region to region, and were dependent on structures of landownership, the responses of rulers, patterns of tenure and the conditions of rural production and marketing.

In Wales, population growth and inflation meant changes in the size of farms and the nature of farming and a transformation of landscapes, and modifications to the ownership of land. It also meant changes in relationships between social strata, patterns of trade, industry and marketing and the way of life in town and countryside alike. The impact of such changes differed from place to place in Wales – regional and local differences in geography, terrain and the character of agriculture remained constants – so that in some parts of Wales, for instance, the building of durable homes that survive to the present day reflected the achievement of surpluses that could be invested in a more comfortable way of life for better-off farmers, whereas elsewhere this 'rebuilding' would have to wait until the later seventeenth and eighteenth centuries. But everywhere a remodelling of society and settlement took place, at the same time as the gap between rich and poor widened. The gentry class that achieved social and political dominance in Wales was made up of those who profited most in these economic conditions, which were fuelled further by opportunities to buy up the lands of crown and Church, and by legal changes which, in those parts of Wales where Welsh land law survived in the early sixteenth century, made the consolidation of landed estates and larger farms more durable.

Having said all this, it is very difficult to say how many people there were in Wales at any particular time. Working out local populations from medieval records is guesswork, though some guesses for towns are worth attempting; and we do not possess the sufficiency of parish registers that allow sensible reconstructions of population levels and rates of birth, death and family formation in the way that can be undertaken for parts of England or France. We are left with records of national taxation and religious censuses that are very tricky to interpret. Still less do we have the kinds of records that would let us work out accurate series of prices for food, animal products or domestic goods.

There were certainly fewer people in Wales in 1450 than there had been in 1350 or 1300. A wetter climate, and pressure of population on what the land could produce, probably meant a fall in population even before the successive plagues that started with the Black Death in the middle of the fourteenth century and continued in the later decades of the century. It is impossible to say how great the additional impact of the Glyn Dŵr revolt was, despite its physical destructiveness and the social dislocation to which it gave rise, but it certainly made no difference to the general pattern of contracting numbers. It is probable that the number of people began to rise some time after 1480; by the mid-sixteenth century, even if quantification is imprecise, population pressure and its impact on economy and society is unmistakable. A good guess at the population of Wales, based on the first Tudor tax records, would be that in the 1540s there may have been something like 225,000 inhabitants. For the 1660s we have records of the

Restoration Hearth Tax, when officials tried to count the number of hearths and chimneys in each house as measures of relative wealth, and these suggest, at another informed guess, around 370,000 people. After this date there may have been little change until the 1700s and the early phases of industrialization.

The population rose because more people were being born than were dying, and population growth seems to have been made possible because, for a time, food was cheap and life a little healthier. Once the rise began it was sustained, despite the fact that there were years when the harvest failed, or disease struck, and the death rate overtook the rate of baptism. We can trace some of these difficult years in the few surviving parish and town records, even if we cannot be more precise in charting vital statistics from decade to decade, and have to assume growth broadly in phase with the overall English trend. The late 1550s, during the reign of Mary Tudor, were bad years; Monmouthshire parish registers suggest that the same was true of 1572 and the late 1580s. The mid 1590s were appalling throughout England and Wales, and the evidence of a high death rate is present in registers for Conwy town; later on, the five or so years before 1622 and the later 1630s were times of hardship. It is not likely that these periods of harvest crisis and depression were accompanied by mass starvation or represented long-term crises of subsistence, but food must have been expensive enough and in sufficiently short supply to weaken resistance to disease in young and old especially.

Comparing mid-sixteenth- and mid-seventeenth-century tax records for parishes we can get some idea of relative population growth and variations in the density of population. Throughout the period, population was sparsest, naturally, in the hills and mountains and densest in the rich mixed-farming lowlands of the borders, and south and west coastal plains. On the other hand, as a generalization, population growth seems to have been greatest in upland and pastoral areas, although the actual experience varied from community to community.

Most people in early modern Wales depended on the land for their way of life. Even those who lived in the small market and port towns lived lives that were intimately associated with the cycles of the rural economy, since towns functioned mainly as a market place for the produce of the surrounding countryside and as a centre for the crafts

that met everybody's needs for manufactured goods. The Welsh
countryside produced oats, barley, rye and wheat; its coastline, fish;
its hills and valleys, grazing for sheep and cattle, and resources of
woodland and meadow. Its inhabitants were mostly involved in
farming – some combining the precarious lives of small farmers or
graziers with work as labourers on the farms of the better off or as
rural craftsmen or weavers. Even the gentry, whose income came
mainly from rent, tended to manage farms that provided for their own
households and sometimes produced animals and crops on a
commercial scale. These realities provide a sense of continuity
throughout the sixteenth and seventeenth centuries, but they should
not disguise the fact that the life and economy of the countryside
altered in significant ways, with the fall and rise of population the
main engine of change.

A new landscape

The reduced population of the later medieval countryside, followed
by rising numbers in the sixteenth century, shaped the rural landscape
of Wales as we ourselves know it; these forces simultaneously created
the social structure of rural society that was the context for
industrialization and which lingered until the second World War.
Internal demand, and the requirements of English markets, made
cattle and sheep the mainstay of Welsh farming, especially in the
uplands, while the way of life of the southern lowlands and north-east
became locked into patterns of trade dominated by Bristol and
Chester, just as much as central Wales and the March looked towards
Shrewsbury and London.

A period when land was cheap and labour expensive was followed
by a century in which land became more and more expensive and
labour cheap, as the population grew faster, probably, than at any time
hitherto. The remodelling of rural society and landscape that began in
the later fourteenth century was continued after 1540.

Most of rural Wales is today a landscape of isolated farms and
enclosed fields, with open moorland grazing evident above hedged or
walled pastureland. Villages – even hamlets – are rare. The countryside of lowland Gwent and Glamorgan, the eastern borderlands, and
Pembrokeshire below the Landsker, has its share of single farmsteads,
but in these areas where Anglo-Norman settlement had created

manorialized communities, villages are common, many associated with a parish church and sometimes the site of a castle. Farmland is organised in smaller or larger enclosed fields. In 1500 both rural worlds looked different. In the manorial lowlands, while there were many enclosures, much of the cultivated land lay in unhedged open fields, though these were seldom of the scale or regularity of the two- and three-field systems of the English Midlands. Beyond, where Welsh land law and inheritance customs remained in operation, although in decay, the predominantly upland landscapes featured their own open fields on patches of good corn land, and small hamlets and farm groupings of an irregular shape were not uncommon. On the higher summer grazing land, seasonal shelters – *hafotai* – provided protection for farmers who continued to practise transhumance agriculture. The way of life of both worlds was undergoing rapid change. In the Wales where Welsh law remained customary (until the Acts of Union), declining population and rebellion had depopulated many of the hamlets occupied by unfree bond tenants; at the same time freemen's landholdings, because of the effects of repetitive sub-division amongst successive generations of joint heirs, had often become too small to be economic. Both processes created a land market in which those with money could profit, accumulate estates and larger farms, amalgamate strips in open fields, and shape the modern landscape of dispersed settlement. Those who did well in this market in the fifteenth century, richer burgesses from the towns, wealthier freemen and Welsh gentlemen (*uchelwyr*), men who held office in the Principality or under the Marcher lords, laid the basis for the gentry society of Tudor and Stuart times. In the Englishries, areas dominated by the non-native Welsh and subject to English land law, lords of manors ceased, in the later fourteenth century, to exploit their demesne farms directly, thus creating opportunities for letting. Similarly, depopulation reduced the number of tenants and smaller freeholders, offering opportunities for the sharp-eyed to acquire and combine holdings into larger farms. The fifteenth century saw the evolution of this process, sometimes accelerated by the dislocation wrought by the Glyn Dŵr rebellion, and, with the consolidation of holdings and the leasing of demesne pasture and arable land, came the gradual enclosure of the open fields. Once again, the heirs of those who did well in this land market, whether they were of ancient gentle stock, lucky freemen or local officials, would be the local rulers in the sixteenth century and after.

The rise in population that ensued accelerated this remodelling of rural society and the reorganization of the countryside. More fuel was added to the land market with the dissolution of the monasteries after 1536 and the subsequent releases of crown land. The ending of partible inheritance, whereby land was divided up among all male heirs rather than passing intact to the eldest son, made it easier for estates that had been precariously built up under Welsh customary law to be protected from one generation to the next. By 1600, little was left of the traditional Welsh clanlands and their associated hamlets; and in the manors, while there were still remnants of the open fields, some of which might linger on for another century or so, a hedged landscape was the rule. Population pressure triggered land hunger in Tudor Wales, and this led to a new phase of colonization of what had hitherto been common grazing, waste or wood. The colonizers might be the aggressive rich, or poor families desperate for a place to settle and farm; the process might be silent and seemingly uncontentious, or it could lead to howls of protest and unease between rich and poor, ruler and ruled (evident in the complaints of the Radnorshire and Montgomery freeholders against gentry engrossers in 1573), but it was inexorable and, as it proceeded, it enabled the expansion of the cattle and sheep economy that typified pre-industrial Wales and undermined the ancient transhumance way of life. Some *hafotai* became permanent farmsteads, others were abandoned.

The pace of change was not uniform in either society. Wales remained a nation in which patterns of farming, ownership, and social structures varied from parish to parish. If the Vale of Glamorgan was predominantly enclosed by 1500, common fields survived in Pembrokeshire in the 1590s and beyond, in the Englishries of Gower in the middle of the seventeenth century, and on the Gwent levels in the 1840s. It is generally the case that such activities triggered little popular protest – complaints by the 'poor tenants' of Rosemarket that Moris Walter of Haverfordwest had disinherited thirty or forty poor householders, which led to the depopulation of the village through the consolidation and enclosure of arable land for pasture, are unusual. There is in fact little evidence of enclosure for such a purpose causing depopulation – in contrast to communities in the English Midlands.

Where consolidation took place, it was often initiated by gentry landowners and was probably supported by the larger tenants who stood to gain from more efficient farming methods. Delayed enclosure, or the failure alongside enclosure to create larger farms, can be explained sometimes by under-capitalization in what remained a poor and underdeveloped economy, or by fragmented land-ownership that inhibited reorganization and consolidation. This may have been the case in English Gower. In the uplands, beyond the villages and manors, the attack on the waste might be more or less extensive – for some communities common grazing remained a plentiful and accessible resource in the seventeenth century. The chronology of the restructuring of agrarian society is not always clear, but it is certain that it took place, and that, in the process, a new rural social structure was born.

The new social structure

Several features of the new order in the Tudor and Stuart countryside of Wales stand out. First, a greater gap had opened up between the relatively well off and the poor; society had become more polarized than it had been in the early- to mid-fifteenth century. This has a lot to do with the way in which larger farms had replaced smaller units, and with the development of gentry estate ownership.

Smaller farmers in the later Tudor and early Stuart period must have been very vulnerable to fluctuations in the weather and prices. They were farming at subsistence level and most may have tried to augment their income from work on larger farms, or from rural crafts. At the other end of the scale, there were families whose farms were large enough, even in a bad year, to be profitable, who we could consider to be operating on a commercial basis, generating surpluses to invest in more land or animals, to lend to poorer neighbours, or to invest in better living standards.

Detailed local studies of farm size and community structure are few and far between, although much is possible from estate records and rentals and there will be opportunities to refine our understanding of change over time in the fifteenth and sixteenth centuries and to make some comparisons between this material and tax records. Getting information about the economy of the individual farm, and life in the household, is more difficult since the wills and inventories that would allow us to look at the middling and upper ranks of parish society are few until the early seventeenth century. In Gower, between 1580 and 1620, the 156 inventories that have been analysed to this end emphasize the small size of the majority of farms: the value of 89 of these inventories came to under £30; one third of these were worth £10 or less. At the lowest level, the inventories probably represent the way of life of thrifty labourers with a few acres of land. It is possible that those who left estates of £60 or more were operating on a significantly bigger scale than the majority of farmers in these communities – they account for 71 of the inventories in the sample.

In north-east Wales, according to Nia Watkin Powell, a yeoman or tenant farmer might hold twenty to forty acres, although there were also many smaller farmers with about fifteen acres. In sixteenth-century Montgomeryshire a quarter of the holdings were under fifteen acres; 37 per cent between fifteen and thirty acres and 12 per cent over fifty acres.

Other than the gentry, the large and middling landowners who represented perhaps 5 per cent of the population, rural society was characterized around 1600 by the presence of a minority of substantial farmers, occasionally describing themselves as yeomen, more often, especially if they were of ancient Welsh stock, wanting to be seen as gentlemen. These, with the true *rentier* gentry, were the leaders of society at the parish level. Below these were families with middle-sized farms, men and women who would be more vulnerable to the harvest, capable of producing modest surpluses in good times but at risk when times were difficult or when they came under pressure from their landlords to pay a higher rent or accept a lease on shorter and less favourable terms. At the lower end of the scale in the rural community were those who farmed on a very small scale and would have needed to supplement their incomes in other ways, and labourer or cottager families who may have held, at most, a couple of acres or so. Although one must be careful of generalization in the face of patchy local information, the general tendency was for the weaker in the middle ranks of rural society to be squeezed both by the movement of prices and consequent gentry initiatives to remodel land tenure in their favour, and by more substantial farming families increasing their share of the land at the expense of their poorer counterparts.

The discussion that took place in the 1530s and early 1540s about how Wales was to be ruled involved some soul-searching as to whether the gentry were wealthy enough to be given the key office and role of justice of the peace in county government. Even at the end of the sixteenth century there were anxieties – expressed by commentators such as George Owen of Henllys in Pembrokeshire – that too many poor 'gentlemen' were getting on to the bench, men who lacked the land, reputation and status to act as guardians of order and security. The truth was that Welsh gentlemen were of predominantly modest wealth in the 1530s, and that many of them remained so a century later, at least in comparison with their equivalents in an English shire. This was certainly the case at parish level, but when one looks at the county communities that developed under Tudor patronage the success of those who stood at the apex of rural society is unmistakable; and in some parts of Wales, for example Glamorgan and Monmouthshire, there were élite families whose wealth and homes marked them out as plutocrats.

In the early seventeenth century the families who occupied the leading roles in local government at county level, and vied for control of parliamentary seats, were small in number – some two dozen in Glamorgan, thirty or so in Caernarfonshire. They had come by their fortunes in diverse ways, and had diverse origins. Many had their origins in native families of noble or freeholder stock, and had begun their rise by doing well out of the fragmentation of traditional Welsh clanlands and bond vills; others had started out as colonists in the boroughs and intermarried with Welsh families, investing the profits of trade in land. Others still, especially in the south-east, had ancestries that went back to English settlement in the twelfth century, although by the close of the Middle Ages, generally through intermarriage, they had acquired convincingly Welsh pedigrees. The knights and squires of the Welsh countryside – Morgans of Llantarnam, Wynns of Gwydir, Boldes of Conwy, Mansels, Stradlings and Carnes of Glamorgan, Maurices of Clenennau, Bulkeleys of Anglesey – were representatives of a ruling class that had profited from office, fattened itself on Marcher, Church and Crown land, and found their local dominance cemented by the new roles that they were given by the state following Union legislation.

Houses in the landscape

For the ordinary Welshmen, the economic and social dominance of this group must have been symbolized by the presence of the homes of such families in the landscape. In fact, one the best signs of stratification in Welsh rural society is the evidence of houses in the countryside. The rise of the gentry, and their wealth, was portrayed to their dependents, their tenants and the world by their houses. Few of these were in fact 'great' houses, whether built anew in the sixteenth and early seventeenth centuries, or modernized castles, although these were to be found in Glamorgan and Monmouthshire, especially, and to a lesser extent in the north-east. This was a society in which the possession of a house with an upper floor or two, several fireplaces and chimneys and internal stairs readily differentiated the successful (and, hopefully, hospitable) owner of the *plasty* from those who looked up to him. Houses of the lesser gentry were often also impressive, surely, to the majority of Welsh families who lived in conditions that showed no improvement on medieval housing. Much is made of 'rebuilding' in the countryside under the Tudors and Stuarts, beginning in the east of Wales in the late fifteenth century and spreading both westwards and down the social ladder over the following centuries. In its earliest phase, visible in the eastern borderlands around 1500, this meant the construction of fine cruck-framed timber hall-houses (frequently improved a century or so later by the insertion of a floor and stairs, and the addition of a kitchen or parlour). From 1550, in the Vale of Glamorgan and in Gwent, an equally marked development is the appearance of 'sub-medieval' stone-built storeyed farm-houses. In the uplands of eastern and central Wales, rebuilding tended to be later for the majority of farmers; in Cardigan it did not happen at all until the later eighteenth century. Over much of Wales, then, a modest vernacular storeyed farmhouse was a mark of social dominance; where rebuilding took place on any scale in our period it was a sign of the affluence of parish gentry and yeomanry, their profits from farming and rent enabling them to stand out from the crowd. For the common farmer and below in the advanced areas, and for even the better-off farmer over much of central, north and west Wales, rural housing remained poor in quality, and probably continued in the medieval stone-hall and open-hearth tradition. The evidence, such as it is, is that furnishing and interior

decoration were equally humble for most people – beds and tables are
rare in surviving inventories, and Eurwyn Wiliam points out that
farmhouse furniture surviving today tends to be of the eighteenth
century or later. The wealth, domination and control represented by
houses such as Gwydir or St Fagans, Althrey or Plas Mawr, Tretower
or Golden Grove must have been awesome: their occupants may have
claimed to be heirs to a long tradition of patronage, kinship and
clientage in the wider community but, in practice, the families who
lived in such houses represented the new economic and political
power that structured the bonds of society.

The poor

For the rural élite and, increasingly, the lesser gentry and better off
yeomanry, economic and social success was reflected in the improved
comfort and privacy of storeyed houses. At the bottom end of the
social scale the position of the 50 per cent or more of families who
ranked as the poorest farmers, cottagers and labourers, was bleak.
Certainly none of their houses survive – and many homes can have
been little more than temporary shelters. A key feature of the society
which emerged in the sixteenth century, one that frightened the state
and those in authority, was the growth in numbers of the very poor.
Except in isolated cases their numbers are impossible to quantify,
even using seventeenth-century records, but their existence worried
town councils and country justices alike.

George Owen's description of 'the common sort of people . . . the
greatest number and not the gentlemen, serving men or townsmen'
reflects the harsh way of life which a gentleman might perceive the
lower orders to live. He guessed that there were 3,000 young people
herding cattle in his native county, put to this work at the age of ten or
twelve

> and turned to the open fields to follow their cattle, when they are
> forced to endure the heat of the sun in his greatest extremity to patch
> and burn their faces, hands, legs, feet and breasts in such sort as they
> seem more like tawny Moors than people of this land. And then, with
> the cold, frost, snow, hail and wind they are so tormented, having the
> skin of their legs, hands, face and feet all in chinks and chaps . . . that,
> poor fools, they may well hold opinion with the papists that there is a
> purgatory.

The lower classes bore the marks of their status on their bodies, in their clothing, in their housing. Theirs were lives of continual labour. They were the victims of population growth and inflation, the result of a society in which there was a pool of cheap labour, their wages further depressed by harsh social legislation. They were the victims of the pressure on common land, younger sons who failed to find a farm or a trade in their parents' communities, forced by circumstances to wander in search of employment, at risk of being rounded up and placed in houses of correction or, if they were regarded as vagrant or able-bodied, whipped and sent back to their place of origin. Tudor legislation, especially the Poor Law statutes of 1597-1604, recognized both the deserving poor – those who were in poverty through no fault of their own – and the able-bodied poor. It was the latter that were most feared – 'rogues, vagabonds and masterless men' who were to be arrested, punished and sent back to their native parishes. Welsh records show that the authorities were as alarmed by vagrants, and the threat of disorder and crime which they posed, as their counterparts in England. The Council in the Marches certainly perceived the poor to be on the increase in the 1570s. We must be careful, though, since the signs are that the migrant poor were less of a problem for authority in Wales than in parts of England. While there is plenty of evidence to suggest a concern for order, and worries about the quality of gentry justices, by and large Welsh society in the later sixteenth century was peaceable and stable; and the oppressed did not resort to violence against their rulers, as the poor among the men of Oxfordshire did in the 1590s, and the Midlands poor in 1607. Gentry faction fighting, which could erupt into threats and violence, was more of a social irritant than lower-class unrest. Certainly, on the Denbighshire evidence, thefts of corn by the poor increased when times were very bad, and it was in such years that begging became a problem for the courts. The impression remains that wandering gangs of beggars were an occasional rather than a persistent issue,. Voluntary charity may have done much to help, and the pastoral nature of Welsh farming, together with the continued existence, despite a century of pressure, of resources of open waste and common, provided chances for survival that limited growth in their number.

Towns and urban society

It was probably the case that the towns of Wales bore the brunt of the 'problem' of poverty, since these were the natural place of refuge and opportunity for those set on the move by lack of work and land. The measures taken in Swansea in the 1560s to control the problem by collecting a poor rate, setting up a house of correction, distributing food and clothing and providing apprenticeships for children, provide a rare glimpse of efforts to deal with the issue, and show, as other records hint, that the fear that moved the authorities to harsh treatment could be tempered by charity and constructive efforts to help the indigent.

The number of people who lived in towns in Wales was small. Depending on how we define a town in a Welsh context it is possible that the larger towns in 1550 (the ten or so with around 1,000 inhabitants or more) accounted for perhaps 15,000 out of a total population of about 225,000. Like the countryside, towns exhibited extremes of wealth and poverty. The town houses of the greatest gentry – the Boldes's Plas Mawr in Conwy, for instance – stood in stark contrast to the shelters of the poor. Urban social structure was marked by a broad base of those living near or below the poverty line, by the existence of a middle band of tradesmen and craftsmen, and by the dominance – increasing in the sixteenth and early seventeenth centuries – of a gentle and mercantile élite. In 1652, a petition to the Pembrokeshire justices by the mayor and corporation of Haverfordwest spoke of the town having 2,000 souls, for the most part 'handicraftsmen and day labourers'.

With a reshaping of society and economy in the countryside came, more slowly, a recovery in town life. Social polarization in rural society appears to be mirrored by both the strengthening of urban oligarchies and an increased role for gentry families in urban society and politics.

When John Leland visited Wales during the reign of Henry VIII he found little that was positive to say about many of the towns he visited. The notes he made about them are eloquent evidence of the small size of Welsh boroughs, and of depopulation and depressed economies. Of the thirty-eight towns he refers to, the comments on thirty were not very complimentary. The 'old town' of Kidwelly, for example, was 'near all desolated', seemingly because of the decay of the haven of Gwendraeth Fechan. However, he added, 'Carmarthen hath increased since Kidwelly Haven decayed.' Newport in Monmouthshire got a mixed report. Leland regarded it as a 'big town', but the fairest of it was 'all in one street', adding, 'the town is in ruin'. Some he saw would continue to dwindle and to lose any semblance of urban life and society; for others the late sixteenth century and after would see either adjustment or renewed growth.

By English standards Welsh towns were small. As we have seen, Leland considered many to be in physical decay, with fewer people than they had once had, their houses modest and their inhabitants impoverished. The fifteenth and early-to-mid sixteenth centuries may have been difficult times. There were more towns in Wales by 1300 than the economy of the countryside could justify, many having been set up for military rather than economic reasons as centres of control and administration. Change in rural society inevitably meant change for urban communities in a context where the health of towns depended, by and large, on the needs of the surrounding country population and the success of markets and fairs. If the predominant economic factor in the fifteenth century was that there were fewer people in the countryside it is hardly surprising that most towns, even in the 1550s, seem to have had fewer inhabitants than two centuries previously. Only a very few – those like Carmarthen or Brecon, which assumed a greater administrative importance in the later Middle Ages and stood also on the most important trade routes – actually grew in this period.

It appears that the expansion of agriculture, under way in the early sixteenth century, had a delayed impact on most towns; the consensus is that there was no genuine growth in the economies and populations of Welsh market towns and ports until the 1560s. For some, the later sixteenth century remained a period of readjustment as trading patterns shifted and local economies adjusted. In the 1560s and 1570s, even Carmarthen experienced problems, as did other towns where weaving had been an important industry, because of the shift of the cloth industry to the countryside. Lesser west Wales boroughs such as Tenby and Pembroke were eclipsed by the dominance of Carmarthen and Haverfordwest. By 1600 there are clearer signs that markets were reviving generally and towns becoming more confident, signified by a rash of new town and market halls and grants of charters, and supported by the social and economic role that local gentry played in their political and social life. The late Tudor account of Cardiff, by Rice Merrick, is both detailed and affectionate, and gives a sense of small-scale commercial and social confidence. He describes 'a very well compacted' town, 'beautified with many fair houses and large streets' with a 'fair' town hall and shambles (meat market), 'fair and large streets, and buildings accordingly' with 'little or no vacant or waste ground within the walls, saving for gardens, and those very small, because it is so well replenished with buildings'.

George Owen was the most detailed and accurate contemporary observer, and supplies vivid pictures of Pembrokeshire life in the 1590s. He acknowledged three market towns in his native county, Haverfordwest, Pembroke and Tenby, with Haverfordwest 'one of the greatest and plentifullest markets that is within the marches of Wales, especially for the plenty and goodness of victual'. He recognized Haverfordwest's regional dominance, but thought that Pembroke and Tenby could be improved if cattle were brought there to market. In addition, Owen understood what had happened to many smaller towns and market centres. The markets of St Davids and Fishguard were 'small and bad', while those at Cilgerran, St Dogmael's, and Llawhaden, among others, had ceased because of poverty and poor location.

By the 1660s we can see evidence of real growth in numbers in the case of the more important towns, those that were well placed to serve land or sea trade, or served relatively prosperous rural districts. The table below gives some idea of the relative importance of towns.

Urban Populations *circa* **1550**

Over 2,000 people	Carmarthen
About 1,500-2000	Brecon, Wrexham, Haverfordwest
About 1,000-1,500	Cardiff, Kidwelly, Swansea, Tenby, Denbigh, Caernarfon
About 500-1,000	Monmouth, Pembroke, Usk, Abergavenny, Beaumaris, Conwy, Welshpool, Knighton
Under 500	Radnor, Cowbridge, Montgomery, Cardigan, Aberystwyth, Chepstow, Builth, Hay, Newport, Llanidloes, Presteigne, Ruthin, Llantrisant

Meanwhile, the early seventeenth century maps drawn by John Speed provide reasonably accurate visual evidence, for the first time, of how

Welsh towns were laid out, suggesting that they had changed very
little in shape since the fourteenth century, even if their walls or
castles were in decay. Many of these maps show how tenements that
had been occupied in the 1300s or so had become vacant and
remained unoccupied in the 1620s. In most towns, when numbers
rose, they could readily be accommodated within the walls of the
medieval settlement or in the small suburbs that had been laid out,
usually before 1350, in the shadow of town defences.

Occupations

The relative fortunes of the towns are a good index of the way in
which the economy of Wales as a whole was changing, especially
after 1560. Key features were the expansion of cross-channel and
overseas trade, linked to a growth in investment in shipping; the
expansion of inland trade, especially the growth of exports of cattle
and sheep, both through Shrewsbury and the border markets to
London and across the Bristol Channel to Bristol and the south west;
the gradual flight of the cloth industry out of the towns to the
countryside where it was freed from restrictions imposed by guilds
and town councils, accompanied by a gradual shift in the location of
production from the south to the north of Wales; and the development
of a local coal industry in western Glamorgan and Carmarthenshire.

It can be argued that the growth of the cloth and woollen industries
may be another reason why the 'problem of the poor' may not have
been as acute for the authorities in Wales as in English corn-growing
counties and their market towns. Cloth making was, primarily, a
dispersed and domestic industry providing employment for women
and children, as well as for men who might otherwise have become
poor migrants. It was an industry that suited areas where there was
plenty of grazing land, sheep to provide wool, water and labour.

Cloth and wool were the mainstays of the pre-industrial Welsh
economy and, in 1600, the largest and wealthiest towns were those
that faced outwards to England and beyond, either ports or towns that
sat on major cross-border lines of communication. This may have
been a world in which the rural economy was underdeveloped
compared to that of lowland England, and in which even the gentry
leaders of society were frequently compared unfavourably in terms of
wealth and way of life with their English counterparts but, for the

Welsh as for all western Europeans, it was nonetheless an age of expanding geographical and mental horizons. Wales traded with France, Spain and Ireland, as well as with the Midlands and the south-west of England. During the sixteenth century the northern port of Beaumaris lost its links with France as the attractions of coal from south Wales pulled French and Breton vessels to the wharves of Haverfordwest, Carmarthen, Swansea and Cardiff. These small ships brought in salt, wine and other luxuries in return for cargoes of coal, lead, corn, friezes, hides and butter. Tenby and Pembroke played a diminishing part in this trade as the larger towns came to dominate. Beaumaris did, however, retain its links with Ireland, and this trade was important also to the south-western ports, which imported timber, salt, fish, tallow, cloth, wool and livestock. The ports and creeks of south Wales were, above all, part of the regional market dominated by Bristol and, during the later sixteenth century, they developed their own ship-owners and fleets, important primarily in the coastal trade, while English and French vessels dominated foreign trade.

Many townspeople were also farmers, and towns themselves had their own corn lands, meadows and pastures. Within town walls there were strong echoes of a rural way of life. Nevertheless, even in these small towns, urban society differed in structure from that of the countryside. Wealth tended to be concentrated in towns; the more important towns such as Caernarfon could, in the 1540s, claim to be much wealthier in aggregate than the countryside that lay round about. Moreover, urban social structure, as in Britain and Europe generally, was marked by the presence of a broad base of those living near or below the poverty line, by the existence of a significant middle class of tradesmen and craftsmen, and by the dominance of a small gentle and mercantile élite, which, in the larger towns – Cardiff say, or Haverfordwest, or Wrexham – seems to have become narrower and more exclusive as time went on. The Welsh gentry saw profit and status from investment in the urban land market as much as in the countryside. The opportunity to compete for the seats allocated to the boroughs by the Acts of Union provided an incentive to seek to dominate town governments and patronage networks, while the Reformation created opportunities to fasten on to former Church and chantry land. Below the gentry and the richer merchant families, many townspeople earned a living through meeting the needs of the town itself and the folk who lived in the countryside beyond. There were weavers and shoemakers, brewers and butchers, tradesmen and craftsmen of all kinds. In some towns, although cloth-making had become well established in the countryside, weaving remained an important industry, and weavers' guilds important social institutions.

These strata within the urban population can be clearly seen in the case of Swansea, one of the few Welsh towns to possess a series of records which enables close analysis of its social and occupational structure. In 1601, merchant and gentry families represented the urban élite; below these came tradesmen, craftsmen, shopkeepers, and farmers, representing a quarter or so of the whole population. Another quarter of the population, some forty families or more, were too poor to contribute to the taxation levied in that year, and benefited from charitable relief provided by the corporation. A further forty families or so seem to have hovered just above the poverty line, their menfolk eking out a living as colliers and labourers, or as the poorest of the shopkeepers. The town's government and trade were controlled by the merchants and gentry. They supplied the burgesses who enjoyed exclusive trading privileges and controlled the corporation – an oligarchy that seems to have become narrower as time went on. Haverfordwest, another relatively well-documented town, shows similar social characteristics. Both towns give us a good idea, too, of the range of occupations to be found in the larger Welsh towns in Elizabethan and Jacobean times. Haverfordwest had glovers, felt-makers, weavers, tailors, hatters, cordwainers and shoemakers – all of them organized into guilds. There were tuckers, tilers and other workers in the building trades. An assessment of 1619 also mentions coopers (2), bakers (2), a butcher, a cutler, a shipwright, four bargemen, two colliers and two barbers. Seventeen labourers are specifically mentioned, as are seven mercers and a merchant.

CULTURE AND BELIEF

The *mentalités* of the gentry changed in the fifteenth century and beyond. As demography, economic change and political opportunity reshaped the structure of this class, so too it reshaped their mental horizons – at least insofar as we can judge from the testimony of its leading representatives. Over time, the values of the medieval *uchelwyr* were overlain and slowly supplanted by the perspectives of the English upper ranks with whom they aligned themselves. The transition from a society which valued kinship and descent more than landownership as an index of status to one in which reputation was founded increasingly on landed wealth as the visible mark of degree was slow but inexorable, though it was not concluded by 1640. The allegiance of the gentry to the Crown, and the duty that they accepted under the state to maintain order, justice and good governance, was reflected in the minds of the greater gentry by the adoption of a doctrine of service, accompanied by a demand for the skills which administration and legal responsibilities required. The medieval concept of *bonedd*, in which the gentleman was a man of good descent and of independence who valued kindred and displayed courage, liberality and magnanimity, had to be modified in a more competitive society in which birth and pedigree were not enough to maintain social status, position and office. While gentlemen accepted a picture that the social hierarchy was divinely ordered and static, experience and the rise and fall of estates and fortunes jarred with traditional assumptions. On the one hand, therefore, the gentry, in all their degrees, delighted in their pedigrees and the documentation that went to prove ancestry; on the other hand, social mobility and the entry into their ranks of *parvenus* who had done well in the land market, trade and the law insisted that the ability to live, behave and look like a gentleman was the real mark of worth. The documentation of descent obsessed Welsh gentlemen but pedigree ultimately became less a proof of lineage than of title.

Alongside the intrusion of reality into the social assumptions of this heterogeneous class, came the adoption of Renaissance concepts of civility, as they were understood by the English aristocracy and gentry, and therefore the need for a humanist education. Eventually this meant that the wealthiest and most proud, at least, discarded the Welsh language and culture for the Latinate and English values of the society they had joined.

What might these changes have implied for the lesser gentry and the lower orders in Welsh society? Medieval society was less differentiated in terms of wealth. It was a world in which agnatic affinity – the ties of kinship – is thought to have provided a social cement that bound kindreds together and placed on the strong the duty to defend the rights of the kin and the community, and to offer protection and hospitality. These values may have been more embedded in poetry than in day-to-day life, but they clearly had a significance for a broad swathe of society. As land and money became more important than blood, as ancient land tenures and inheritance customs dissolved and were abolished, as economic individualism encouraged the success of the *rentier* gentleman, as communal rights in land were abrogated by expropriation, engrossment and the modernization of tenurial relationships, as Tudor law and order got a grip on clientage and faction, the poor man's perception of his betters must have changed, however much the poets continued to eulogize the hospitality of the gentleman's *plasty*. When Welshmen followed the gentry into the Royalist armies of the Civil Wars they did so as tenants obligated to, and dragooned by, their landlords rather than as the dependents of the leaders of their clans. The older values may have lasted longest amongst the poorer gentry and freeholders of the uplands, north, and west, but by 1640 the county gentry had adopted the culture and outlook of their English peers, including the obligatory Grand Tour. They were as likely to speak Italian and French as Welsh.

Educational opportunities – English and Welsh

One feature of town life which is hard to quantify, but which seems to be borne out by tax records, probate records and other sources, is the extent to which towns which were dominated in the fifteenth century by families of English origin and speech had come, by the middle of the sixteenth century, to have populations where Welsh names predominated. This had been true of many smaller towns much earlier, but the larger boroughs, especially the towns built or strengthened by Edward I, had been foreign enclaves and instruments of colonization, as well as attempting economic hegemony. By the reign of Elizabeth I, in the aftermath of Union and in the reign of the fifth Tudor monarch, the penal laws and the apartheid they sought were dead and buried. People with Welsh names were also, to an extent, re-colonizing such areas of English settlement as the Vale of Glamorgan, Gower Is-coed and the Gwent lowlands. The language of most Welsh people was Welsh, but at the same time the towns were the only significant centres of formal education, and the schools of Tudor and Stuart Wales offered a curriculum taught in English and modelled on the humanist teaching of the English grammar schools.

This education could be afforded mainly by gentry families, some of the better-off farmers, and the merchants and more affluent craftsmen and tradesmen of the towns. It was an opportunity restricted to males, and it cost sums of money that few could afford. By and large, it was not available to the monoglot Welsh communities who made up the majority of the population. This provides another insight into the changing nature of Welsh society: the association of its affluent strata not just with an ideology of service to the English state but, increasingly, with cultural values that were English and European, rather than those rooted in the attitudes and habits of *uchelwyr* predecessors. The majority of the Welsh had little access to anything other than the most elementary of schooling at the parish level – and here we can only guess at the extent to which the local clergy or poor schoolmasters provided a basic education and the rudiments of Welsh literacy. It has been suggested that Tudor Wales saw a decline in the ability to read and write in Welsh, as the Welsh language came to hold less appeal to the better off. There were a few scholarships for children of 'poor' families – but, in this context, poverty was surely relative. When we talk of an increase in provision for formal education in Wales what we really mean is a growth in numbers of grammar schools in the towns of the northern and southern coastal belts and the borders. The interior had little to offer, and it was the sons of gentle and yeoman families, in particular, who experienced a grammar school education and the chance to progress to Oxford and Cambridge or the Inns of Court. When the wealthiest of the squirearchy sent their sons to public schools and the universities, and themselves spent much of their time in London and the county towns of the March or in their Welsh town houses, they acted as the role models for their lesser brethren for whom the urban grammar schools were the means to the cultural attributes that blazoned their social affinity.

The sixteenth century was the age of the print explosion, one that marks the transition from an oral and visual culture to one based on reading and the book. As Glanmor Williams has noted,

In the printed book, burgeoning nationalism, the power of the monarchy, the influence of the middle classes in town and country, the rise of the vernacular languages, and the rapid spread of literacy, all found their most powerful expression…

For a monoglot Welsh speaker such a development can have had little significance, for the printed books that came into Wales from English and Continental presses were rarely in Welsh. The overall impact of print was to support Latin and English as the media for schooling, for intellectual and scholarly communication, and for the popular consumption of almanac, broadsheet and chapbook. Hence the literature that the Wales of the Renaissance produced was seldom in Welsh but in English and Latin – poetry, history, genealogy and devotional works. It was a rich tradition but it marginalized the language of the majority and left little space for the maintenance of the native literary tradition that flourished at the close of the Middle Ages. If a Welsh man or (occasionally) woman read – as probably at best 20 per cent of the population could do c.1600 – it would be in a language that was not his own. There was little as yet in print in the language of hearth and home.

Moreover, the Welsh literary tradition that had reached its zenith in the late fifteenth and early sixteenth centuries can only with caution be described as a 'popular' tradition since it was primarily praise poetry for the benefit of gentry patrons and hosts. In the mid sixteenth century, poets such as the 'supreme elegist' William Llŷn were still producing fine verse, but the best were conscious that most of what was produced was conventional and tired, and that the society which had underpinned it was collapsing. While this tradition lingered into the seventeenth century it was by then out of tune with the anglicized taste of the leaders of society. Rather than the *cynghanedd* of the bards, it is possible that the free-metre carols and *cwndidau* which appealed to the lesser gentry and yeomanry take the reader closer to a popular cultural form. These were genres that included the metrical psalms of Edmwnd Prys and the religious verse of Vicar Prichard, but most was anonymous folk verse dealing with the everyday emotions inspired by 'weather, love, longing, folk life'.

Welsh poetry of any kind was preserved orally and in manuscript rather than print, but gradually Welsh prose did reach the presses as the result of the efforts of a minority of humanist scholars who were both proud of their tongue and eager to evangelize their brethren.

Belief

If the upper echelons of society and the lower orders became increasingly separate in language and culture, so the association of the majority of the gentry with the new Church that went hand in hand with the Elizabethan nation state created an additional gulf between rulers and ruled in Welsh society.

It has been conventional to view the late medieval Church as 'remote and conservative', its parishioners as 'illiterate and superstitious'. Nonconformity has left its mark on our view of the condition of Holy Mother Church on the eve of Henry VIII's break with Rome. It is easy to share the assumptions of a Luther or an Erasmus and criticize the instrumentalism of a sacramental religion based on good works, thereby ignoring the richness and complexity of the religious system that structured the medieval experience of life and death, and missing the gap that was left in people's lives when the altars were stripped and the symbolic world of medieval religion dismantled. We need to be more aware that, as Eamon Duffy has demonstrated, the late medieval religious outlook was shared by the élite and the common people alike. He criticizes the notion that the teaching of the clergy was poorly understood and only partly practised, and that, as a result, 'paganism and superstition were rife'. If we overemphasize the real institutional difficulties of the medieval Church in Wales – the poverty of its clergy, the absenteeism of its bishops, the desuetude of its monastic houses – we will likewise undervalue the vitality of religious belief and miss the fact that there were other ways for the essentials of religion to be communicated to the parishioner apart from the sermon. There was a rich matrix of church decoration, carpentry, glass and painting, popular prayer and hagiography to inculcate traditional belief. It took decades for the Elizabethan Church to make a Protestant nation out of the English; in the case of Wales, the Reformation was even harder to impose because the language of the liturgy, the instrument that above all structured and symbolized religious belief, was English.

Despite the catastrophic impact of the Glyn Dŵr rebellion on the economy of the Church in Wales there is powerful evidence that late medieval Roman Catholicism was, for the Welsh, a vibrant faith shared and understood in much the same terms by all sectors of society. One sign of this is the wave of church building and restoration that developed from the 1460s and gained strength in the first decades of the sixteenth century. In this period, churches large and small, in town and in the countryside, acquired new stained glass, crosses, fonts and roods; they were physically extended by the addition of porches, towers, lady chapels and transepts, and were decorated with colourful cycles of wall painting depicting the Passion and the saints. Without lay piety and lay cash this renewal could not have been afforded, and it has to be supposed that it was something which was wanted and supported by ordinary parishioners as much as the better off. At the same time the popularity of pilgrimage to shrines local and international, the emergence of Welsh religious drama, and the strength of a literary tradition that produced texts in Welsh of extracts from the Scriptures, manuals of instruction, hymns and prayers and the Lives of saints, and devotional verse in strict and free metre, is evocative of a rich devotion shared by all sectors of society. Clerical deficiencies were made good by various visual and oral means of representation and symbol, and we should be cautious about equating poverty and ignorance, popular belief and credulity.

The Reformation that was imposed on the Welsh produced little serious protest; there were no popular rebellions as there had been in Yorkshire under Henry VIII and in Cornwall in 1549 (elicited by an incomprehensible English *Book of Common Prayer*); only a handful of Protestants and Roman Catholics were martyred. Nonetheless, something of the emotional shock that must have been present is witnessed by poems that regretted the dismantling of chantries and altars and the expropriation of plate and vestments (under Edward VI), and welcomed the restoration of the Mass (under Mary Tudor); presumably these reflect the concern of their patrons and give some clue to wider attitudes. Eventually, everything that conveyed the meanings inherent in the word or symbol of traditional devotion was removed or broken: rood screens and altars, images of saints, vestments and lights, the very sound and music of Rome. Wall paintings were whitewashed and a simple Communion table stood in the nave. The Prayer Books of 1549, 1552, and 1559 and the Bible were in English. Protestantism was a religion of the Word, and without an educated, preaching clergy, and without texts in the language of the faithful, it could not communicate and evangelize. The fabric of Catholic belief had been taken away and only the rise of Nonconformity would replace this gap in people's lives, despite the best efforts of humanist evangelists.

All this was accepted because there was no alternative. Even if they regretted what had happened, there were no other options for the majority of the leaders of society – their position depended on their loyalty to the Crown and obedience to the state. That meant obedience, too, to the ruler's Church. For a good number of them, the dissolution of the monasteries had been a means to land and wealth. Many gentry families had a direct stake in the Church through the impropriation of livings. A few were noted recusants – the humanist Sir Edward Carne of Ewenny, who had been Mary Tudor's ambassador to Rome, is a notable example. The growing number of gentry who read and spoke English at least found the texts of the Church of England accessible. Under Elizabeth I their position was, in Glanmor Williams's words, one of 'indifference, unease and compromise', while eventually the solidity of the Tudor settlement and the Protestant establishment ensured that the Protestant humanist scholars who lobbied for a Welsh liturgy and Bible would have the upper hand. The evangelists recognised the problem for the Church if it wanted to make Protestants out of a nation that lacked trained, or even resident, clergy and where, inevitably, Catholic practices and traditional folk belief lingered on. In 1563, Parliament authorized a Welsh-language Prayer Book. This was published in 1567, together with a New Testament translated by William Salesbury and Richard Davies. In 1588 the Welsh got William Morgan's Bible and the *Book of Homilies*. Gradually, the universities turned out clergy who could read and preach in Welsh, while literate in English and Latin. By 1600, at least a minority of the gentry and clergy accepted and could promote the Reformation. In this context, early Puritanism – whether of the fiery nature expressed by the Elizabethan John Penry or the milder version to be found in towns that looked towards England – was the interest of a tiny minority, even in the 1630s. Recusancy was perhaps more of an issue, but the 800 or so minor gentlemen and yeomen who admitted to the old faith at the turn of the century, while they may have been the tip of a larger body of Roman Catholic

allegiance that worried the authorities, were isolated and unrepresent-
ative. On the eve of the Civil War, Crown, State and Church were the
bedrocks of the loyalty of most of the Anglican gentry who ruled
Wales, even if it could not be claimed that their Church had
embedded itself in society at large, and if there were border squires
who feared that the innovations associated with Archbishop Laud
represented creeping Catholicism which would therefore promote the
radical preaching of Puritans such as a Wroth, Cradock or Erbury. It
could be said of the English of the early seventeenth century that they
were Protestants, but not necessarily accepting Calvinists. It could be
said of the majority of the Welsh that they conformed to the official
Church, but were not necessarily accepting Protestants. They lived in
a 'dark corner of the land', condemned by the authorities as
backward, conservative in belief and illiterate.

Yet the Welsh did ultimately become 'the people of the Book'.
Anglican, anglicized, capitalist squirearchy lived a life disconnected
from the lives and language of the tenantry and small freeholders,
whose lives in turn had a different rhythm and weave from the more
cosmopolitan culture of the little towns that looked outwards to
England. The fragmented Welsh language ultimately derived strength
and grew in vigour because of the existence of a Welsh Bible, and the
growing religious devotion that it would feed. It became a 'sacral
language', supportive, once the majority of Welsh learned to read, of
Dissent rather than of the established Church; it was the basis for
another version of a Welsh identity, growing on the eve of the
industrialization that would recolonize and remake Wales and the
Welsh yet again.

Wales and Britain

It is ironic that as rulers and ruled in Wales grew apart in culture
and belief, and native literary expression entered a long decline, the
mythical components of the history that the Welsh had forged and
shared over a thousand years became integral to the way in which the
new Protestant 'British' state of Queen Elizabeth defined itself in
relation both to continental cultural traditions and the international
politics of Counter Reformation Europe.

The status of the Welsh at large in Tudor and Stuart society
developed in marked contrast to attitudes to the Irish, who came to be

demonized as a primitive and dangerous Roman Catholic, pro-Spanish 'other'. The result was that many Welsh people left Wales in the sixteenth century and after, pursuing advancement in trade, the law, learning and at court. They took with them a story of their own origins (origins of which the Tudors were themselves perfectly conscious); by the 1580s this had become thoroughly absorbed into official ideology and its cultural expressions.

If the identity of the Welsh who lived in Wales was fractured and divided by class and language, their diaspora influenced attitudes to Wales and the Welsh among the English. Through this diaspora Wales, from being perceived as a foreign and dangerous land, came to be regarded as a country integrated with England not just politically but in social and cultural terms. Unlike Ireland and Scotland, it was 'mostly harmless'.

Inevitably, we know more about the careers of the better off who left Wales than of the lower orders, but it is important to remember, first, that migration was nothing new after 1485 – even if it gained a new dynamic – and, second, that it must be seen in the context of wider patterns of mobility within the British Isles that put Scots, Irish, Welsh and English on the roads and the sea-lanes. Economic pressures created subsistence migrants – the poor whom Tudor rulers feared; economic opportunities, fuelled by the general expansion of inland and coastal trade, led many others to seek their fortunes away from home. In the sixteenth century, ordinary Welshmen were familiar characters in London and the provincial market towns and ports; their odd, explosive accents and their stereotyped character traits presented the basis for the stage Welshman of the late sixteenth and early seventeenth centuries.

The presence of large numbers of non-threatening Welshmen in English communities was one factor in reshaping perceptions of Wales and the Welsh. It was enhanced by the fact that the most successful became extremely prominent as merchants, tradesmen and lawyers in Elizabethan society. Figures such as Richard Clough of Denbigh, who got himself apprenticed to Sir Thomas Gresham's deputy, or Thomas, Robert and Hugh Myddelton, became rich, well-known and influential – successful in London, and capable of investing their wealth in land and patronage in their home area. The greater Welsh gentry families contributed their share as servants of the state. Sir Edward Carne's career encompassed a mission to plead Henry VIII's cause to the pope, and a finale as Mary's ambassador to the Holy See. Sir John Perrot served on the Privy Council and in Elizabeth's government in Ireland. In James I's reign Sir John Herbert became second Secretary to Robert Cecil.

Other Welshmen did well in the Church, at university, in the law, and as soldiers. Under Elizabeth I, Thomas Young occupied successfully the sees of St Davids and York; under Charles, John Williams became bishop of Lincoln, Lord Keeper, and archbishop of York. John Aubrey's grandfather, William, was professor of Civil Law at Oxford in the 1560s, where, in 1571, Dr Hugh Price of Brecon founded Jesus College. Charles I's general-in-chief of Engineers was the Welshman, Charles Lloyd, while maritime adventurers included Sir Robert Mansel and Sir Thomas Button, the latter searching in vain for the North-west Passage.

Many other young Welshmen founded their careers on English educational opportunities. Some 2,000 Welsh students are known to have attended Oxford and Cambridge between 1570 and 1642; we know of 700 Welshmen who trained at the Inns of Court in the century before 1640. Inevitably, the acquisition and absorption of English language, education, legal training and cultural tastes had an impact both in mediating English perceptions of Wales and the Welsh, and, through the influence of those who returned to Wales, in eroding native cultural traditions. Intellectuals such as William Camden and George Owen were proud of the way the Welsh élite had grown in learning, manners and grace, even while an attachment lingered towards genealogy and pedigree.

The most learned of the Welsh played a key role in the construction of the new idea of Britain that was promulgated by the Court's thinkers and litterateurs. This came about not simply as a response to the fact that the Anglican Church was a precarious implant, the dynasty itself being challenged both internally and externally, and imperilled by lack of an heir, but also as part of the active creation of a national moral, religious and literary identity designed to buttress Queen, Church and state. Sidney's *Defence of Poetry* and his *Arcadia*, and Spenser's *The Faerie Queene* represent the highest expression of this myth making, works which grafted Italian literary models onto Protestant and national value systems. In *The Faerie Queene*, Spenser (the author of xenophobic propaganda justifying the conquest and expropriation of the Irish) fuses Italian romantic epic, medieval chivalric romance and allegory, the British myth that had descended through Geoffrey of Monmouth and Malory, Aristotelian models of moral virtue, neoplatonic mysticism and the prophecy of the Book of Revelation to construct a Protestant vision of the values he believed should inform religious and state policy. Elizabeth I, prefigured as Una, Astraea, and Gloriana, is presented as guardian of the nation state and regenerator of the primitive Church. In this projection of the authority of the Queen and the destiny of a nation, the British Arthurian cycle was central. It made possible the assertion of a distinct British identity, linked to Rome and to early-Christian Britain, traced through the genealogies of the Welsh kings to reach its apotheosis in that son of prophecy, Henry Tudor, and the Tudor dynasty, and the *Ecclesia Anglicana*. Although challenged by Polydore Vergil, the intellectual consensus lined up behind Geoffrey of Monmouth, to be defended and promulgated by Welsh scholars such as Sir John Price, Sir David Powel (author of the *History of Cambria, now called Wales* of 1584) and Humphrey Llwyd, as well as John Bale and William Camden among the English humanist historians. The notion of an historic British identity was integral to the perceptions of John Leland and Michael Drayton, and it flowed naturally into the poetry associated with the Elizabethan court of the 1580s and 1590s. In this context influential Welshmen naturally viewed the Tudor dynasty and state as enlargements of the historic Welsh identity, and hitched their wagons to a Crown that had given self-government back to Wales and confirmed the authority of the local rulers.

Possibly the most remarkable exponent of the story of Britain as an ideology for the new imperial state was a London Welshman from a Radnorshire family, John Dee, whose father served at Henry VII's court and who claimed kinship with the Tudors and a lineage that reached back to Rhodri Mawr. Dee was the most famous and most influential of a host of Welsh scholars who impressed the English. The tutor of Robert Dudley, earl of Leicester, the Christian Cabalism of this scientist and mathematician fused with his interest in Arthurian matters to produce a mystical vision of a 'British empire'. His library was huge, with over 4,000 books, and became the resort of courtiers and poets, navigators and mathematicians, historians and antiquaries, but most notably, of Sir Philip Sidney and his circle. Dee's ideas were at the core of a politico-religious programme which proclaimed the foreign expansion of Elizabeth's England at the same time as it saw the Tudors as the ancient British line returned to power and restoring the ancient British Church. Dee's neo-platonism underlies Spenser's vision of Gloriana. His anti-Papal and anti-Spanish ideology gave Raleigh and other Elizabethan navigators and privateers legitimacy in their attacks on Spanish America and in their hopes of colonization. The publication by Humphrey Llwyd in 1594 of the story of Prince Madoc's adventures in America, together with associated Welsh tales weaving in Roman Emperor Magnus Maximus (*Macsen Wledig*), Emperor Constantine and Helen, provided a ready weapon against Philip II's Spain.

While Dee's mathematical genius was of enormous practical importance to navigators and privateers, his neo-platonist magic fell rapidly out of fashion. As early as 1583 Dee was attacked by the mob as a conjuror and devil-dealer (though he himself claimed to speak with angels), and his laboratory at Mortlake was sacked. He was condemned by John Foxe and was an obvious target for Puritans. He died in poverty in 1608. The sacred visions he shared with Cecil and Sidney, Spenser and Leicester had had their moment; their appeal faded, but the loyalty that Welsh gentlemen and intellectuals had given to Elizabeth was readily transferred to James I, likewise a descendant of Henry Tudor. James himself saw the assimilation of the Welsh as a model for his own nostrums of the unity of Scotland, England and Wales. This loyalty was transferred again to Charles; it was the Church and the state that he inherited to which the gentry owed their own power and rule. In 1642 what Puritan leaders there were in Wales fled as the majority of the gentry aligned themselves with the King and dragged their tenantry into war.

CHAPTER 3

Between Two Revolutions: Wales 1642-1780

PHILIP JENKINS

In 1642 the landed élites which ruled Wales responded over-whelmingly to their king's call for help in putting down his obstreperous parliament. At this time the lords and gentry could still count on the solid – if not enthusiastic – support of the common people, who were their clients and their tenants. The landowners could also rely on the bards and poets to sing their praises as loyal defenders of the Crown, and on the Anglican clergy to pray for their successes, and both the poems of praise and the prayers for success were likely to have been in the Welsh language. Still in the mid-seventeenth century, the powerful men and women who owned the great houses and estates generally spoke Welsh as well as English, and saw themselves as the flower of Welsh culture.

A few of the Welsh who fought in the Civil Wars would live on into the new century, and survive to see the first stirrings of a completely different world in which so many of the old assumptions would melt away. Though the old élites, the landed classes, kept a firm hand on political authority, and indeed grew ever richer, the foundations of their authority were being systematically undermined, to the extent that some radicals portrayed them as alien occupiers. The old power system based in the manor-house, the castle and the church came under increasing assault as the eighteenth century progressed.

Ultimately, the most important change, and the foundation of all that would follow, was the transformation of the economy. Though there was no single or overnight event that we can call an industrial revolution, industry, economic modernization, commercial expansion, and the growth of towns all had a major impact on some regions of Wales, which began a period of prolonged expansion. By the 1760s, the pace of change was accelerating with frightening speed. The industrial boom called into existence a whole new range of occupations and social categories, and reshaped networks of trade and transportation. We even find the first industrial magnates potentially rich enough to challenge the great landlords.

Cultural change was no less explosive. While in 1642 Welsh was the common language for the whole society, by 1760 only a few major landlords or squires could muster anything beyond a few conversational phrases. Obviously, the new élites had no interest in sponsoring bards and traditional Welsh culture, which withered rapidly during the early eighteenth century. As language became a critical class division, so did religion. Traditional Church loyalties were strained to breaking point by the rise of new religious movements. Protestant Nonconformity and later Methodism reshaped the whole thought-world of their believers. While language was not a contentious issue between Anglicans and Dissenters in the seventeenth century, it increasingly became so in later decades. This development threatened to leave the established Church in the unenviable position of an English Church serving a Welsh population, with the parson as a kind of private house chaplain to the landlord.

Around 1770, we hear the first suggestions of the genuinely subversive idea that perhaps the *real* Wales was to be found not among the élites, but in that mass of the ordinary people who spoke the old language, and who were increasingly likely to belong to dissident religious sects. From this point of view, the traditional landed rulers of society were outsiders, invaders, and the parsons were their paid hirelings. At first, this revised notion of Welshness was confined to a few intellectuals and cultural activists but, by the end of the eighteenth century, their ideas found an audience exactly in the burgeoning towns and industrial centres that were emerging as the nerve-centres of the new 'improved' Wales. Issues of language and religion were indissolubly linked to themes of ethnicity, class, culture and, ultimately, of nationality.

IMPROVERS

Seventeenth-century Wales was notorious for its poverty and remoteness, and countless satires mocked the land for its steep crags and thorny shrubs, its neck-breaking roads, its stereotypical thistles, goats, leeks, and (inevitably) cheese. Of course, this parody neglects some real centres of prosperity and flourishing mixed agriculture along the southern coastal fringe and through much of the border country, but Wales seemed extraordinarily unlikely to play an important role in the economic development of the British Isles. The country had every possible disadvantage. In fact, Wales survives as a distinct entity exactly because of difficulties of transportation and communication which made most of the country inaccessible from England. However, these same features also created fundamental and quite intractable internal divisions.

Wales was an agglomeration of many different societies and regions. They lacked an urban centre to unite disparate areas, or at least, the centres which did exist were all to be found across the English border. Wales had no natural capital and, until the mid-eighteenth century, the largest centres were market towns like Wrexham, Swansea, Haverfordwest and Brecon, each of which had a population of only 2,000 to 3,000, paltry by the standards of provincial England. Though the Welsh liked to give towns like Carmarthen the title of 'the London of Wales', English visitors understandably found these claims ludicrous. In 1642, no town with a population of 500 was to be found in the large, empty quadrilateral bounded by Cardigan, Builth, Ruthin and Caernarfon. Without a Welsh city, the country's regions still looked towards English metropolitan centres, chiefly to Chester, Shrewsbury and Bristol.

Economic life in Stuart Wales depended on exporting agricultural produce within these metropolitan regions, chiefly cattle and wool, but corn became a leading item of southern trade by the 1650s. Though there were some scattered industrial ventures, mainly in flannels, stockings and other textiles, this was overwhelmingly an agricultural economy. Welsh trade and commerce largely depended on coastal shipping: though Welsh roads were proverbially among the worst in the British Isles, it is easy to forget how people avoided these problems by using the sea routes, often from one of the dozens of tiny harbours that dotted the Welsh coastline. The 'Severn Sea' trade was critical for towns like Cardiff, Swansea, Carmarthen, Tenby and Haverfordwest, and their hinterlands, and the four Bristol-oriented shires of the south coast enjoyed the liveliest commercial life in the whole of Wales. North Wales similarly looked to Chester as its regional capital, especially the three substantial towns of Wrexham, Denbigh and Caernarfon.

From the 1680s onwards, the Welsh economy began a process of rapid change, and the first half of the eighteenth century was a bustling time in much of the Principality, even before the much-studied take off of the iron industry in the 1750s. Though coal and iron enterprises dated back centuries, a new surge of growth about 1690 followed the discovery that iron could be smelted by means of coke, rather than charcoal. This gave enormous advantages to areas like the Swansea Bay region in which coal supplies could be found conveniently near port facilities. In 1689, moreover, Britain began its long series of wars with France, with all the demand that implied for iron, copper and brass. Thankfully for the Welsh economy, lasting peace would not be restored until 1815. Also critical was the establishment of a new political tranquillity in Ireland following the wars of 1689-90, as so many of Wales's commercial links lay across the Irish Sea. Whatever the wrongs of the 'Protestant Ascendancy', the long decades of Irish prosperity were a great boon to Wales.

From the 1690s, new companies began to exploit the lead and copper resources of west Wales, and Sir Humphrey Mackworth began a massive expansion of iron and coal enterprises in the Neath area. He soon became the crucial figure in the Welsh industry of his day. Mackworth conceived the daring notion of an interdependent economic region, in which lead or copper ores would be shipped from west Wales or Ireland to Neath, where they would be smelted, thereby expanding the market for his local coal. Mackworth's enterprises were also daring in technological terms: by 1700, his coal-mines were using steam engines and tramways, and his miners digging ever deeper shafts. He looks very much like the prototype of the great entrepreneurs who made the fortunes of Victorian Wales, and his example inspired his neighbours – or, to be more exact, made them very jealous. But by about 1710, other landlords were enthusiastically promoting their own coal-mines, iron-works and copper-smelting enterprises. By 1730, Swansea had become the metallurgical centre that it would remain for two centuries, and industrial communities emerged across western Glamorgan and eastern Carmarthenshire, roughly from Aberafan to Carmarthen. Already, Swansea had become a major port for the export of coal to the south-western counties of England, as well as Ireland and France. Wales was also providing one sixth of British pig-iron.

Industry also had its negative side. Already by 1710, Neath and some of the villages around Swansea were facing some of the appalling problems of pollution and environmental destruction which always accompany the smelting of lead and copper. Fights over water and natural resources gave an extra edge to long-standing faction battles between gentry families, who mobilized their tenants and workers to mob and riot against their competitors. But for better or worse, parts of Wales had entered an era in which industry was decisive for economic life.

By the standards of the later industrial revolution, the developments of the Mackworth era were on a petty scale but, even so, they had ramifications through the whole economy. Industrial growth increased the need for food production, and thus for agricultural 'improvement' – which became as fashionable a word in the early eighteenth century as 'development' would be in the late twentieth. Though regularly denounced as primitive by English observers, agriculture in parts of Wales developed quite rapidly, with lime fertilizer being used effectively along much of the south coast. New rotations allowed the cultivation of crops which could feed livestock through the long winter, and prevent the need to slaughter a portion of the herd at the start of the winter (this practice explains why the Welsh word for November is *Tachwedd*, 'slaughter'). Welsh farmers were early pioneers of turnips, which provided the long-needed winter fodder. In the later seventeenth century, grazing was improved by the introduction of clover, while in Georgian times, the southern coastal counties experimented with new sown grasses. Change was piecemeal through the early eighteenth century, but the Breconshire Agricultural Society, established in 1755, was the first of a wave of county-based organizations which systematically promoted innovation.

Improvement encouraged the growth of middle-class and professional groups which hitherto had been so scarce in the Welsh social landscape. This was a great era for attorneys and stewards, who could manipulate old feudal privileges in order to help their employers exploit water and mineral rights, while asserting the lord's right to encroach on common lands. In farming matters too, expertise was at a premium: stewards could be highly professional, improving estates by consolidating holdings, promoting larger farms and encouraging the use of leases. Change also tended to be cumulative: the more individuals there were with industrial or commercial expertise, the more managers and engineers, the larger the skilled workforce, the more likely it was that future opportunities would be exploited, and that industrial growth would carry on unchecked.

The economic boom of the first half of the eighteenth century had geographical effects far beyond the immediate west Glamorgan area. In fact, well before the industrial breakout of the great years of iron-making, Wales was already reshaping itself into a modern society, with widespread European and transatlantic connections. It was also creating service networks and even a rudimentary leisure industry, and it was acquiring the professional middle class which Wales had never really had hitherto. The population grew from perhaps 380,000 in 1670 to just over 480,000 by 1750.

We can see the process of improvement at work across the country. The opportunity to exploit mineral wealth raised the value of land in hitherto poor counties like Cardiganshire, and as Aberystwyth flourished through its ore exports, the town came to dominate Cardigan Bay, displacing older competitors which slid into genteel decay. In 1726, Daniel Defoe found Aberystwyth 'enriched by the coals and lead which is found in the neighborhood, and is a populous, but a very dirty, black, smoky place . . . However, they are rich, and the place is very populous.' Before this time, it would never have occurred to English tourists to apply phrases like 'rich' and 'very populous' to Welsh towns, which they generally despised. Other industrial centres grew independently elsewhere in Wales, with the brass and copper industries of Holywell, tinplate at Pontypool and textiles at Dolgellau.

The eighteenth century was a great age for the Welsh ports: while large centres like Swansea benefited from the growth of imperial commerce with America, Africa and the West Indies, the towns of Cardigan Bay had trading links across the Irish Sea. By 1720,

Caernarfon had even begun a respectable trade in slate, though the industry was still tiny in comparison with the enormous development at the end of the century. Commercial success was enhanced by privateering ventures during wartime, in other words, by licensed piracy.

Welsh towns were not merely getting bigger, they were also gaining an air of civilization to accompany the new prosperity, to satisfy the aspirations of both the established gentry and the new middling classes. As Defoe noted, 'politeness' and English manners tended to follow trade: the people of Swansea were 'more civilized and more courteous than in the more mountainous parts . . . But here as they seem to converse with the rest of the country by their commerce, so they are more conversible than their neighbours.' Civility had many manifestations. A Welsh printing industry developed at Carmarthen in the 1720s, and at Cowbridge in the 1770s; we also see the spread of cultural societies, book societies and libraries, and a well-recognized entertainment circuit was travelled regularly by theatre companies and lecturers. There were even attempts to rid the streets of the most gruesome threats to public health and comfort, and improve public hygiene. Cardiff, Swansea and Bridgend all tried to mimic London paving and lighting in the 1760s and 1770s, and many towns acquired impressive new public building – Montgomery's town hall stands today as a good example. Masonic lodges provide a useful index of the dissemination of a town-based social and political fad, in which professional and middle-class groups participated alongside landed gentry. The first Welsh lodge appeared at Carmarthen in 1726, and fourteen more followed between 1741 and 1770, all founded in towns, mainly in the south. The progress of improvement is suggested by Cowbridge, which stood in perhaps the most prosperous and gentrified landscape in Wales, and which was long known for its grammar school and gentry social gatherings. In the 1760s and 1770s, its attractions included races, a book society, an assembly room, and a masonic lodge, and by 1774 the town was praised for its 'broad and handsome' main street. Monmouth, too, aspired to improve itself to attract respectable visitors from near and far.

By the 1780s, every large or medium-sized town could offer at least one substantial inn, and the appearance of new inns and improved roads encouraged the opening of Wales to tourism, following the discovery of the 'picturesque' by the English upper classes. In 1770, Rev William Gilpin published his pioneering account of a tour in quest of the 'picturesque beauty' of the Principality, beginning a genre of similar travel memoirs that would endure for a century. Welsh towns took advantage of new tourist fads like sea-bathing and spas, which made leisure centres out of Swansea, Aberystwyth, Tenby and Llandrindod Wells. As in modern days, historical monuments like medieval abbeys and castles offered added attractions in otherwise fading centres like Caerphilly, Kidwelly and Harlech. Defoe believed that 'there are more tokens of antiquity to be seen everywhere in Wales than in any particular part of England, except the counties of Cumberland and Northumberland'. Only a few observers noted the irony that the Welsh were proudly displaying as their national heritage structures originally built to suppress their ancestors: in this vein, Thomas Pennant famously characterized Caernarfon Castle as 'the most magnificent badge of our subjection'.

The pace of development accelerated from the middle of the century, mainly due to factors far beyond the borders of Wales. By far the most important element was the successive wars and international crises in which the British nation-state found itself engaged between 1740 and 1815. These events increased Welsh commitment to an imperial/colonial economic framework that thrived on naval successes, and which drew the Welsh towns into a war economy based on the production of iron, copper, tinplate, lead and brass, and the coal needed to sustain these industries. The main beneficiaries were established towns like Swansea but, from the 1760s, iron production moved into the uplands of Glamorgan and Gwent, especially around the ancient parish of Merthyr Tydfil, which up to this point had been a remote pastoral landscape. Between 1759 and 1765, however, some of the most famous names in the history of the iron industry appear in this region, with the establishment of the works at Dowlais, Plymouth, Tredegar and Cyfarthfa. Another rash of new works was created during the American war twenty years later, and yet another with the French wars of the 1790s.

Already by the 1780s, the south Wales iron industry was dominated by the families who would be legends of Victorian industry, names like Crawshay, Guest, Hill and Homfray. Moreover, the coal industry was carried along on the coat-tails of iron: as iron production advanced, so did extraction of the coal on which smelting depended. More demand for coal meant seeking out deeper seams, which could only be obtained with adequate drainage, and that, in turn, needed better steam engines. Steam power had been known in Wales since the days of Humphrey Mackworth but, by the end of the eighteenth century, we find the first of the efficient new Watt engines.

Industry demanded a much better communications system than anything Wales had known before. Improvement in this sphere began in the 1750s, with new roads spreading out from Shrewsbury to the leading towns of mid- and north Wales, such as Wrexham, Welshpool and Mold, and the emergence of turnpikes in the south. Sometimes, the incentive for improvement can be seen as a near-desperate response by industrialists anxious to link their remote eyries in the Welsh uplands with markets and with raw materials. In 1767, it was a Merthyr ironmaster who sponsored the development of a new road from Cardiff to Merthyr Tydfil. Canals promised a more effective solution to the dilemma of transporting heavy cargoes. In 1766, the first Welsh canal was built at Kidwelly, though there was then a delay before the major expansion got under way in the 1780s. Naturally. all were located in the powerhouse region of the south-east, roughly between Swansea, Brecon and Newport.

The rapid expansion of industry and communications promoted the development of towns on a scale far larger than anything ever seen before in Wales: by 1790, Swansea, Carmarthen and the brand-new community of Merthyr-Dowlais all had 6,000 to 7,000 residents apiece, and a number of other ports and industrial centres in the uplands were beginning an impressive growth in population. The population of Wales grew from 480,000 in 1750 to 587,000 by 1801. These trends fundamentally reoriented Welsh social geography, with far-reaching implications for culture and politics. In particular, the emergence of Swansea and Merthyr Tydfil meant that, for the first time, the Welsh economy was emancipated from the domination of English cities like Bristol. By the 1780s, we find the first distinctively Welsh urban network based on Welsh towns and Welsh urban élites. Professional communities and financial services developed apace in Welsh towns at the end of the century, mainly in the southern industrial regions.

Though modernization seemed to be racing ahead, obviously Wales did not suddenly become an urban industrial nation. Even in 1801, the counties of Glamorgan and Monmouthshire comprised only a fifth of the population of Wales, and not until the expansion of the coal industry after 1840 would industry achieve its absolute dominance of the Welsh economy. Still, the growth of industry did have its effects through much of the country: on farmers selling their produce or livestock to the new industrial towns, with their ever-expanding need for butter and cheese, potatoes and meat, for wool and flannel shirts; on rural villages whose young people began migrating to the strange settings of industrial Wales, leaving painful labour shortages in their home areas; and of course, on the workers who now depended directly upon wages earned in the monstrous iron furnaces and the hellish pits. Already in 1780, the contours of nineteenth-century industrialism were taking shape.

ENTHUSIASTS

Though the eighteenth century was a heady time for the Welsh economy, most histories of Wales devote at least as much time to describing the nation's religious experience in these years as they do its economic fate. This emphasis is true for most periods, from the time of the Roman Catholics and recusants under the Tudors to the early Puritans and Nonconformists of the seventeenth century, from the rise of Methodism in the eighteenth through the transforming revivals of the Victorian era. It sometimes seems as if Welsh historians are obsessed with religious controversies and denominational differences. At one level, this emphasis reflects the attitudes of those scholars in the nineteenth and early twentieth centuries who did so much to define that history, as authors were often clergy themselves, or else their whole social and political outlook was coloured by their religious beliefs. So much of the politics of Victorian and Edwardian Wales was shaped by the fundamental split between Church and chapel. But in the seventeenth and eighteenth centuries, there were plenty of other reasons to concentrate on the religious context of life. For most of the period, the established Church not only dominated spiritual life, demanding attendance at its approved services, but also controlled many other aspects of existence that we today would divide among a dozen other institutions and official agencies. The Church was the main arm of social welfare and poor relief. It regulated education as well as matters of marriage and probate, while Church courts decided local conflicts between neighbours. The clergy could be enormously influential figures in the local community, which was required to support the religious establishment through compulsory tithes, a virtual 10 per cent tax on all produce. Any change in the organization or ideology of the Church necessarily had a huge impact on the wider society.

Seventeenth-century Welsh politics revolved around attitudes to the Church: should it be a hierarchical national structure with bishops, as orthodox Anglicans believed, or should the deciding voice be in councils of ministers, on Presbyterian lines? Or, still more radical, should the nation do without a national Church at all, and move towards independent congregations made up of voluntary communities of believers? Each view had far-reaching implications for the powers and authority of the state, and the rights and status of individual believers. In each case, too, the matter of organization was closely linked to that of toleration. How far could the community enforce beliefs, and should it do so with the support of the state? This was a knotty question for all Protestants, who believed in the supreme importance of the Bible as interpreted by the individual believer, unassisted by priests. Throughout this period, religious activists of all persuasions promoted the growth of schools where ordinary people could learn to read the Bible, and thus become better Protestant Christians. The problem was that, left to themselves, people tended to find in the Scriptures all sorts of lessons, religious, social and political, some of which seemed like the darkest heresy to conservatives. If the Bible was the highest authority, what room did that leave for a Church? Or, perhaps, for a king or a landlord? And if that question seemed over-dramatic, the experience of the mid-seventeenth century showed that religious controversies could overthrow a social order. No line separated religion and politics, matters of Church and state.

Before 1642, the main religious division in Wales was between mainstream Anglicans and a handful of Roman Catholic resisters, who were mainly concentrated in Monmouthshire and Flintshire. The Civil

Wars, however, allowed the sudden growth of new radical Puritan sects, whose members became the ancestors of the Dissenters or Nonconformists who played so vital a role in Welsh culture and politics into modern times. When the king's party was defeated in 1648, the new regime fostered the growth of new Puritan congregations, some of which rejected the whole idea of a state Church, and adopted heretical theological ideas. Through its Commission for the Propagation of the Gospel in Wales, the government supported networks of itinerant preachers funded from confiscated Anglican properties. The aim was to spread radical Puritan ideas throughout the 'dark corners of the land', and what corner could be darker than Anglican, royalist, gentry-dominated Wales? Even more frightening for the traditionally minded was that the most radical sects, like the Baptists and Quakers, were well represented in the armed forces which ruled the country in the 1650s. If there was one thing worse than a heretic, it was a heretic with a cannon.

Through this decade, there was a steady drift to ever greater religious extremism, and moderate Puritans were outraged when they were outflanked on the Left by the new sect of the Quakers. Across Wales, Quakers stood up and preached against the ministers during church services; they refused to pay tithes; they declined the traditional signs of social respect, addressing their superiors as 'thou'; and they asserted the superiority of the inner spirit to the Scriptures themselves. Shockingly, some of those who performed these anarchic acts were women. The representatives of the old order might wish to curb these excesses at all costs, but they were excluded from power: the mighty had been cast from their seats.

To understand just how radical these times were, we might look at the case of one man who represented an entirely new type in the political history of Wales, in that he exercised vast power on a basis quite different from that of the traditional landowner: indeed, a career like Vavasor Powell's (1617-70) would have been inconceivable in any previous era. He was born in Knucklas, Radnorshire, the son of a petty gentleman, and he became a schoolmaster. In ordinary times he might have risen no further, but these were extraordinary times, and astonishing mobility suddenly became possible for a person on the right political side. By 1640, Vavasor had become a militant Puritan, and he served as an army chaplain for the Parliamentary forces in mid-Wales.

After the Wars he became a radical millenarian, expecting that Christ would come soon to rule the earth for a thousand years. Vavasor was a major sponsor of the Propagation scheme to convert Wales by itinerant preachers, and throughout the 1650s his followers represented the extreme radical wing of the Puritan cause. These were armed saints, with the power to enforce their will against the squires and parsons who had hitherto dominated the Welsh countryside. Even after the Stuart kings were restored in 1660, Vavasorian congregations continued to meet illegally in Radnorshire, Breconshire and Glamorgan, and many members were former captains and colonels. Understandably, government supporters found it hard to distinguish between congregational gatherings and reunions of Roundhead veterans: were they praying, or plotting a new religious revolution; seeking a kingdom in heaven or on earth?

Vavasor and his allies did not think in terms of the future – how could they, as the world was so obviously about to end? – but they planted better than they knew, and a century or two later, Nonconformist congregations still grew from the old Puritan roots. In 1763, the local Anglican clergyman in Merthyr Tydfil tried to explain to his bishop just why there were so few loyal Church followers in his area. He had no doubt that things had gone terribly wrong during the civil war years: 'Before the Grand Rebellion', he wrote, '[they] were not so many, but in those unhappy times of usurpation multiplied apace, took firm footing, and overspread this part of the country every way.' When industry emerged in eighteenth-century Wales, it was generally in areas like these, where Church power had never been strong, and where the Puritans had made such strides in Cromwellian times. Radical Nonconformity had a long head start in evangelizing the emerging industrial towns.

The experience of the 1650s remained a lively memory in Welsh politics for two hundred years. For the heirs of the Puritans, this was a kind of godly golden age, but for the old gentry and Anglican clergy, it was the ultimate nightmare, the rule of the devil. When Charles II returned in 1660, the old élites were restored to power too, and they spent the next half century trying to root out the Puritans, who were now also called Dissenters or Nonconformists. In the process, the persecution left Nonconformity with a deep and lingering hostility towards the landed and clerical élites, resentments which would still galvanize political action in Victorian times. They also took their revenge in more recent times, when Nonconformist historians established the fiction that Wales between about 1660 and 1740 was enduring a kind of dark age, a time of social and political stagnation, a deep spiritual sleep which only ended with the Methodist revival.

This was no mere battle for the political upper hand. The Anglicans were trying very sincerely to wipe out the very name of the sects, the Presbyterians and Independents, Baptists and Quakers, and to some extended they succeeded. Most of the Quakers migrated in the 1680s, fleeing to a haven in Pennsylvania, where they built their Welsh Barony, their new Merion, Radnor, Haverford, and Gwynedd, adjacent to the 'Welsh Mountains'. By 1700, Welsh Quakers and Baptists made up perhaps a third of the new colony's 20,000 white settlers. The founders of the new Welsh Tract hoped that 'we might live together as a civil society to endeavor to settle all controversies and debates amongst ourselves, in a gospel order, and not to entangle ourselves with laws in an unknown tongue ... to preserve our language, that we might ever keep correspondence with our friends in the land of our nativity'. William Penn even wanted to call his whole new colony New Wales, before he was overruled by the king. No wonder that the ever-optimistic Welsh claimed that his name indicated Welsh origins as well as sympathies: surely, it must be *pen* (head)? But even if they were disappointed in the colony's name, the exiles could not be dissatisfied with the outcome of Penn's venture, which marked a crucial phase in the Welsh diaspora.

Though removed from the British Isles, Welsh radicals flourished in their new environment, and many became prominent in American public life. In the first half of the eighteenth century, cantankerous country Quakers like David Lloyd opposed any authoritarian tendencies in Pennsylvania's provincial government with all the zeal with which their forebears had challenged the Stuart kings at home. Most of the colony's doctors in the eighteenth century were Welsh, as were such élite Philadelphia dynasties and financial magnates as the Morrises, Lloyds and Cadwalladers. The present writer is based at the Pennsylvania State University, which was founded in 1855 by a fifth-generation Pennsylvania Welsh Quaker with the pristine name of Evan Pugh, and the Evan Pugh Professorship remains the highest honour which the institution can bestow. The Welsh share of

Pennsylvania's population fell steadily during the eighteenth century, to perhaps only 5 per cent by 1790, but Pennsylvania had definitively become what it would remain into the twentieth century, namely a nucleus of Welsh cultural as well as radical sentiment. In the 1720s, stonemason Ellis Pugh published his *Annerch i'r Cymru* (Salute to Wales) in Philadelphia, while that city's St David's Society is today the oldest extant ethnic society in the United States. Even the Baptist tradition, which has been so immensely significant throughout American history, largely traces its origins to Welsh exile congregations founded in south-eastern Pennsylvania between 1682 and 1700. This early settlement of Pennsylvania laid the foundations for what would be a long and deeply rewarding relationship between Wales and America.

Though Dissent survived in Wales, the threat to the established order had been contained, and the Dissenting population remained static from the end of the century, around 7 per cent of the whole. Their influence was also geographically limited, as their main centres of strength were in and around towns closely connected with English centres like Bristol: over two-thirds of Welsh Dissenters lived in the three southern shires of Monmouth, Glamorgan and Carmarthen. Outside the south-east, Dissent had virtually no presence in most of rural Wales. Even after the Dissenters were granted toleration in the early eighteenth century, their numbers contracted because toleration was very different from equality: a Dissenter could not hold political office or attend one of the universities, and a family had to suffer the stigma that prevented it from social advancement. New generations tended to drift back into the Anglican Church, especially if they had any social ambitions. Nonconformist congregations themselves became sober and respectable bodies, led by learned ministers, but the groups had a bad habit of falling apart over theological disputes which seem petty and incomprehensible to later generations.

It seemed that the Church had restored its position, if not its monopoly, but religious enthusiasm tended to break out where and when it was least expected: and we should recollect that 'enthusiasm' in this age was not a complimentary word, but rather suggested what today we might call cult-like fanaticism. At the end of the seventeenth century, an Anglican group began a campaign to spread schooling and literacy among the poor, with a view to making them better Christians through Bible-reading. These charity schools were particularly successful in the south-west, where they were supported by pious gentry, including Sir Humphrey Mackworth. In this area the charity schools were brilliantly promoted by the Anglican cleric Griffith Jones of Llanddowror, who made this educational movement the seed-bed of a religious revival. Jones was the mentor of several other clergy who experienced emotional conversions in the 1730s, and who went on to launch the religious revival which was perhaps the most important single cultural event in eighteenth-century Wales. This group included Daniel Rowland of Llangeitho, who was a young Anglican curate when he was converted by Griffith Jones about 1735, a year when Wales seemed to be ignited by the Holy Spirit. Rowland went on to become one of the two or three greatest Welsh preachers of the century, and he made Llangeitho a 'Methodist Mecca'. It may be coincidence, but the areas in which the revivals were burning most brightly by 1740 were exactly those regions of the south where Jones's charity schools were also being founded. As in the 1650s, popular religious schooling expanded alongside the work of wandering evangelists.

One of the greatest of the new evangelists was Howell Harris (1714-73), who seems almost like a reincarnation of Vavasor Powell, if we can so mix our religious traditions: at least, he had Vavasor's brilliant talent for infuriating friends and terrifying foes. Born in Talgarth in Breconshire, Harris became a schoolmaster, like Vavasor had done before him; in early-modern Wales, this was the natural occupation for a bright and bookish young man without the money or connections to succeed in the established Church. Like so many others, he was converted to an emotional evangelical faith in 1735, and he began his own forty-year career of preaching throughout Wales. He contacted Daniel Rowland and, with some other enthusiastic preachers, in 1742 they founded an Association which was the Welsh counterpart of the new Methodist movement in England led by the Wesleys and Whitefield. This body institutionalized the emerging revival, which came to be known as Welsh Methodism. In 1752 Harris built at Trefeca the amazing 'castellated monastery' that would house the followers who had joined his revolutionary religious community, his communist 'family'. Among other innovations, religious. social and cultural, Trefeca became an early centre of Welsh printing, as well as a seminary for preachers.

At many points, Harris's career reminds us of the long-established traditions of religious radicalism that we can find in the Welsh landscape. Consider for example the upper Wye country on the Breconshire/Radnorshire border, just west of Hay on Wye. Among other things, this part of Wales includes the oldest standing Nonconformist chapel, at Maes-yr-Onnen (1696), as well as the rich associations of Trefeca. This region was a Dissenting stronghold at least from the 1640s, and Nonconformists settled here in eras of persecution because it stood on the frontier between different counties and dioceses, so that confused jurisdictions made it more difficult to organize effective legal sanctions. Hay and Llanigon were the bases for a Baptist church that ultimately spread its influence over much of west Wales. From the 1650s onwards, there was a strong Vavasorian Baptist tradition here, in addition to Quaker groups, and the government often had to deal with alleged plots and conspiracies centred around Hay. In 1696, the Independent congregation built their chapel at Maes-yr-Onnen, and in the 1720s the pastor of this congregation ran a school where the pupils included such later evangelical dynamos as Howell Harris and William Williams of Pantycelyn: it was in Talgarth churchyard that Williams was converted through Harris's preaching. The old Dissenters raised in the traditions of the Interregnum were thus a link to the newer radicalism of the next century, and this area long continued to play a central role in the history of enthusiasm. Perhaps it was not just ignorance which led to the country people of Caernarfonshire calling the new Methodist preachers *pengryniaid*, or roundheads. In the 1850s, yet again, the 'school for prophets' at Trefeca would once more send out preachers to launch a searing national revival.

From the 1730s, a national revival was inspired by the preaching of Rowland, Harris and Williams, part of the general religious upsurge across Europe and North America. Throughout the eighteenth century, the Welsh movement was rooted in the established Church, and many of the most devoted preachers and reformers were themselves Anglican clergy, but the movement very soon developed ideas and practices which made this relationship very difficult. From its earliest days, Methodism emphasized dramatic inner conversion and passionate enthusiasm, values far removed from the sober learning of either the Anglican Church or traditional Dissent. Usually through

hearing sermons, converts believed that their sins had consigned them
to eternal fire and damnation, from which they were now saved.
When, in 1773, Thomas Charles heard Daniel Rowland preach, he
described his experience in this way: 'The change a blind man who
receives his sight experiences doth not exceed the change I at that
time experienced in my mind . . . I had such a view of Christ as our
high priest, of his love, compassion, power, and all-sufficiency as
filled my mind with astonishment – with joy unspeakable and full of
glory.' In the immediate thrill of conversion, the appropriate response
was usually wild enthusiasm far removed from concepts of rational
religion, but familiar from accounts of ecstatic religion in all parts of
the world. Typical behaviour included repeated shouts, ejaculations or
rhythmic chants of prayers, coupled with groaning or weeping. In the
late eighteenth century, Welsh revivals were often characterized by
'jumping':

> In the course of a few years, the advocates of groaning and loud
> talking, as well as of loud singing, repeating the same line or stanza
> over and over thirty or forty times, became more numerous, and were
> found among some of the other denominations in the principality . . .
> Several of the most zealous itinerant preachers in Wales recommend
> the people to cry out *Gogoniant* (the Welsh word for Glory), Amen,
> etc. etc. to put themselves in violent agitations; and finally to jump
> until they were quite exhausted, so as often to be obliged to fall down.

Once the realization of salvation came, in a moment of horror and
relief, the only response was to abandon previous evils, and to live a
new life based on personal godliness, coupled with missionary
endeavour towards the still unconverted. New believers struggled
against what they saw as sin in all its forms, and Howell Harris
declared that 'There appeared now a general reformation in several
counties – public diversions became unfashionable, and religion
became the common talk.' This could even mean preaching against
the sins of the rich and powerful, and at Monmouth in 1740, Harris
took his life in his hands when he denounced the assembled lords and
squires of the county for their 'balls, assemblies, horse-races,
whoredom and drunkenness'.

Enthusiasm was to be kept alive by means of new organizational
structures, which critics saw as a subversive parallel framework

within the established Church, beyond the control of bishops and parsons. Each of the charismatic leaders had his following, organized into religious societies, which became a fundamental social institution in much of Wales. Already by 1740, the movement had become a potent sect within the larger Church. Like all new religious movements, the evangelicals succeeded by appealing to groups who did not feel that their needs were met by existing arrangements, namely adolescents and young adults, and especially women, who made up a sizeable majority of many early Methodist societies. Preachers were judged by their spiritual qualities, not their class background: in 1764, Anglican critic Evan Evans complained that the new ministers were drawn from 'weavers, smiths, shoemakers, tailors, and the very meanest handicrafts'. With this cross-class appeal, the revival offered a tremendous sense of excitement and emotional involvement, and it blazed through the country: by 1750, the major centres were heavily concentrated in several areas: around Llanddowror; between Llangeitho and Tregaron; near Trefeca; and in the Vale of Glamorgan. By the 1780s, the Methodist surge was sweeping over regions hitherto untouched by Dissent, especially in the north and west.

The Methodist position in the Anglican establishment became steadily more difficult as mainstream clergy grew ever more hostile to this church-within-the-Church, and the remaining Methodist parsons were increasingly isolated. Still, there was a reluctance to take the natural step, and to secede as a separate denomination, and the decisive break did not come until 1811. Once this long overdue move was accomplished, the established Anglican Church found itself in a grim position as a shrinking minority community, though still holding all the traditional powers to demand tithes and enforce Church law. Church powers actually increased in these years, as governments tended increasingly to appoint clergy as Justices of the Peace, making the local parson both a temporal and spiritual shepherd over a flock that largely rejected the legitimacy of his authority. Much of nineteenth-century Welsh politics would be concerned with resolving this paradoxical position.

BARDS AND DRUIDS

In matters of culture and language, too, the world of 1780 was very different from that of 1642, and here again the differences were tied up with social class. Though the lower and middle classes continued to speak Welsh as their primary language, by the early eighteenth century most of the élite took entirely to English. Henceforward, Welsh culture would become the possession of new and more humble social categories, with their distinctive social and religious preoccupations.

At first sight, the pace of change was not rapid. Throughout the period there was never any doubt that Wales constituted a radically distinct society. In 1780, as in 1642, at least 90 per cent of the people of the thirteen traditional counties spoke Welsh with some fluency, and the usage spilled over the border into Herefordshire and Shropshire. The people also tended to use the old Celtic custom of patronymics, so that the son of David William was John David, and his son was Henry John. Only very gradually did families adopt the English custom of surnames, so that the descendants of Henry John all assumed the name of Jones, and the replacement of patronymics by surnames was a process under way from the sixteenth century through to the nineteenth, beginning with the upper classes and moving progressively down the social scale. A permanent surname was commonly the first acquisition of a rising family on the make.

In 1642, Welsh people of all classes were still clearly conscious of belonging to a distinctive culture, but this did not translate into political activism, still less nationalism. Geography did much to ensure this: then as now, the most obvious schism in Wales is that between north and south, a point clearly indicated by the progress of the Civil Wars in Wales, which involved two distinct and barely related series of campaigns. The process of industrialization in Wales likewise involved two quite unrelated centres, one in the south-eastern shires, with another north-eastern focus in the counties of Denbigh and Flint. Below this fundamental division, we have already seen that Wales lacked an obvious capital, and its main regional divisions were related to English towns. Nor were there any 'national' structures or institutions to define or characterize Welshness, nothing which might overcome geographical obstacles. There was neither a Welsh parliament nor a separate Church, not even a metropolitan to co-ordinate the activities of the four dioceses, no 'Archbishop of Wales'.

Welshness therefore depended on language, and the associated culture. Around 1640, Welsh continued to be well known and used at all levels of Welsh society, up to the wealthiest aristocrats, who often emerge as fervent cultural patriots. Even the Earl of Worcester, one of the wealthiest aristocrats in England or Wales, was one 'who does not hesitate to speak Welsh and to cherish and magnify it in a clearly British manner', while Sir Edward Stradling of Glamorgan was 'the chief cherisher of our Welsh language in south Wales'. Also in Glamorgan, during the 1630s, the wealthy gentry family of Lewis of Van employed three tutors for their children, one each for the Latin, French and Welsh tongues. Not until the end of the century did the Welsh gentry and aristocracy cease to patronize manifestations of traditional Welsh culture such as bardic poetry or the music of the harp. Like their predecessors for many centuries past, the great Welsh poets pursued their ancient task of praising the generosity and heroism of their noble landed patrons.

Under the Stuarts, Welsh cultural patriotism was intimately bound up with the values of the Anglican landed élite, and with Church-and-King politics. From Elizabethan times onwards, the Church in Wales used a Welsh Bible and liturgy, and some of the most active defenders of traditional poetry and literature were themselves senior clerics. One of the greatest was Humphrey Humphreys, who served as bishop of Bangor from 1689 to 1701, who was described by the great scholar and linguist Edward Lhuyd as 'incomparably the best skilled in our antiquities of any person in Wales'. Humphreys received the appropriate tributes from the bards, he patronized a circle of Welsh antiquaries among his local clergy, and he even carried out his episcopal visitation in Welsh. Welshness was neatly integrated into Protestant ideology, as antiquarian-minded clergy claimed that the Protestant Reformation was only restoring the authentic religious ideas of ancient Wales, before they had been trampled underfoot by conquering Anglo-Saxon Catholics. Welsh scholars and antiquaries devoted themselves to historical scholarship, and in the process of analysing the past, the antiquaries would produce some remarkably radical manifestations of national resentment, as the story they recounted so often involved the crushing of Welsh national aspirations by English and Norman overlords.

Between about 1680 and 1720, the Anglican clergy secured a virtual hegemony over the traditional culture of Wales, and some of the most influential works of Welsh scholarship were written by clerics like Theophilus Evans, author of *Drych y Prif Oesoedd* (The Mirror of the Early Ages). Another parish clergyman of enormous ability was Ellis Wynne who, in 1703, published *Gweledigaethau y Bardd Cwsc* (The Visions of the Sleeping Bard), one of the greatest works of Welsh prose. Griffith Jones of Llanddowror boasted that the Welsh language was 'unalterably the same, is now perhaps the same she was four thousand years ago; still retains the beauties of her youth, grown old in years, but not decayed'.

Yet even at this height of patriotic achievement, the age of Edward Lhuyd and Elis Wynne, matters were changing fundamentally. Élite support for Welsh culture was withering at an alarming rate, partly because old families were drawn to the rival attractions of London, and already in 1682, a violently anti-Welsh tract called the *Wallography* noted with satisfaction how 'the native gibberish' was receding in the market towns, while ''Tis usually cashiered out of gentlemen's houses . . . the *Lingua* will be English'd out of Wales'. This was premature, but demographic changes soon made this 'cashiering' a reality. Across Wales, old families were dying out in the male line, and their estates inherited by relatives from Cheshire or Somerset, who had little sympathy with local traditions: Humphrey Mackworth himself was such a new man with new ideas, a Shropshire squire who acquired a Glamorgan estate by marrying the heiress of an old Welsh line. Some estates passed to absentees who left the great houses in the care of stewards.

Nor did the new masters share the same enthusiasm for appointing Welsh-speaking clergy, and the age of Welsh-speaking bishops now drew to a close: when Bishop John Wynne of St. Asaph died in 1727, he was the last native speaker to serve a Welsh diocese until 1870. Eighteenth-century Church leaders varied in their determination to eliminate Welsh, but one lawsuit over the issue of Welsh-speaking clergy produced an assertion of linguistic imperialism that remains shockingly stark. When one diocese was asked to appoint a Welsh-speaking cleric, the response was simply that 'Wales is a conquered country, it is proper to introduce the English language, and it is the duty of the bishops to endeavour to promote the English . . . It has always been the policy of the legislature to introduce the English language into Wales.'

Lacking élite patronage, the old bardic order faded away in the first quarter of the eighteenth century. By the 1720s, it was increasingly apparent that the old high culture was in grave danger. Old musical notations were already incomprehensible, the instruments were all but extinct, and the difficult poetic metres were fading from memory. A sense of cultural betrayal may explain why Elis Wynne was prepared to condemn Welsh landed society so sharply: the demons of hell are made to say that 'We remember hardly one estate not founded by some oppressor or murderer or arrant thief, leaving it to others as oppressive as themselves, or to lazy blockheads or drunken swine. And to maintain their prodigal pride, vassals and tenants must be crushed' In 1735, John Rhydderch complained of the scarcity of competent poets, finding only 'apathy, faintheartedness and cowardice', and he noted 'the decline from the language and art of our grandfathers', in the days when 'the noblemen were formerly very helpful to the matter'. Welsh radicals had a convenient ideological weapon to hand, in explaining such a betrayal, in the concept of the landlords as the heirs of the Saxon and Norman exploiters who had overthrown free Wales, and this kind of polemic appears widely in the later seventeenth century. A popular movement against the Duke of Beaufort's land enclosures in Monmouthshire was justified in terms of ancient Welsh (and indeed Romano-British) rights usurped by the Norman conquerors English radicals complained of the 'Norman Yoke' imposed by lords and churchmen; their Welsh counterparts faced a 'Saxon Yoke'.

Of course, the desertion of the magnates did not mean that the old culture perished, but it was transformed, and it lost its firm roots in the conservative ideology of the squire and parson. Support now came not from the great manor houses but from quite humble individuals, petty office holders or obscure parish clergy. The best-known activists were the four Morris brothers of Anglesey, the greatest of whom were Lewis and Richard Morris, both civil servants. Incidentally, they represented the first generation of their family to use a surname, as opposed to a patronymic. For decades, the Morrises sought out the remnants of the old poetry and music, ransacking gentry libraries: they developed a network of correspondence among the surviving poets and historians of the day, and circulated their remarkable findings about ancient Welsh literature and music. Reporting the discovery of the sixth-century battle poem the *Gododdin*, Lewis Morris boasted in 1758 that it was 'equal at least to the Iliad, Odyssey or *Paradise Lost*'. In 1751, Richard Morris was the prime mover in creating the first Cymmrodorion Society among the London Welsh: this was a focus for intellectual and literary activism in London and Wales, and served as the model for many other cultural and political organizations in the next century. Members of the Cymmrodorion were urged to speak as much as possible 'in the ancient British language', and the society tried to cultivate links with Wales-over-the-seas in Pennsylvania in the hope of keeping the language alive on those shores.

The loss of the oral tradition of bardism meant that any revival would have to rely on the printed word. Fortunately the work of the Morrises coincided with an upsurge of publishing in the Welsh language. Between 1660 and 1710, 215 books appeared in the Welsh language, compared to an impressive 330 between 1710 and 1730, suggesting that there was a sizeable reading public prepared to support Welsh scholarship. Before 1730, the vast majority of this literature was religious in nature, but literary and antiquarian works began to appear in some numbers. In the 1760s and 1770s, the Cymmrodorion circle published many of the most important works of medieval Welsh poetry, arousing the interest of sophisticated English observers in quest of Gothic antiquity or Celtic romanticism.

Dictionaries and grammatical texts became a vital weapon in preserving the Welsh language from disintegration into mutually incomprehensible dialects and, between 1720 and 1780, Welsh acquired an entirely new degree of stability and even academic respectability. One sign of the new linguistic pride was the *Dissertation of the Welsh language*, published in 1771 by Rev John Walters of Llandough, whose book declares the vital necessity of the language as the basis of Welsh patriotism. As such, it marks a new and more aggressive stage in the revival, and it shows how far the culture had been detached from its old connections with the landed élites. Walters has nothing but contempt for those lords or squires who despise the native tongue: these, 'being Welshmen by birth, have lately commenced Englishmen'. Those who tried to exterminate the language could not be true Ancient Britons, but were instead 'aliens (Normans, Flemings, etc) that have by intrusion formerly got footing in the country'. Though not expressed in terms of class conflict, such a statement had radical implications, as these 'aliens' could be none other than the landlords and their agents. Though Walters's words can be seen as isolated and even extreme at the time, such sentiments became far more commonplace with the radical cultural and political upsurge of the 1790s, and they became something like orthodoxy for Liberal Nonconformists in the nineteenth century.

Yet not all the enemies of the old tongue were 'Normans and Flemings', for in just these years, Welsh culture received another devastating blow, and this time from a quite novel direction. From its early days, the evangelical revival demanded a complete reformation of manners and behaviour among its followers, and this zeal was now turned against the popular culture of traditional Wales, against the musical gatherings and competitions, against harpists and fiddlers, poets and rhymers, sports and dancing. A special target was popular ritual celebrations like the 'Mabsant', in which each church commemorated its founding Celtic saint, and often, indirectly, its pre-Christian roots. Methodist leader Thomas Charles boasted how 'The revival of religion has put an end to all the merry meetings for dancing, singing with the harp, and every kind of sinful mirth which used to be so prevalent amongst young people here.' The traditional musical skills were 'entirely destroyed and abolished'. Even at fairs, which were normally rowdy affairs, Charles was happy to see 'a decency in the conduct and sobriety in the countenances of our country people'. Other observers viewed the change as nothing less than catastrophic. In 1802, Edward Jones complained in a much-quoted passage that 'The sudden decline of the national minstrelsy and customs of Wales is in a great degree to be attributed to the fanatick impostors or illiterate plebeian preachers who have too often been suffered to overrun the country'. Jones reported meeting 'several harpers and songsters who actually had been prevailed upon by those erratic strollers to relinquish their profession from the idea that it was sinful . . . Wales, which was formerly one of the merriest and happiest countries in the world, is now become one of the dullest.' In their passion to create a pure Bible-based society, the evangelicals devastated an ancient rural culture which had survived centuries of political upheavals: the new nation would be Welsh in language, but on the cultural terms imposed by the neo-puritans. This was a sweeping revolution in sensibility, for better or worse, an authentic cultural reformation.

By about 1770, it seemed that Welsh culture would be rigidly divided between the elevated ideas of the intellectuals and antiquarians on the one hand, and the evangelical world of hymns and sermons on the other, with authentic popular traditions altogether wiped out. But matters would take quite a different turn, due in large measure to the work of one man who created a new cultural synthesis drawing on both high and popular elements. In the last quarter of the century, Iolo Morganwg invented nothing less than a national Welsh religious and cultural tradition based on democratic rationalism, with roots supposedly as old as Moses and the Trojan war.

Iolo Morganwg (Edward of Glamorgan) was the bardic name of Edward Williams (1747-1826), a Glamorgan stonemason who was a friend of John Walters. Iolo synthesized existing trends in literary and antiquarian thought to create a bogus Welsh mythology not entirely laid to rest in our own time. Iolo's questionable contribution must be seen in the light of the development of Celtic scholarship since the golden days of the 1690s, when Edward Lhuyd had emerged as one of the finest archaeological and linguistic scholars in British history. Lhuyd showed that Welsh was one of a Celtic family of languages and, as such, the Celts could claim literal and cultural descent from the Gauls described by Caesar, with their warriors and seers, their bards and druids. The druids in particular were fascinating, as leaders of a mystical pre-Christian order with access to who knew what forms of ancient wisdom? They enjoyed a vogue as worshippers of Nature and Reason, precursors of the rational religion of the Enlightenment. And, it was claimed, they had worshipped at stone circles like Stonehenge. Druids made their first significant appearance in modem Welsh historiography in 1723, in Henry Rowlands's book on the rich ancient monuments of Anglesey, *Mona Antiqua Restaurata*. Rowlands tried to reconstruct a whole druidical religion, an enlightened creed that included 'the theory of Nature, astronomy, geometry, medicine, and natural magic'. If there had been such a thing, then it was the rightful inheritance of the Welsh, 'we, the remains of the British nation, who have sole interest in the honour of this ancient Celtic tongue'. Was not druidic worship commemorated everywhere in Wales where there appears the place-name element *llwyn*, or 'grove'?

Caesar said the Celts had druids and bards: Rowlands supplied the druids, Iolo Morganwg provided the bards. Iolo claimed to have made contact with poetic circles in the Glamorgan hill country, who he identified as the last survivors of the ancient bardic tradition, and who held local *Eisteddfod* competitions. Incidentally, these representatives of Welsh culture were definitely plebeian men, artisans and hill-farmers, and often Nonconformists, nothing like the loyalist bards who had once wandered between the great houses of Wales. For them, as for Walters, Welsh culture had become the property and birthright of the common people. Iolo's own contempt for his supposed betters among the gentry emerges from his bitter remark: 'Hang foxhounds and those kind of sad dogs called foxhunters, who import foxes into the country for the savage sport of hunting them, or breaking their tenants' gates or fences, and otherwise injure them. Fortunately for the world, they sometimes in breaking down a five barred gate break their own necks. Amen. So be it.' In religious matters, he belonged to the most radical sect of the day, the Unitarians: what else was a rational neo-druid to do in the eighteenth century?

By the 1780s, Iolo was making sensational claims about what he had learned from the poets of the hill country and found in their libraries. He declared that the bardic order had maintained its traditions in remote rural areas and that he had been initiated into it. In support of this notion, he offered written accounts of bardic meetings and decisions tracing back over the centuries. In reviving the bardic craft he also attempted to show its druidical roots, and plundered Rowlands mercilessly. The druids were only part of a one-man industry of forgery and invention that offered helpful evidence about every aspect of the history of Wales, and especially his cherished Glamorgan, from prehistoric times into the eighteenth century: but if people had accepted the genuine finds of the Morrises, why should they not believe his fabrications?

By the 1780s, Iolo had devised the whole farrago of robes and stone circles that are so powerful a component of the modern Eisteddfod movement and, in 1792, he began initiating enthusiasts into his druidical circle, the *Gorsedd*. The druid craze reached new heights in the decade following the French Revolution, when new democratic concepts of Welsh nationality came into being, taking particular root in the new industrial areas: in this, as in so much else, Iolo foreshadowed, and in part invented, the radical Welsh culture which came to fruition in the early nineteenth century.

Between 1793 and 1815, the perils of war overseas persuaded many English tourists to focus their attentions on Wales instead, and the land they found was radically different from what it had been a century or so previously: at once more progressive, dynamic and altogether more prosperous. Who could have foreseen in 1640 that travellers might come to Wales to see the new economic order which was about to transform the world? Yet the social and industrial changes the travellers witnessed were as nothing compared to the cultural transformation. At least for the more sensitive and romantically inclined, the Welsh language and its associated culture had ceased to be an embarrassing 'gibberish' doomed to extinction, and become instead an evocative symbol of immeasurable antiquity. If the Welsh economy was pointing the way into the nineteenth century, then the nation's culture seemed rather to be directed towards the mists of pre-Roman Britain, to the contemporaries of the biblical patriarchs. This intoxicating cultural vision could not fail to reshape the sense of Welsh nationality, among the élites as much as the common people.

In the 1780s, the structures of political power in Wales were much as they had been for two centuries, but now they were becoming steadily more difficult to reconcile with social realities. Wales was governed by Members of Parliament elected largely by farmers rather than by shopkeepers or industrial workers, or even ironmasters, and justice was administered by squires and rectors. Matters grew worse as the sharpest population growth occurred in just those areas in which gentlemen of any quality were scarce on the ground, in upstart communities like Merthyr and Dowlais. One obvious solution was to adjust the franchise, to redistribute parliamentary seats and offices to take account of the new situation, but such a flexible approach aroused fears that power would be transferred away from the landed classes, and from the Church to Dissenters. The prospect was so horrible to the established order that they defended the increasingly untenable *ancien régime* for five grim decades, until forced to agree to reforms in the 1830s. By that point, however, social conflicts had gone too far to be resolved by an easy accommodation. An economically vibrant nation, its economy rooted in expanding industrial towns, was beginning to assert the rights of its Welsh speakers and religious Dissenters, in other words, of the *real* people of Wales.

CHAPTER 4

'As Rich as California . . .': Opening and Closing the Frontier: Wales 1780-1870

Neil Evans

Imagine flying over Wales in the late eighteenth century. This is not a totally absurd idea. Benjamin Franklin had already flown a kite in a thunder-storm to demonstrate the scientific spirit of the age and the Montgolfier brothers were flying a hot air balloon. There would be familiar features. The highest ground has never been forested, and the upper slopes, as well as the moorlands, had long been cleared of trees to provide wood for fuel, tools, shipbuilding and smelting. But there would have been more trees on the lowlands than now and the middle slopes were still covered with deciduous trees. The fields would have contained more grain. Most basic commodities had to be produced near to where they would be consumed. Ships were the most effective means of communication and trade: particularly, they linked the agricultural areas of south Wales with Bristol. In summer we would see herds of cattle on the hoof to London and other English markets. The money that returned in exchange for them paid rents and injected much-needed cash into the regionalized economies of Wales.

Some of the settlement pattern would also be familiar to us. There were many scattered farms based on enclosed fields. On the lowest ground, salt marshes often fuzzily framed the coasts, like Traeth Mawr in the armpit where the Llŷn Peninsula joins the body of Wales. To cross it required a guide with local knowledge of how to avoid the deadly quicksands and incoming tides. Prominent in the landscape were country houses, many symbolically isolated from the local community by parks. Mark Girouard has called them 'power houses, the houses of a ruling class'. Within these houses the wealth that accrued from the ownership of land was transformed into political and social power. They were concentrated in lower-lying areas like the Vale of Glamorgan, the Welsh borders and the Teifi Valley: inevitably there were transmission losses in the highlands.

What would strike us most would be the absence of people. In 1750 there were 489,900 people in Wales and in 1801, 587,345 – about a fifth of the present total. They were fairly evenly spread, concentrating where soils were richer and climates less harsh but with no fundamental imbalance. Even in 1801, Glamorgan and Monmouthshire, the main seats of the developing industrial revolution, contained only 20 per cent of the population of Wales. In 1750 towns would have been relatively hard to see. Swansea, Carmarthen and Wrexham were the biggest but none contained more than 4,000 people. Cardiff rejoiced in a population of 1,800. By 1801 Merthyr would be the largest town in Wales: but its 7,705 people were scattered over a large parish. Swansea's 6,099 would have looked as numerous from the air, and they certainly lived in what was more conventionally a town. The smallness of the towns was in marked contrast with England. In no region of England were towns as small and thin on the ground as in Wales. It had no capital such as the Scots had in Edinburgh.

Industrial concentrations were also hard to detect. Wool manufacture was the most widespread industry but it was almost invisible apart from the weaving sheds attached to many farms and in the bloating of towns like Dolgellau, Llangollen and Newtown. In south Cardiganshire and the Halkyn Mountain in Flintshire we would see the spoil heaps and headframes of lead mines. Coal was worked in many areas but did not deeply score the landscape. By the 1780s some of it was used to smelt iron in the upper reaches of the valleys of Glamorgan and Monmouthshire but iron masters had first been attracted into the area by the availability of wood for making charcoal to fuel small furnaces and forges. It took around a third of an acre of woodland to smelt a ton of iron. This had imposed such limits on iron smelting that it could not concentrate anywhere. It was migratory and established wherever there were small deposits of iron ore. The furnace at Dolgun outside Dolgellau served a forge at Borthynwg six miles away down the Mawddach estuary. They could not be closer as they would have encroached on each other's supplies of wood. The thickest scatter of industry was in the Swansea-Neath area where coal reached the surface near the sea. It was thus easy to export, and led to the development of smelting industries. The copper to feed these furnaces crossed the channel from Cornwall which had no coal.

To imagine the same flight nearly a century later is even less preposterous. Balloons had by then been used for military observation in both the American Civil War and the Franco-Prussian War. Powered flight was only thirty years in the future. Many artists trying to capture the size of nineteenth-century towns adopted the bird's-eye view. It seemed the only way to convey the vastness of the towns of the Victorian age, particularly if the purpose was to advertise the growth and prosperity of an area to prospective investors.

The view of Wales had changed significantly. In upland areas dry stone walls and fences clung to mountain sides, even on slopes which looked almost perpendicular. The commons and waste lands had been eaten away by them. On the lowest ground the same process had taken care of many of the salt marshes. At Traeth Mawr there was a large swathe of reclaimed agricultural land and a new town, Porthmadog, had emerged from the morass. On the north-Wales coast was a series of resorts absorbing the contents of the better-stuffed pockets of Lancashire. Along the south Wales coast lay complexes of enclosed docks at Newport, Cardiff, Swansea and Llanelli (and even a small dock at Porthcawl), unknown a century before. Tree cover had been reduced by the impact of industry, with its demands for wood for pit-props and building materials, as well as for development land. As yet there was little attempt to replace them with new growth, so we are approaching the all time low of tree cover in Welsh history. Industry had produced a cluster of small towns and villages on the north Wales coal-field, and others were studded into Snowdonia for the extraction of slate. Blaenau Ffestiniog, Llanberis, Bethesda and the Nantlle Valley communities were now around the peak of their growth, with about 10-12,000 people in each. Of course it was in south Wales that the greatest changes would be apparent. The population of Wales had doubled between 1801 and 1851, and in 1871 it stood at 1.4 million. Increasingly these escalating numbers concentrated in south Wales; 33 per cent in Glamorgan and Monmouthshire in 1851 and 42 per cent in 1871. Wales still lacked really large towns; if we follow the census in 1871 Merthyr was still the largest town in Wales, with almost 52,000 people. But our aerial view would reveal seamless growth out from Cardiff into its new suburbs of Roath and Canton. Adding these to the figures (as the census omitted to do) already made it the largest town in Wales, with over 57,000 people. If there were no towns in Wales which compared with Manchester, Birmingham, Leeds and Sheffield, there was a great concentration of small towns and industrial villages. By some measures, Glamorgan and Monmouthshire were amongst the most urbanized counties in Britain in 1871 and only London, Lancashire and Durham had crossed the urban threshold earlier than Glamorgan. The towns, wired together by railways which cut into the landscape, were the new political and social dynamos. What had happened in the human communities below to so change the landscape?

INDUSTRIAL REVOLUTION, 1780-1850

The fission chamber of Wales was the strip of moorland and valleys stretching from Hirwaun to Blaenafon: eighteen miles long and up to three miles wide. By the 1840s it held 150,000 people, busy manufacturing iron. It was the greatest concentration of iron production on the face of the earth, with the largest single works at Dowlais employing 5,000 people when Lancashire cotton factories rarely numbered their employees in more than hundreds. Cyfarthfa was the second biggest works in the world and only three miles away. Britain was the leading industrial power in the world and 40 per cent of its iron was made here.

The transformation was started by outsiders, the founders of the great dynasties which would dominate the area like the Crawshays of Cyfarthfa and the Guests of Dowlais. They plugged this remote and sparsely populated area into the growth machine of the British Empire. Expansionary wars created huge demands for munitions. Merchants and manufacturers from London, Bristol, Yorkshire and the Midlands moved here to fulfil their contracts for iron. Though the industry started in the warlike eighteenth century, by the time of its peak in the mid-nineteenth century it had shifted towards more peaceful uses, especially making rails. The nineteenth century was more pacific, and widespread economic development created a demand for iron for civil engineering projects. The money to finance this ongoing growth increasingly came from the previous profits of the works themselves rather than from inward investment. Coal suitable for coking, limestone and ironstone all outcropped near the surface. Geology gave the area a basic advantage.

It is just as well, for it had no other advantages. Merthyr is 500 feet above its natural outlet to the sea at Cardiff, and carrying heavy loads of iron goods through the tortuous tracks of these heavily-wooded valleys strained the backs of pack animals and ruined road surfaces. Canals made the expansion of the district possible. Most were started in the 1790s, before the future of the area was secure. They were notable feats of engineering, with the Glamorgan Canal needing a 'ladder' of sixteen locks at Abercynon for the steepest part of its climb. The most important were the Monmouthshire and Glamorgan canals which divided the heads of the valleys strip into two portions centring on Newport and Cardiff, with horse-drawn tramroads and branch canals completing the network. Canals also linked the region with Breconshire, from where agricultural produce was collected to feed the growing numbers who had no visible means of subsistence.

A sparse local population meant there were also problems with assembling a work-force. Keeping it in such frontier conditions was also a challenge. Paying workers relatively high wages – certainly well in excess of those of the impoverished agricultural labourer – attracted the people needed. The huge population growth that Wales was undergoing ensured there were plenty of potential employees. Skilled workers came from the Midlands or from the rural fringes of Merthyr, where artisans, often with radical religious and political ideas, were drawn in. There were always shortages. The skilled were held with contracts (breaking them landed a man in jail), and others with long pays and debts accumulated at company stores. There was little option for the ironmasters but to create shops in such areas as there were few existing local facilities, but paying workers only each month or six weeks, and allowing them to run up debts to the company in the meantime, was a useful means of controlling their movements. Workers were always in short supply in areas like this, even in the absence of periodic, vicious slumps. That is one reason why the iron industry also drew on women for heavy manual labour;

in some areas around 10 per cent of the work-force was female, and young children were also drafted in to undertake 'suitable' tasks. From the 1820s some of these workers came from Ireland, where population growth on a vaster scale than that in Wales was not matched by similar economic growth. There was a certain amount of conflict from the beginning, with a significant riot at Rhymney in 1826 followed by others throughout the period, particularly after Irish migration accelerated under the pressure of the 'Great Hunger' of the later 1840s.

Ironmasters also had to provide houses. Initially they used farm-houses and out-buildings but soon there was little alternative but to build themselves. Their model was the rural farmhouse – as opposed to the labourer's cottage – which was swiftly modified and re-produced in large numbers. So the basic standard of housing was substantial and, for many, better than the hovels they had left behind in the countryside. But no provision was made for sanitation or drainage, and thousands of people adopting the waste disposal habits which suited a less dense rural population quickly created a health disaster. Houses were built in peculiar ways and combinations to suit the sites which were available, and often had no draught of fresh air to ventilate them. And they were crowded. Ironmasters generally built well initially and then overfilled their creations because of the shortage of houses. Lodgers were added to large families, and taking them in was often a condition of being let the house by the company.

Outside this strip, south Wales remained undeveloped, apart from the area around Swansea and Neath which had the most rooted traditions of industry in Wales. Coal export and metal smelting, well-established before the industrial revolution, expanded in line with the new developments elsewhere in Britain. Large firms also dominated: Swansea, like Merthyr, was in the thrall of four major concerns which did everything to manufacture copper, from extracting coal to shaping the final product. It was never on the scale of iron manufacture; at its peak there were barely more than 3,000 copper workers (around a twentieth of the numbers in iron and coal), but they created many subsidiary jobs and the product had a high value. The central, deep-lying part of the coalfield remained largely dormant and unexploited. Indeed, coal was still in the main a subsidiary product used to smelt iron or copper, though Swansea had an established export trade and one began to develop in the lower reaches of the valleys of Gwent from the end of the Napoleonic Wars. Here, in what shocked observers called the 'black domain', were capitalists who lived on the knife-edge and had insufficient margin to temper their power with the kind of paternalism that the best of the ironmasters and copper masters deployed.

What kind of life was possible for the workers who were so rapidly brought together in this unfriendly and neglected environment? It was clearly a new world – but one which many artists depicted as a variant of hell. Explosive growth attracted many tourists and social observers: several who came to Merthyr were clearly offended by its lack of a conventional urban form, especially of a centre. It was really four ironworking villages grouped loosely around another village. Visitors looked only at externals, and the lack of a focus for the whole community was too readily taken as a symbol of the internal arrangements of the place. External signs of social stress, like weekend drunkenness, pointed in the same direction.

Within the walls there was less to worry about. Public houses and beer-houses proliferated, but are too often approached by historians through the avenue of the later temperance movement. They are seen as evidence of social pathology. Week-end drunkenness was one of the ways of coping in Merthyr and the other ironworking communities. But public houses were also the centres of a culture which drew nourishment from the revived Welsh eisteddfod. Iolo Morganwg, inventor of the Gorsedd of Bards, and of much else of significance in Welsh culture, spent his later years in Merthyr. Ballads were sold on the streets, and sung there and in the public houses. These ballads were full of the ordinary things of life: love, romance, marriage and the trials of existence. Some of this culture was brought from the countryside, most obviously the language. A survey undertaken in Merthyr in the 1840s showed that 90 per cent of the population spoke Welsh. Communities punished straying husbands by the kind of *ceffyl pren*, or traditional horse-effigy, procession which characterized the country-side. Women gathered in the streets, around the springs and pumps which provided the precarious water supply of these new communities. In the process they 'gossiped': that is they regulated much of the behaviour around them. Being the subject of gossip was to be feared, and these exchanges helped set standards. From the beginning there were 'tidy' people as well as those who surrendered to the conditions.

Religion flowered in these new communities, creating a cultural revolution. Across Wales chapels were built at the rate of one every eight days in the period 1800-1850. Behind the statistics are months and years of fundraising, collections from poor people and making do in temporary rooms (often in public houses) until the chapel could be built. Up to mid-century they were spartan places, modelled on rural barns and with hard, scrubbed, wooden seats inside. Ministers were rarely trained, and there was no one as superior as the university-educated clergymen who presided over the established Church. Nonconformist Sunday schools provided one of the major available sources of instruction, and not simply in religious matters. Basic literacy was taught and many were introduced to a world of fantastic stories, inspirational behaviour and moral guidance. Even hostile Anglican observers found much to admire in the Sunday school. Ieuan Gwynedd Jones gets us to the heart of things when he observes that Nonconformity '. . . did not confine [people] to the narrow horizons of the hills'. In Birmingham in 1851 there were seats available in places of worship for just over a quarter of the population. In south Wales, three quarters could be seated. It is one of the mysteries of nineteenth century history to explain why so many observers saw an area with so much religion as a threat to the social order.

Part of the answer lies in the nature of this religion. It was Dissent. It was outside the official state Church which was meant to cement the social order, even if most Nonconformists failed to draw the political implications from this at this time. Anglicans did it for them. The Church was a hierarchy extending from God through the monarch and the bishops to the clergy, and finally to the congregations. In Nonconformity the congregations made the important decisions, like appointing ministers, and believed in a much more direct route between God and the individual soul. Perhaps, strictly speaking, they were not democrats but they looked enough like it to frighten the gentry, the ironmasters and superficial observers.

Some Nonconformists made the politics implicit in their religious beliefs explicit. When radicalism began to appear in the 1790s, it was in areas which had been well colonized by Nonconformists. The upland areas of Glamorgan had been a favourite place for them after the upheavals of the seventeenth century. There, the supervision of a resident gentry and clergy was largely absent, unlike the situation in the Vale where they had such a strong presence. Merthyr had a substantial plantation of Dissenters which would bear fruit in the coming decades.

But there was a more basic politics, intimately related to the everyday demands of life, to attend to first. Industrial workers in eighteenth-century Wales, and the population of market towns, had frequently taken action to regulate the price of flour and grain, the essential commodities in the diets of the poor. As the market came to rule in the domain of food prices they defended the idea of a 'just price', more than which it was unethical to charge. Historians have called this an idea of 'moral economy'. Crowds would seize grain, sell it at what was considered a fair price, and hand over the proceeds to the merchant. In other instances, when there were local shortages, exports would be prevented: *fear* of starvation, rather than the actuality, ruled. Magistrates often looked on benignly, both because they had little love for the upstart 'badgers' who made money out of scarcity and partly because, without a police force, it was difficult for them to intervene. Troops were far too blunt – and tardy – an instrument to be of much use. Magistrates often bought up corn and sold it at a loss, or persuaded dealers to reduce their prices to avert disturbances.

The first widespread wave of food riots had swept over Wales in 1739-40. By the 1790s, they were endemic. The growing size of the industrial population made more people vulnerable to variations in the price of food. Even for the well-paid copper workers of Swansea, who rioted in 1793, grain represented half of their spending. Little wonder that they were sensitive to its price. Huge waves of riots followed in 1795 and 1800, especially, in the latter year, around Merthyr. Mixed in with the normal regulation of prices was the intimidation of shopkeepers and others to make donations to the workers' cause: a kind of Mari Lwyd with menaces, and out of season at that. Now the authorities took a sterner line. Three men, admitted by the judge to be of hitherto unblemished character, were sentenced to death, and two of them actually hanged at Cardiff. There were new elements in the situation. Britain was fighting a war with revolutionary France and judges knew that food riots had played a role in precipitating the French Revolution. The emerging industrial complexes were now of a size that frightened the authorities. Disorder in a tiny market town or industrial village was one thing; disorder in the embryonic complex at the heads of the valleys was another. The authorities backed the market and withdrew from the moral economy. Women often took a leading part in such disturbances, reflecting the way in which food prices coincided with their domestic roles. Now they were abused as prostitutes and unruly women.

Food riots came to a peak in the 1790s and then dropped into oblivion. After 1800 they are increasingly hard to find, with a last fling in 1817-18. Repression, along with the constant price rises of the Napoleonic Wars (which made a mockery of any idea of 'traditional' prices) and the tendency of food prices to fall after 1815, undermined this type of protest. Workers came to see themselves as producers rather than consumers. Perhaps they were influenced by the growing size and importance of the places in which they worked and by the realization that, for all the steam engines and water wheels, without their sweat and muscle nothing would happen there. Huge investments laid ironmasters open to the fear of not making economic returns. The uninterrupted boom ended around 1810, when blockades and economic warfare led to fluctuating demand for iron. In the long era of peace things were even more uncertain, with vicious slumps punctuating the growth of the industry. The cruelty of the iron industry was that it offered prosperity and its trappings: clocks, carpets, crockery and furniture, and then snatched them away into the pawn shop or the debtors' court.

In 1816, workers across the Heads of the Valleys belt went on strike to resist a wage cut, rather than rioting to contest a price rise. Industrial action was inherently difficult in a world bounded by master-and-servant laws which meant one law for the workers and another for the employers. Masters who broke contracts were liable for damages; workers went to jail. Owners had all the suspicion of industrial negotiation which this legal position implied. Members of respectful delegations were likely to be dismissed. If trade unions were created their members could be prosecuted either under the cumbersome procedures of the common law or the sleeker, less draconian, but more effective, Combination Acts of 1799-1800.

In the 1820s strikes to resist wage cuts, and even on occasion to demand increases, became more common and were supplemented by a secret society. In the 'black domain' of the Glamorgan-Monmouthshire border there emerged 'Scotch Cattle'. Members were admitted to it via blood-curdling oaths. Those who revealed the secrets would have their hearts impaled on the horns of the bull. The style came from the ancient traditions of the *ceffyl pren* (wooden horse). Blacklegs and agents who threatened the solidarity of a strike were warned by letter and then by the 'rough music' of the cattle from the hillside. Guns were fired, lowing noises made, metal implements banged together. It was meant to instil fear and it often did. Company property might also be attacked so as to hit small capitalists in their vulnerable pockets. Damaged machinery made a strike hard to break. Those who failed to take these heavy hints were visited in person. The bull would rampage around the china shop of their hard-won, precious property, and destroy it. Normally it was only if a further visit proved necessary that violence was deployed against people. For more than a decade, from the early 1820s to the mid-1830s, such disturbances were endemic. Significantly, they were the work of men rather than of men and women, took place under the cover of darkness and were organized by lodges. Already we are a world away from the open community protest of the grain riot. Clearly, this disturbed the authorities: in the 1830s they would have even more to concern them.

In 1831 the struggle to reform Britain's archaic system of parliamentary representation coincided with an economic crisis. Industrial areas were to the fore in this, as industrialists wanted a hearing in parliament for their newly-important interests. In Merthyr the ironmasters were joined by the shopocracy – the prosperous shopkeepers – and professional classes in their quest for a seat for the town and a system of voting which ensured that people like themselves controlled it. They enlisted the workers as shock troops to threaten the government that violence might result from a failure to grant their demands.

From the start it was a shaky alliance. Workers had been reading radical tracts demanding the vote for all men (few, however radical, advocated votes for women) rather than for the propertied. The economic crisis put workers under further pressure as they were taken

before the local debtors' court for sums owed to shopkeepers. Wage
reductions in the ironworks were the last straw. Proposals to join a
trade union were rejected in favour of direct action against the Court
of Requests and the shopkeepers. This brought troops into Merthyr
and led to a bloody confrontation outside the Castle Inn. Armed
camps were established on the outskirts of the town and, for two days,
reinforcements were turned back. Finally, they came in numbers and
with a professionalism that was impossible to deal with. The rising
collapsed and many went into hiding. At least sixteen people had died
during the battles. Merthyr gained a parliamentary seat, occupied by
the ironmaster Josiah John Guest who was voted for by the
shopkeepers. The workers got a transported leader, in Lewis Lewis –
Lewsyn y Heliwr – and a hanged innocent and martyr in Richard
Lewis – *Dic Penderyn*.

The workers' chance to emulate the middle classes and join the
political game came with the Chartist movement which emerged in
1838. Its demands for political rights for all men were the common
currency of the radical movements which some workers had
supported since the 1790s, and were enshrined in a document called
'the People's Charter'. Chartism exerted pressure on the government
through mass petitions, demonstrations and propaganda. In south
Wales it found its strength mainly in Merthyr and the Scotch Cattle
country to the south-east. In 1839 arming and drilling went on,
culminating in a rising aimed at Newport and other key towns which
would be occupied to inspire other areas of Britain to copy them. A
democracy would ensue. If Merthyr had produced a spontaneous
quasi-revolutionary effusion, this was a rising with revolution
aforethought. It foundered on the weather (men marched in torrential
rain), the discipline of troops expected to side with the workers, and
the failure of some areas like Merthyr to send their promised
contingents. This was not the end of the Chartist story. There were
resurgences of the movement in 1842 and 1847-8, though with
declining support. In 1842, workers in Merthyr joined a general strike
called to secure Chartist demands, liberally mixed in with industrial
grievances. The Chartists involved women in subsidiary roles and
there were female groups in many parts of south Wales. But the main
emphasis was on men. Chartist heart-throb Henry Vincent gave the
game away with the characteristic way he closed his public meetings

– 'Three cheers for the Charter, for our wives and sweethearts – and ourselves!' Chartism marked the emergence of an industrial society in that the target was not just the landlords but the ironmasters and coalowners. It was a kind of politics adjusted to this new world.

'SLOW, DRAGGING CRISIS': 1780-1850

All too often accounts of industrialization are set against a backdrop of an unchanging and 'traditional' rural society. Such a view is encouraged for Wales because it was in this period that its mountains and valleys were first discovered by tourists. Romantics seeking an escape from industry in other parts of Britain celebrated the ancient and rugged mountains of Wales. There seemed to be something primal about them. For purposes of celebration, the people who inhabited the mountains were increasingly ignored or treated as quaint rustic characters. This is a false perspective. The rural areas were as much involved in change and transformation as were those which developed large-scale industrial complexes. Over most of north and mid-Wales the period opened much as it did in south Wales, with an industrial boom. This was widespread, and affected many industries and areas. The Empire stimulated an expansion in wool manufacture, both for the soldiers fighting its wars and for the slaves who produced sugar in its colonies. Weaving sheds multiplied, small spinning jennies gathered into micro-factories, and towns like Llanidloes, Newtown, Welshpool and Dolgellau began to aspire to greater things. Newtown came to be known as 'the Leeds of Wales'. Cloth was sent out of Barmouth and Liverpool to by-pass the Shrewsbury Drapers' Company, which had once controlled the industry in all of north and mid-Wales. Outside these centres, spun wool was manufactured and sent in. By the 1830s Newtown and Llanidloes were on the brink of the factory age.

Elsewhere it was minerals of one kind or another which produced the dynamic. Lead was widely mined, especially in Cardiganshire and Flintshire. Slate began to be produced by large concerns, with waged workers instead of the ramshackle partnerships which had quarried it previously. In the north-east of Wales the area around Wrexham produced a tiny imitation of the heads of the valleys in south Wales.

Iron was manufactured and coal dug to feed the furnaces. Flint, on Deeside, became one of the key sites of lead smelting in Britain. Holywell had a range of industries based on the water power of the Greenfield Valley. In 1801 it was the third-largest town in Wales. But it was in copper production that north Wales really caught the eye in the late eighteenth century.

The discovery of the huge lode that had long been rumoured to exist on the Parys Mountain in north-east Anglesey in 1767 was the starting point. By the 1790s this was the key to the world's copper industry. Copper could be extracted cheaply here in great open-casts, and this enabled Anglesey to undersell Cornwall and control the price of copper. The demand was again related to Empire: a major use was for copper sheathing of naval vessels. The entrepreneur was Thomas Williams, who got the Cornish producers in such a neck-hold that parliament investigated his activities. He refused to be dominated by copper smelters, manufacturers and bankers and set up his own ventures in these fields which added to the massive power he wielded. His empire spread out from Amlwch to Deeside, Lancashire, Swansea and London. At the centre of the web was one of the most densely-settled parishes in Wales in 1801. With 1,000 workers, the same number of houses and 5,000 inhabitants, it was little behind Merthyr and Swansea. Williams had a reputation for fair play towards his workers. As in south Wales some of them were women, the *copar ledis*, who used hammers to remove impurities from the ore and were celebrated for their skill and hard work.

This boom did not last. It was based on cheap labour and small supplies of minerals which were quickly exhausted. Even on Parys Mountain the best of the ore was exhausted by the time Thomas Williams died in 1802. Mining continued there through the nineteenth century but it became a footnote to the industrial revolution rather than an opening paragraph in it. A similar pattern followed in industry after industry between the end of the Napoleonic Wars and the 1830s. North and mid-Wales became pastoralized or de-industrialized. In the modern western world this makes it look like a pioneer rather than a backwater. What survived were tiny pockets of industry which could buck these trends. Iron declined in the north-east, but there the presence of a coal-field meant that other industries grew to replace it; slate could expand as its supplies were massive, and its position as the premier source of roofing in the United Kingdom was unassailed. The woollen industry lost out to Lancashire and Yorkshire. Newtown, Llanidloes and Welshpool struggled on a little longer, but their days were numbered. A wave of industrial growth passed over north Wales, but when it receded it left behind only a few scattered islands which could be called industrial.

This atmosphere of change also affected agriculture. Wales was a land of large estates – owned by landlords – and small farms worked by families, mainly using their own labour. Family labour meant that men and women – as well as children – engaged in heavy manual work. There was strict segregation in this: women were not allowed to work with horses, while the dairy was the preserve of the farmer's wife. But women could be seen at work in the fields – hoeing, weeding, picking stones and involved in harvest work that later generations would find unseemly. There were relatively few agricultural labourers, who were paid wages for working on the land, though their numbers increased as the population rose from the mid-eighteenth century. In a pastoral economy like Wales, many were farm servants hired by the year or half year at a fair and provided with accommodation in a sleeping loft over a barn. These were both men and women, though normally the lofts were segregated. Labourers often aspired to become farmers, and the jump was not impossible, given the small farms and the limited amount of money needed to stock them. However, if the economic gulf between labourer and farmer was not vast, the gap in status and respect was much more substantial.

From the middle of the eighteenth century the prices farmers got for their produce started to rise under the impact of the rising population. This encouraged landowners and farmers to invest in land. The chief means of doing this was to enclose the commons and wastes. Occasionally, investment in the land took on a visionary dimension. William Alexander Maddocks found the cash to realize an old dream of reclaiming Traeth Mawr and grazing cattle on the once treacherous estuary. He built an embankment, created a planned town at Tremadog and, as an unintended by-product, a port at Porthmadog. In mid-Cardiganshire Thomas Johnes planted trees and tried to press new stock breeds on his disbelieving (usually rightly so) neighbours. But most investment had a rather more basic approach: favourable balances in double entry ledgers.

As part of this process, farms got larger and rents rose. Estate surveys were conducted to establish precisely where boundaries lay and whether people had encroached on land without paying rent for it. Land agents took a tougher line with tenants and there were attempts to reduce the length of the leases. Custom had set these at three lives: father, son, grandson; or farmer, widow, son. Now fixed terms became the object, so that more control could be exercised over farming practices. Twenty-one-year leases became more normal, and sights were set on annual renewal. The spirit of rational calculation was entering the countryside as much as the industrial centres, and farmers were learning the consequences.

The underlying social problem in rural Wales was that the population was rising faster than means could be found to support it. Between 1740 and 1840 the population of the rural areas doubled. In many rural parishes by 1840 the population was far in excess of what it is now. People confronted this problem in a variety of ways. Some looked up to the hills for their help. According to custom, people could settle on waste land if they built a house between sunset and sunup, and had a fire in the hearth by morning. The land around, at a radius of the throw of an axe, became theirs too. With communal aid many succeeded in building these *tai unnos* (one-night houses) in the allotted time. They were not always popular with the other inhabitants, who resented the loss of collective open space, and this was a source of tension in village communities. Others found that the only way to survive was to leave, and they went to America or to the closer industrial frontier of the south. This movement did not prevent the population of the rural areas from rising. Substantial as it was, it was not as great as the population growth.

The numbers who could emigrate was restricted by the cost of passages across the Atlantic, and initially they raised the opposition of Methodists who thought that sin was the key problem in the universe and sin could not escaped by flight, however far. But significant numbers did leave in search of land: Merioneth and Cardiganshire, poor rural counties, lost about 5,000 people each to the beckoning of 'Mr Go to America', a figure deplored by the preacher Christmas Evans. Large parts of rural communities were transplanted. Around 240 people left the Llŷn peninsula in the 1790s, to settle in Oneida County on the New York frontier and 67 went from Dyffryn Ardudwy in Merioneth to Racine in Wisconsin in 1841. They travelled as groups and settled close to each other in their new lands. Paddy's Run in Ohio took its tithe from Llanbrynmair. Most of the emigrants in this period came from rural Wales. A few had religious and political reasons for their quest. Morgan John Rhys had dreamed of a Welsh-speaking radical community in the 1790s, but his scheme was eclipsed by the more mundane adjacent settlement of Ebensburg in Pennsylvania. In the 1850s Samuel Roberts was still trying to find a secure home for a Nonconformist people in Tenessee. But it was already clear that the pace of settlement in the American West made this a receding dream. America offered more to Welsh people who went for economic reasons, and perhaps particularly for women, to whom America offered more than the home country did. However, for most people in rural Wales, there was little choice but to remain and confront the problems.

Changes in agriculture were the root causes of many social tensions and protest movements. Enclosure produced its rash of riots, especially from squatters who were displaced. Particularly violent were the disturbances at Llanddeinolen in 1809 when many inhabitants resisted an enclosure of commons and the 'crime' whereby the local landowner acquired land rich in slate. After the enclosure of Mynydd Bach, in Cardiganshire, the house built by an Englishman, Augustus Brackenbury, was three times destroyed in a series of events known as *Rhyfel Y Sais Bach* (The War of the Little Englishman). Women played a prominent role in such conflicts. Farmers had often welcomed enclosures in the early stages, seeing the prospect of larger farms before them. The vision turned into higher rents for increased acreages – and the loss of the use of the commons, for which they had not calculated. In the longer run they had reasons to be displeased with enclosures, even if they were not usually opponents at the time of the passing of the Act.

Rural Wales also underwent a religious transformation as profound as that of the industrial areas. Indeed, in 1851 rural areas were even better provided with seats in places of worship than were the industrial. Merioneth had almost as many seats as people. Chapels dotted the countryside, often in locations which were determined by the presence of more tolerant landlords who would lease land to Dissenters, and often in the gaps between the great estates. A generation grew which was grounded in the words and values of the Bible and would draw on them for both moral guidance and for inspiration to resist the changing nature of their world. A rift had opened between landlord and tenant in many areas, and there was a symbolic expression of it in the large-scale opting for a religion which was not that of the establishment or its local representatives, the landed gentry.

By the 1830s the position in the countryside was critical. The prices farmers got in the markets tumbled. Landlords finally got their leases down to one year. Ballads sung in the countryside pleaded for leases of three *everlasting* lives, so great was farmers' search for security. Other problems piled on top until the weight became unbearable. Tithes became more oppressive. Changes in the Poor Law added to the burden. The new Poor Law of 1834 instituted a system of workhouses in which able-bodied poor people would be supported. In much of rural Wales farmers had often given produce and other help to their neighbours and used informal charity in the place of the compulsion of the rates. The new system was a double imposition. Workhouses were expensive to build, even when parishes were grouped together in poor law unions to share the costs. This was felt in the pocket. There was also resentment at the indignity of such a system, which treated the poor like criminals and broke with the established ways of care. Discontents were many and varied. All that was needed was an issue around which these discontents might crystallize. The rural areas lacked the tradition of political involvement which characterized industrial south Wales and had formed the platform for the Merthyr rising and for Chartism. Protests, instead, formed ranks along the toll roads which had proliferated in south-west Wales since the late eighteenth century.

Turnpike trusts were a means of improving the notoriously bad Welsh roads. A trust improved a road and levied a toll for its pains. But in south-west Wales the trusts covered small areas, consequently there were too many. Moving from the roads of one trust to enter another involved paying a further toll. The main victims were farmers trying to take their goods to markets or bringing in lime to sweeten the acid soils of the area. Carmarthen was surrounded by a dozen toll-gates, and more difficult to penetrate than Fort Knox. Nor were the trusts doing well. Their smallness, combined with lax administration, had led them to the brink of bankruptcy. In their efforts to stave it off the trusts triggered the unexploded bomb that lay beneath south-west Wales.

Efailwen was a village without a gate on a main road connecting the outcrops of limestone on the western edge of the south Wales coal-field with the agricultural hinterland. Putting a gate here in the spring of 1839 seemed like a cute move. The local population disagreed. A public meeting was called 'to consider the necessity for a toll-gate at Efailwen'. In a display of theatricality that would characterize much of the ensuing outbreak, the gate was deemed superfluous and destroyed. The crowd dressed in women's clothes, blackened their faces and gave a rather unmusical but noisy accompaniment to the proceedings. In assuming women's dress they were appropriating a role which women had often been seen to have in pre-industrial societies: that of breaking the law in the interests of their families. For men to do this was both to displace women from the actual disturbances and to claim a justification for their law breaking. The Rebecca Riots had begun. Their memory has recently been revived by farmers contesting the multiple crises of milk quotas, Chernobyl lamb and BSE-infected beef, with a similar resort to direct action against imported beef.

Clearly the deeds of Rebecca were those of a people brought up on the Bible. In Genesis, Rebecca proclaimed that her followers should destroy the gates of 'them that hate thee'. The enemies were the gentry, the major turnpike trustees. The conflict which erupted briefly in 1839 exploded in 1842-3 until, at one point, not a single toll-gate remained standing in Dyfed. This brought attention from London: troops, worried Ministers and even a concerned *Times* journalist, Thomas Campbell Foster. From the beginning it was clear that toll-gates were only one issue amongst many. In 1839 there was an attack on Narberth workhouse, as well as the gate-smashing. In 1843 there was an attack on Carmarthen workhouse. Threatening letters dropped on to gentry doormats, promising decidedly nasty deaths to those who did not reduce their rents. Overall, slightly more than half the incidents concerned toll-gates; the rest were more general in nature and usually more violent. One person was killed but, given the frequency with which shots were fired into the houses of suspected informers and other targets, it is a wonder that the death toll was so low. Rebecca revealed a violent edge to the countryside that some historians have preferred not to see.

From the end of 1843 the disturbances declined. Sympathy in *The Times* led to a parliamentary inquiry into the roads and quickly to legislation to melt the tip of the iceberg of disaffection, even if little was done to address the larger portion of underlying grievances. The farmers became worried when the labourers began to give vent to their grievances. That was just a little too democratic.

Rebecca's hosts did not roam around all of rural Wales. They were mainly confined to the south-western quadrant, with a particular concentration in Carmarthenshire. These were the areas least touched by industry: purely agricultural districts had the worst of the crisis and point to the kind of future that would have been in store for Wales if there had been no industrial revolution. In north Cardiganshire the extensive lead workings raised incomes and provided work. Rebecca was a rare visitor there. In the emerging slate areas of Gwynedd the only visit was a practical joke – acted out in south-Walian accents – in the village of Penmorfa. Radnorshire and Brecon were perhaps too accessible to the industrial complexes of south Wales for a real crisis to build up, though there were some incidents in Radnorshire.

Chartism barely touched the area of Wales most involved in Rebecca's activities, apart from its early planting in Carmarthen town and its substantial presence in the wool manufacturing towns of mid-Wales. By the 1830s, competition was severe, and handloom weavers suffered in Llanidloes, Newtown, Rhayader and Welshpool as much as they did in Lancashire. Political radicalism had entered these towns back in the 1790s, and the mixture of industrial decline and deeply-rooted political traditions proved to produce the kind of conditions which created Chartism. Famous was the incident in Llanidloes in the spring of 1839 when a crowd, with women in the forefront, attacked the Trewythyn Arms after the authorities had arrested some Chartist leaders and taken shelter there. When the troops arrived their commander claimed he had done rather more damage himself on a 'good' Saturday night. That did not prevent the arrest, imprisonment and transportation of several local Chartists. But there was certainly arming and target-shooting going on, and there may have been more to the situation than the bare details of the riot suggest.

Elsewhere in north and mid-Wales Chartists comprised only tiny pockets of enthusiasts in the towns. There were few of them in the north Wales coal-field where they might have been expected, despite the existence of a strong trade union tradition around Wrexham which had been expressed in large-scale membership of the Friendly Society of Coalminers, the union that the Merthyr workers had scorned before their Rising. North Wales had had its cameo of Merthyr in the battle of Chirk Bridge in 1831, when miners had clashed with troops. But in the Chartist years they were largely quiet.

North and mid-Wales therefore underwent their own transformation in the period, even if it was not as dramatic or graphic as on the fringes of the southern coal-field. Governments were understandably concerned about Wales by the 1840s, and Select Committee followed Royal Commission to try to understand the turmoil and find solutions. Merthyr was followed by Llanidloes, Newport and Rebecca. In the first issue of *The News of the World,* in 1843, it was suggested – perhaps ironically – that martial law might be extended to Wales. Would nothing give this turbulent country any peace?

Stability? 1847-75

In the next thirty years Wales seemed to be much more peaceful and stable. No risings shocked the government in London. Had some magic formula for stability suddenly been found? Or was the sudden transformation something of an illusion?

Clearly some things did change. In the iron-working districts, after the Chartist outbreaks, the ironmasters showed more social concern, and the Anglican Church became a more effective body. The huge industrial enterprises had always had a dominant economic role in their communities and provided many basic facilities, but they had usually ignored the social life of the population they had so rapidly thrown together. Paternalism now came to be practised, though much of it was the work of the industrialists' wives and daughters – of mothers of the society rather than fathers. It was expressed in education and the provision of reading rooms: Charlotte Guest, a woman of aristocratic, landed origins, was the pioneer at Dowlais, and she records in her journal that workers were so totally absorbed in reading matter that they did not notice her visit. An early photograph shows her tall figure luminously watching over neat rows of desks behind which sit clean and attentive children. What she pioneered was followed by others like Rose Crawshay at Cyfarthfa. Church-building followed on from this and, generally, frontier communities matured with age. Even Merthyr began to look like a town. It sported a main street with modern shops and came to boast of its array of public buildings. After considerable political struggle the iron-working towns were being cleaned up. Pure water supplies were laid on; sewers and drains were provided. Merthyr began to be built over its cesspits rather than amidst them. Urban death rates were arrested and then began to drop. Industrial towns became something more hospitable to life than the killing jars they had been in the 1840s.

Similar things began to happen in the rural areas, too. Rebecca's fangs were drawn by the government's palliatives, and these were quickly followed by an upturn in the fortunes of agriculture which lasted for a generation or more. Railways began to be built in Wales in the 1840s; towards the end of the decade the south Wales main line began to snake its way along the coast. By the early 1850s it was in Rebecca's country. It helped in two ways. First, it became easier to sell agricultural produce, which was good news for the farmers. The days of the drove road were numbered. Secondly, it became easier for people to migrate out of the rural areas. Mainly, this was good news for the agricultural labourers, who could now move in greater numbers to industrial towns and relieve the pressure of population on resources in the countryside. From the 1840s the population began to fall in the purely agricultural areas. Labourers moved and found opportunities elsewhere.

They moved to new areas of growth. The iron district was reaching its peak of prosperity and the limits of its expansion. By the 1840s local supplies of ironstone were becoming scarce and expensive to work. Leases granted a hundred years before, when landlords did not realize the value of what they were sitting on, fell in and were renewed on less favourable terms. From the 1850s cheap steel production was beginning in other parts of the world, and south Wales found it hard to compete. The heads of the valleys, so blessed by nature with the resources for iron-working, were badly endowed for steel.

The future lay elsewhere. In the 1840s, large-scale working of steam coal began in the Cynon Valley. Aberdare soon became a new boom town, based on coal extracted for sale abroad rather than for smelting iron. From the 1850s the Rhondda Valleys were opened up, along with the whole of the central portion of the coalfield. No longer were there simply two industrial areas flanking an undeveloped area of hills, valleys and trees. By the 1870s we can really begin to speak of the south Wales coal-field in the sense of development over the whole of the area. The new demand was for steam-coal, the pay dirt which lay beneath the central valleys of the coal-field. Only by mid-century had mining technology developed enough to make the coal accessible, and railways allowed it to be taken out in large quantities. It was the best steam-raising coal in the world, and this was the age of the greatest flowering of the steam-engine. Steamships, in particular, needed this coal. The world would have beaten a path to the Rhondda for it. The area was in a similar position to that of the middle-eastern oilfields since 1945. By the 1870s Rhondda coal was being taken to most parts of the world so that steamships could ply their way across the globe. In trials, the Royal Navy again and again proved south Wales coal to be the best for steam-raising. What better advertising could there be? It was like having a particular brand of petrol endorsed by the Pentagon.

As industrialization began to take root in other parts of the world opportunities opened up for Welsh workers with technical skills. In industrial depressions surplus workers were siphoned off to America and Australia. In Scranton, Pennsylvania, Welsh workers were famous because it was a Welshman who had had the necessary knowledge to fire its first furnace in 1840. In Pennsylvania, the skills that the Welsh brought with them made them into foremen rather than workers. They were also in demand as puddlers. It is little wonder that the Confederacy's major ironworks in the Civil War was called Tredegar. Other Welsh workers were drawn to Australia's gold-fields and coal-fields and to a range of American industries like the slate quarries of Vermont. Some went to Russia when the Donetz basin was opened up in the late 1860s. By this standard the flow to Middlesbrough to establish a new steel industry was a modest journey. But, like all these industrial migrations, it eased pressures at home and was a means of negotiating the industrial slumps which had generated so much conflict earlier in the century.

Outside the south Wales coal-field the economic success stories were less compelling. In the north east, the small coal-field which clung to the border produced a range of industries and modest growth which could have been tucked into a corner of the Rhondda and lost, but which shaped the character of the area. In north-west Wales, slate now began its global expansion. The government took the brakes off by removing the duty on exported slate in 1831 and the cheapness, hygiene (thatched roofs harbour rats) and low fire risk of slate in crowded industrial towns did the rest. Ships, canals and railways enabled slate to reach the industrial towns of Britain. Sailing ships, built in large numbers on the coasts of western Wales, enabled slates to reach Europe, the Americas and Australia. Blaenau Ffestiniog and Nantlle were mini Rhonddas and Aberdares rising rapidly in a runaway boom from the 1830s. They were much smaller, but the experience of life was similar.

The stabilization of the iron-making areas, the draining of people from the countryside, and the opening up of new areas of prosperity all help to explain the apparent stability of mid-Victorian Wales. But they are not sufficient reasons for it. Many areas of difficulty remained. Iron-making in decline produced social tensions; new processes were introduced and, as late as 1882, there was a violent riot against Irish people in Tredegar which took place against a backdrop of contested industrial change. If Merthyr's notorious criminal district of 'China' was becoming calmer and past its heyday by 1860, a much bigger and more infamous one was emerging in Cardiff's Butetown. The presence of sailors of many nations made it a much more pulsating vice district than 'China' had ever been, constantly renewed by the comings and goings of the seven seas: and it was on those seas that its reputation spread far and wide. The new steam-coal areas were as much like frontiers as Merthyr in its heyday. Commentators quickly turned their wrath away from the iron workers – now seen as 'steady' – and towards the unruly steam-coal miner. Few public health lessons were learned from the experience of the iron towns. The Rhondda was still built before its sewers, and without building regulations, even if these followed more closely on the heels of development than they had in Merthyr. Only at the very end of our period would the provision of basic social amenities come alongside the growth of new settlements. The same was true in the slate districts, with Blaenau Ffestiniog, built in a naturally healthy location, having a death rate around four times that of an equivalent rural area in the early 1870s.

Nor was there social peace. The Aberdare Valley was rocked by Scotch Cattle letters and a number of violent strikes in the 1850s, some of which led to troops being brought in. In north Wales, quarry workers expressed contempt for managers and told them they could do the job better. A generation later, in south Wales, such defiance would be branded workers' control. In the north-east Wales coal industry there was the same hostility to managers and to coal-miners brought in from across the border. Both were, on occasion, less than gently told to leave the area, frog marched to a station and put on a train. When the authorities sought to punish the perpetrators of a 'running out of town' incident at the Assizes at Mold in 1869, the workers rushed the troops guarding them. The troops opened fire, and two men and two women were killed. There was also conflict in many areas of the countryside. Mid-Wales had been slow to join Rebecca, coming in only on the later stages of the agitation, but it led the way in the mass salmon-poaching protests from the 1850s which became known as the 'second Rebecca'. Violent actions against enclosure also continued in some areas. We can, therefore, exaggerate the tight button of respectability of mid-Victorian Wales.

Of course, the position overall was less threatening. Britain's industrial dominance was unchallenged, and the coming of the railways had stabilized its economy. Living standards rose. Violence and conflict did not disappear but they could now be regarded as being isolated and containable. There was no longer the seemingly irresistible line-up of threats that there had been in the 1840s. There was also a greater air of confidence.

Some of this had come about as a result of the protracted debate over the inquiry into the state of education in Wales, set up in 1846 and reporting the following year. The three commissioners were all Churchmen, and they produced a hostile report on Wales, labelling its inhabitants ignorant, immoral and turbulent, all of which were related to the speaking of Welsh. This Commission followed hard on the heels of many other government investigations in the period and, like them, offered education as the solution for all ills. Only rather grudgingly did it recognize any merits in Nonconformity. Nonconformists might have joined in some of the complaints if only more credit had been given to their achievements over the previous half century or so. Instead, in the 1847 *Report,* chapels were seen as the loci for assignations which underlay the allegedly high illegitimacy rate in Wales. Nonconformity was seen as part of the problem, rather than part of the solution. This massive indictment was good news for printers who must have worked overtime to produce the flood of pamphlets, books and newspaper and journal articles which issued forth to try to sweep the three commissioners away. Anglican and Tory writers joined in the fray to defend them. Charges were rebutted one by one: Wales did not have high levels of illegitimacy; revolution was the result of English influences rather than Welsh; 'foreigners' – English, Scots, and especially Irish – made up much of the industrial population and crime was mainly the work of such outsiders.

What came out of this debate was not simply a response to criticism and a rebuttal of charges, but a redefinition of nationhood, the creation of a new national myth. The predominant way of seeing Wales in the 1840s was as an old and distinguished culture, framed by its beautiful and ancient mountains. This was encapsulated a few years later in the words of 'Hen Wlad Fy Nhadau', which was to become the national anthem. The myth was a laying out, with a view to burial. What was laid on top of it was Nonconformist respectability. The controversy surrounding the 1847 education Report came to be called the 'treason of the Blue Books', after the dark blue covers in which parliamentary reports were published. This was a reference back to ancient Welsh history, 'the treason of the long knives' in which the Saxons had betrayed the Welsh and killed them while they slept. In the course of the argument, Wales came to be defined not by its history but by its religion. The Welsh became the most loyal of the peoples of Britain and their radicalism the most peaceful. To a large extent this new Wales was set against Ireland (and the Irish in its midst), a frame for its Protestant respectability. Its women were the purest in spirit and body. Serious crime was so rare that judges were frequently given the white gloves that symbolized the absence of cases to try. The Welsh people were spiritual, intellectual, honest, hard-working, God-fearing and avid consumers and writers of poetry. The 'Blue Books' controversy played a central role in crystallizing Welsh Victorian values. Though part of the older view of Wales was retained, it was relegated to a corner and covered in a chintz cloth. The Tredegar Independent minister, Evan Jones, (Ieuan Gwynedd), was explicit about this shift in identity: 'Though fond of the "harp of my country," the songs of Zion give me greater delight.'

Soon, real events would enable this image to be transmitted to the world. In 1872 a Welsh male voice choir raised by Caradoc from amongst the miners of Aberdare won first prize in a competition at the Crystal Palace. The idea of Wales as a land of song – but now the serried male ranks of industrial workers rather than more individual efforts with harps – was reborn. Five years later, some miners were entombed at Tynewydd in the Rhondda. As the rescuers hacked through the falls of coal to reach them in a 'touch-and-go' race with the rising water they were heard to be singing Welsh hymns. Queen Victoria regularly telegraphed for news. The idea of the singing, respectable miner was born. Just over sixty years later John Ford would twist it onto celluloid and have his miners singing on their way home from the pit.

Once the image was constructed there were renewed efforts to make the people live up to it. The nagging fear in Nonconformist breasts was that some of the charges of 1847 may not have been treason but truth. Ieuan Gwynedd, key defender of Wales against its detractors, started the first magazine for women, which advised them to pay particular attention to their husbands' collars. He and his successors dispensed much advice on morality and decorum. Women were discouraged from doing heavy manual labour. Decent family life was seen as requiring the constant presence of a woman presiding over the home. Education and day schools were promoted by Nonconformists. Hitherto, they had given most of their attention to chapel-building and Sunday schools. The Anglicans had played a more prominent role in providing day schools and were less afraid of accepting government grants than were Dissenters. Nonconformity had to rethink its relationship with the state and accept the need for subsidy. Only in the 1870s, with the board schools, would Wales have something approaching an educational system, and that too impressed many people with the sense of order and discipline that it produced in unruly children. Religious people had always frowned on drunkenness but now they came to frown on drink itself. Teetotalism, an import from America to the extreme fringes of Nonconformity in the 1830s, became respectable and more mainstream by the 1870s. The eisteddfod, central symbol of the revival and renewal of ancient Welsh culture, was wrenched away from the public house and placed firmly under the control of the chapel. Oratorios by Handel became the staples of Christmas concerts in the chapels. The local eisteddfodau were crowned with a National Eisteddfod from 1858 onwards, the railways making possible the gathering of people which it required. The eisteddfod was the pinnacle of Wales's distinctive manifestation of Victorian respectability.

The social turmoil of the 1830s and 1840s now transmuted into Liberal politics. At the end of the Rebecca riots there were many protest meetings and much drawing up of lists of grievances. This was the beginning of a long political apprenticeship in the countryside. In the industrial towns, Chartism provided a similar foundation. In turning the old aristocratic Whig party into the Victorian Liberal Party the capture of working-class support was a key element. In 1848, in the context of revolution and nationalism in Europe, the crucial leader, Henry Richard, rose from the bogs of Tregaron to prominence in the international peace movement. In the following decades Wales was warrened from end to end with pressure groups demanding peace, temperance, sabbatarianism, education and the disestablish-ment of the Church. They clamoured for the attention of candidates at the hustings. In 1867 the government opened the door a little by extending the franchise in the towns to include some working-class voters. Merthyr's electorate multiplied tenfold overnight, though elsewhere the changes were less dramatic. This was enough of a chink to allow a large Liberal boot to be inserted. In the elections of 1868, twenty-three Liberals were elected in Wales. Most were in fact old Whigs rather than new Liberals: landowners and Anglicans who had sympathy for Dissent and political liberty as a family heirloom. Only three Nonconformist middle class MPs were elected but they proved to be the pattern of the future. The victory of Henry Richard in Merthyr was achieved because of the power of working-class votes. Richard employed a nationalist and class language against the gentry but they (and even more his ironmaster and coal-owner allies) knew that his bark was very much better than the bite that the workers had taken in 1831. By the 1880s Henry Richard's kind of candidate was sweeping all before him. It was, of course, 'him' in every case. But the demand for votes for women began to be heard in the aftermath of the 'Welsh Revolt' of 1868. A few women, like Rose Crawshay, won places on local government bodies but they were almost curiosities. Yet it was also the beginning of another, even longer, political apprenticeship.

Workers completed their transition to order by establishing trade unions in the key industries of slate and coal. In coal the impetus came from outside, with the Amalgamated Association of Miners hailing from Lancashire and having a Lancastrian, Thomas Halliday, as its leading light in south Wales. The early 1870s were punctuated by three huge strikes which mark the rise, success and downfall of the Union. They gave south Wales a reputation for trade union militancy, not for risings. Halliday stood as a candidate for Merthyr in 1874 and, though he finished bottom of the poll, he garnered almost 5,000 votes, sending a signal about the possibility of working-class representation. A decade later, the Rhondda miners received it, and elected William Abraham, known by his bardic name of Mabon, who was Halliday's Welsh-speaking lieutenant. In 1874 the slate workers, with no outside intervention, formed a union. Controlling virtually all British production of slate, they had little need to consult more widely in the way that the miners did. North-east Wales also had its union explosions, while there were tentative attempts at negotiation in some of the south Wales ports. Of all these unions only the quarrymen's union would endure, but enough had been learned to ensure that unions would be very much a part of the future in Wales. While unions probed the limits of cross-class alliance, there was no denying that the workers had joined the national community dominated by Nonconformity and its political expression in Liberalism. The nineteenth century is often celebrated for its inventions – railways, telegraphs, steam printing and steamships. Together these things helped forge peoples into nations, perhaps one of the most remarkable of nineteenth-century inventions.

CONCLUSION: ANATOMY OF THE NEW WELSH NATION

Wales had clearly become a more cohesive entity over the century we have examined. Railways made it possible to travel across it in ways never dreamt of in the past, and even to move from north to south. There were strong binding ties. The most basic were the human ones fashioned by migration. Not all the population moved, and links of emotion and memory bound the country together. The coming of the penny post in 1840, along with literacy and the telegraph, meant that links could be maintained and reforged. Visits home became possible because of the railways. In the last quarter of 1844, 1,706 money orders were bought at the Post Office at Merthyr to send home almost £3,000 to distant families.

The rural and industrial areas were also bound together by institutions, feelings and language. In this period there was virtually no change in the proportion of people speaking the Welsh language. The numbers of Welsh-speakers and English-speakers both rose, and many industrial areas were Welsh-speaking. The Welsh-language press shifted towards the coal-field in pursuit of its best market. Nonconformity remained a common experience for most people in Wales, even if it was never all-embracing. Many were never seduced by its charms, while a substantial Roman Catholic minority emerged, and was the more noticeable for its concentration in Cardiff, Swansea and Merthyr. Liberal politics also bound Wales together, with a clear assertion of the distinctiveness of Wales and its people. Henry Richard proclaimed in 1868 that the Welsh people were those who spoke Welsh and inherited its culture. They were the Nonconformists and the people of the cottage, not of the mansion. This excluded some, especially the gentry, the Irish and the English, but it covered the bulk of the Welsh people. A hand was extended to the English through the efforts to establish English-language chapels for them and, in a sense, to bring them inside this Welsh nation.

In these respects, Wales presented a united front to the world. It was never a total integration of people with shared values and experiences but it was the greatest degree of national unity that had ever been established in the history of Wales up to that point – and since, for that matter. We are still trying to come to terms with the ways in which the thinking about Wales forged in this period influences us, for good and ill, in the contemporary world.

One aspect of this Wales that we have reacted against violently in recent years is the increasingly sharp lines that were drawn between the sexes in the Victorian period. This is not, of course, to say that there was equality before the serpent of industrialization slithered and hissed its way through the garden of Wales. Women had distinct and inferior jobs at the beginning of this period: they had well-defined roles in agriculture and were confined to spinning rather than weaving in the woollen industry. We do not find them amongst the puddlers and forge-men in the ironworks. But there was little sense that women were not suited to heavy manual work and none at all that they should not be full participants in the winning of a living for the family. By the end of the period this was less and less the case. Heavy manual work was seen as challenging femininity, and in the ironworks it was increasingly rare. In coal-mines, underground working for women was banned by law, though few women had worked beneath the surface in Wales. Manual work lingered most pervasively in the rural areas, where we find greater proportions of women in paid work than in the industrial areas by the end of the period. Women were excluded from many of the public roles which developed in the period. They made up much of the chapel congregations but were expected to be silent and ask their husbands for religious guidance. When an occasional woman, like Cranogwen, preached it ruffled many denominational feathers. Women had been at the forefront of food riots but were rarely in trade unions and given only a supporting role in strikes. Men in drag usurped some of their traditional roles in protest movements from the 1830s. One everyday expression of these changed relationships is the funeral, which became increasingly a 'gentlemen only' affair in this period. Women were seen as being hysterical and easily succumbing to emotion.

But if women's position within society changed it did so within the framework of family structures which were more stable. Two vivid descriptions of family life from the beginning and the end of our period show a good deal of continuity. The tourist S. J. Pratt described the family economy of a fisherman in Barmouth in the 1790s. It was clearly a precarious existence, based on a remarkable range of different kinds of work done by all members of the family. Each member had to sacrifice personal happiness and desires in order for the unit to survive. With appropriate adjustments this is the same kind of situation which one woman born in 1858 recalled from her childhood in Cefnmawr, near Wrexham. As the eldest child, she did the family washing and looked after younger children, while going out to earn occasional crusts and pennies. Once she was old enough – at the age of eight – to go out and earn her keep she was sent to do so as there was now another child to assume her role in the family. As an unpaid domestic servant she was no longer a mouth for the family to feed. Soon she would be useful enough to earn a pittance, but by our standards she was remarkably young to be denied the emotional support of family life. In the industrial areas, child labour and women's work ensured that similar patterns were maintained. Only the more certain wages and improved living conditions of the mid-Victorian period, and more widespread and longer-term education, along with the changing perceptions of women produced by religious attitudes, would begin to change this and offer greater opportunities to individuals, allowing them the possibility of dreaming personal dreams even if the means to fulfil them remained painfully restricted. One indicator is the spread of ready-made clothing; it was less often made by the family, so allowing more scope for dedicated following of fashion, and individual styles.

If one of the consequences of the changes we have been considering was to bind Wales together more tightly, and to define it as different from the outside world, these changes also tied it firmly to that world. Railways held Wales together for those prepared to negotiate the timetables and the difficult north-south routes. They also bound it much more firmly to England than in the past. People crossed the borders in large numbers, which had implications for the nature of Welshness in the future. The controversy over the 'Blue Books' was driven by the desire to celebrate the achievements of a distinctively Nonconformist Wales, but it was also deeply influenced by the desire to look respectable in English eyes. The exaggerated decorum of the period has to be understood at least partly in this way. Welsh people were also linked to the United States and Australia by ties of migration and by the ships which plied their trades from the ports of Wales. In Cardiff this resulted in bringing many of the peoples of the world into Wales itself. If Wales shrank and became more cohesive, so did the world in general. In 1873 Jules Verne sent the fictional Phineas Fogg *Around the World in Eighty Days*, crossing the Atlantic in a ship based at Cardiff. In 1890 the real American journalist Nellie Bly managed it in just seventy-two days. Railways, steamships and the telegraph – the Victorian internet – tied peoples together, leading to both aspirations for world peace and, in the future, increasingly violent wars.

The dual revolution of the nineteenth century – industrialization and the quest for democratic rights – transformed Wales, its image and consciousness. At the end of the eighteenth century Welsh people would have thought of themselves as an ancient British people, inheritors of a continuous culture and proud of a country they were increasingly being told was beautiful. Outsiders would have seen them in the same way, particularly emphasizing the surroundings, which attracted small numbers of robust tourists to view them. Many of them elected to write a book about it to inform others of the delights that few would see for themselves. Wales rose in the estimation of the world because of the enthusiasm for wild scenery that marked the Romantic movement. But it had to share the spotlight with the Scottish Highlands and Switzerland, and there is little doubt that they got more of the applause. We have seen that, by the later nineteenth century, Nonconformist respectability had overlaid this conception of Wales so as almost to smother it. Welsh self-conceptions were of an economically prosperous, politically radical, religious and cultured people. The culture stressed music rather than the intricacies of Welsh poetry, and some of this image was transported to the world through choral successes at the Crystal Palace and the singing miners of the Rhondda. The image has persisted. When, in one of Woody Allen's films, a new York taxi driver hears a reference to Wales he asks if it means 'the fish or them singing bastards'! Others would know of Wales through the communities of transplanted Welsh people in their midst. They clung to chapel and language, at least for a generation, and kept themselves much more apart than most British immigrants in America or Australia. They might also have seen another side of Welsh life in the 'saloons Cymreig' of Pennsylvania. Some would clearly have remembered the Welsh record for militancy and radicalism as the folk memories of the 1830s were reinforced by industrial militancy in the early 1870s. Otherwise, people would know of the scenery and history of Wales, as expressed in ruined castles and abbeys, in greater numbers than before as railways opened up the country to something approaching mass tourism. All these things shaped the rest of the world's perceptions of Wales. Two generations later Richard Llewelyn combined all these elements and had an international best seller in *How Green was My Valley*. He codified what the world 'knew' about Wales.

Wales was remade for the modern world. Heavy industry became not just its key material support but also a central aspect of Welsh identity. In the last generation the images of Wales created then have been so hollowed out of their supporting reality that they have collapsed. Contemporary Wales faces a similar challenge in the redefinition of its identity to that faced in the Victorian age; but it is in the nature of modernity that the solutions will have to be very different from those of the past.

CHAPTER 5

BANQUETING AT A MOVEABLE FEAST: WALES 1870-1914

BILL JONES

'There is no better guide to the future than the records of the past,' wrote Joseph Davies, the Secretary of the Incorporated South Wales and Monmouthshire Coal Freighters' Association, in an article in the *Western Mail* of 1 January 1914, which predicted a gloriously prosperous future for Cardiff. 'As a prologue to a forecast of the next forty years,' he continued,

> it is as interesting as it is valuable to take a glance at Cardiff of the early seventies as compared with the Cardiff of today. The first and best measure of our progress is the growth of the population. Today the inhabitants of the city of Cardiff are estimated to number 182,000; in 1871 they numbered 47,500. In trade, our coal shipments in 1871 totalled 2,979,000 tons; in 1912 – omitting Penarth and Barry – 10,102,700 tons . . . The wealth of the city has advanced even more rapidly. Wages are far above those of the seventies. Shopkeepers, professional men, and merchants enjoy incomes which forty years ago men in a similar position would have regarded as beyond the dreams of avarice. Colleges and schools, libraries and parks, churches and chapels, telegraphs, telephones, and postal facilities, commercial exchanges, and means of transit and conveyance within the city and to all parts of our own and other countries have so added to the comforts and amenities of life, so changed the basis of life and of business, that one finds it difficult to imagine a Cardiffian in 1870 looking forward to the present year of grace and anticipating conditions anything approaching those under which we live.

There were many in Wales in 1914 who shared Davies's optimism for the future and marvelled with him at the dazzling progress and expansion that had occurred during the previous forty or so years. Spectacular in their own right, the previously unimaginable transformations to Wales's largest settlement that so entranced Davies also symbolized wider tidal waves of change which engulfed Wales and remade it into a modern, vibrant, dynamic society. Population growth, unparalleled economic buoyancy and especially the worldwide importance of its industries (above all, coal), increased national awareness and the development of national institutions, political assertiveness, and sporting prowess: all of these fused potently to burst Wales out of the margins of British life and signal its emergence as one of the world's leading nations.

As well as being years when Wales experienced dramatic and rapid change, the period between 1870 and the outbreak of the first World War also saw crucial developments which had profound implications for the future. Some of them are still evident today at the dawn of the new millennium, and most of them are etched into the historical consciousness of many Welsh people. There was a relentless increase in coal production in south Wales, and its coal exports came to dominate the world market. There also occurred great shifts in the demographic, political and social structure of the country. These were the years which saw the final metamorphosis of Wales from a rural, agricultural society into an urbanized, industrial one, crammed for the most part into the valleys and ports of the south. Between 1870 and 1914 the almost monolithic power and control over Welsh life that a landowning aristocracy had enjoyed for centuries was greatly eroded. The Liberal Party became predominant, though only to be itself seriously challenged and undermined by increased industrial militancy, class conflict and the rise of labour towards the end of the period. By 1914 there were more Welsh speakers in Wales than ever before, yet the growth in their number occurred during a period when they ceased to be a majority in the country. There were also key innovations in the fields of popular culture with the emergence of mass participatory and spectator activities – this was the golden age of rugby, of brass bands and of the great choirs. This period also saw the first flush of the consumer industry in Wales, signifying the shift from domestic production to the purchasing of food and other commodities. In so many areas of life in Wales there were inexorable trends towards uniformity and concentration of experience, processes which Jay Martin has characterized of the same period in the United States of America as 'The massing of forces and the forging of masses'.

These epoch-making developments can be traced in the arresting events which mark the history of these years. There was the great 1904-05 religious revival, for example, with its scorching emotional intensity and its unparalleled, albeit temporary, conversion of thousands to the ways of God; or the disturbances at Tonypandy in November 1910, when seemingly random rioting and looting of shops in the cockpit of industrial militancy of Wales camouflaged a much deeper struggle for control of that community. The changing nature of Wales can also be well illustrated by the lives and careers of some of the key personalities of the period: David Lloyd George, Wales's most successful politician; Owen M. Edwards, the great educationalist and editor, whose driving mission was to teach Welsh people about their history; or Arthur 'Monkey' Gould, Wales's first ever rugby superstar. All these events and faces are pieces of the jigsaw that make up the 'big' picture of the history of Wales during these years. This picture provided the context which helped to shape the way the people of Wales led their lives.

Yet the impression of a country which witnessed momentous change should not be exaggerated. Threads of qualification need to be woven into this tapestry of unparalleled transformation. The changes that occurred were uneven, they lacked universality and there were strong currents of continuity. Not all of Wales, for example, experienced economic expansion and the generation of wealth: indeed one of the key features of the history of Wales in these years is the exacerbation of regional imbalances in terms of resources and dynamism. Though it dominates the picture, industrial Wales was not *all* of Wales. Just as important, and speaking in very broad terms, for the mass of the people of Wales some aspects of daily life changed little. In the 1870s, as in the second decade of the twentieth century, crucial factors such as the quality (or rather the lack of it) of working and living conditions and health made life a precarious balance between survival and failure. This was still the case despite important reforming initiatives in public health and public amenities. In some respects these shared struggles and realities overrode the divisions that were increasingly becoming a feature of Welsh society. In this sense, Wales was a vortex of both conforming and conflicting forces which impacted on its people. This chapter ranges over some key features of the history of the people of Wales between 1870 and 1914 in order to explore the central themes of concentration, of diversity and disparity, and of continuity and change. It also seeks to uncover some of the richness and complexities of lived experiences in Wales between 1870 and 1914. It begins by examining profiles of people in Wales, their living conditions, and their relationships, desires and tensions.

WE, THE PEOPLE

The most basic point to make about the history of the people of Wales between 1870 and 1914 is that by the end of the period there were considerably more of them. The population of Wales as recorded by the censuses rose from 1,412,583 in 1871 to 2,420,921 in 1911 (by 1914 it had increased to an estimated 2,523,000). On the eve of the first World War, then, there were over a million more people living in Wales than there had been forty years earlier – indeed there were more people living in Wales than ever before. There were also sizeable numbers of people who had been born in Wales but were now living outside its borders, in the 'Greater Wales' to which late Victorian and Edwardian commentators so often referred. Outmigration increased in scale during the latter part of the nine-teenth century. Welsh people from a variety of geographical and occupational origins were motivated, for a host of diverse reasons, to settle in a widening range of destinations. In 1900 about 265,000 natives of Wales were living in England, concentrated in the industrial heartlands of the Midlands and the north, and in the London area. To many people at the time, Liverpool, with its opulent Welsh chapels and its Welsh-dominated building trade, was the capital of north Wales, and its wealthy, self-confident and dynamic middle class exerted significant leadership in Wales's political and literary life. The London Welsh, of course, had worn that mantle for centuries, and continued to do so at the same time as former Cardiganshire agriculturists continued to make milk production in the city almost synonymous with Welshness. There were also at least another

200,000 Welsh people living overseas. The majority of them had made the United States their home, but there was also a marked Welsh presence in some of the cities and industrial, mineral and agricultural belts of Canada, Australasia and South Africa, as well as on the pampas of *Y Wladfa* (The Welsh Colony) in Patagonia.

The richness and complexities of the experiences of Welsh people who lived and worked beyond Wales, and the ways in which they sought to accommodate both the ties of the old country and the demands of the new, are a significant part of the story of Wales during these years. Nevertheless, those Welsh who crossed Offa's Dyke were moving against the tide. Much of the increase in the population of Wales itself was the result of inmigration from outside Wales. Throughout this period the magnetic work opportunities created by Wales's booming industries made it a country of immigration, not emigration. Some have maintained that during these years south Wales was absorbing population at a rate second only to that mecca for the modern world's movers, the United States of America. These newcomers had diverse origins and, as a result, Wales took on an increasingly cosmopolitan character. By far the largest group was English immigrants, the bulk of them from the counties adjoining Offa's Dyke and the south-west of England. In 1871, 9.6 per cent of the population of south Wales came from English counties; by 1891 the figure had risen to 16.5 per cent. Irish people had been moving in for much of the nineteenth century and continued to do so, though in smaller numbers, in the late Victorian and Edwardian period. They were joined by a variety of people from virtually all the continents of the globe. It was estimated that, as a result of immigration from the 1880s onwards, over forty nationalities lived together in Cardiff's multi-cultural and multi-national dockland. Elsewhere in south Wales the built environment bore testimony to Eastern European, Jewish, Spanish or Italian immigration: numerous Catholic churches, the synagogue in Merthyr, Alphonso Street in Dowlais and many an Italian cafe.

Growing ethnic diversity and the congregating of different nationalities was, geographically, effectively confined to the industrial areas of the south. Important in its own right, this trend also illustrates a much wider development, immense in its social and cultural implications. There was an extraordinary change in the distribution of the population. The twin forces of industrialization (above all the phenomenal growth of the coal industry) and urbanization (which was closely but not exclusively linked to industrial expansion) created a host of new towns and villages in the south Wales valleys. But they also created a new Wales, one in which divergences between different parts of the country were becoming increasingly marked. In 1801, 80 per cent of Wales's population lived in the rural areas; by 1911 only 20 per cent did so. In 1851, 20 per cent lived in towns of over 5,000 people; by 1891 the figure had risen to 50 per cent and to nearly 60 per cent by 1911. By 1901, one third of the population lived within a twenty-five-mile radius of Cardiff. In 1881, 38 per cent of the people of Wales lived in the county of Glamorgan; by 1911 the proportion had risen to a staggering 55 per cent. By then, too, the population of Rhondda alone was greater than that of any other Welsh county apart from Carmarthenshire and Monmouthshire. Nor was this growth steady throughout the period. The most intense period of expansion in terms of coal production, population, inmigration and even housebuilding was in the first decade of the twentieth century. Between 1901 and 1911 the population of Wales increased by 400,000, about 130,000 people moved into the colliery districts of Glamorgan and Monmouthshire, and the south Wales coal industry took on an additional 70,000 workers.

The spectacular growth of population in the coastal ports and coal-field settlements of the south was due to natural increase, immigration, and inmigration of people from elsewhere in Wales, especially the rural areas. Historians disagree over the extent to which the movement of people into the burgeoning colliery districts of south Wales was exclusively or even primarily a *Welsh* movement, and when inmigration from outside Wales came to predominate. Recent work reveals that the influx into, and settlement of, the valleys was an immensely complex and intricate phenomenon and, moreover, one which often involved a series of moves, as new collieries were opened up in previously unsettled areas. But there is no doubt that by the end of the nineteenth century at the latest, people from outside Wales were the majority among those moving into the southern industrial areas, a development which, as we shall see, had profound linguistic as well as social and cultural consequences.

Although the pace and scale of expansion in the south resoundingly dominates our history, it should also be remembered that there were other growth points in Wales between 1870 and 1914. Denbighshire and Flintshire, which possessed coal and steel industries and a more diversified economy than the south, also experienced growth, as did the slate-quarrying districts in north-west Wales. Under the impact of the growing importance of tourism, itself largely a result of the building of railways, places like Llandudno, Colwyn Bay, Rhyl, Aberystwyth and Tenby continued to grow throughout the period. The fortunes of the rural counties of Wales, however, and especially the agricultural districts, present a stark contrast. Hard times on the land because of the agricultural depression of the 1880s and 1890s, and a fall in demand for labour as a result of much greater concentration on pastoral farming in the face of cheap grain imports from abroad, stimulated agricultural labourers (but not farmers) to move away in search of work elsewhere. Rural Wales was losing its natural population increase and several counties experienced a decline in population. Many people who were born in Anglesey, Brecon, Cardigan or Montgomery, in particular, would spend their lives outside the county of their birth.

The concentration of industry into the south-east and the crisis on the land also created further regional divergences in the demographic profile of the Welsh people during these years. The ratio of men to women, marriage rates, birth rates, age profile and family size were all affected and they helped shape the lived experiences of men and women. In 1871 there were more females than males in Wales (706,535 as compared to 706,048). Ten years later the position had been reversed, and the imbalance in favour of males became more marked as time went on: in 1914 there were 1,231,739 males and 1,189,182 females (965 females to every 1,000 males). Yet there were major regional and county variations and disparities, and in some respects such variations are more important than changes in the average returns for Wales as a whole. A comparison between Cardiganshire and Rhondda marks the extremes, but the basic pattern represented a real rural-industrial divide. In Rhondda in 1891 there were 1,314 men to every 1,000 women; in Cardiganshire in the same period there were 776 men to every 1,000 women. Partly due to the sex imbalance, in Cardiganshire in 1911 only 37 per cent of women aged 20-40 were married, compared to 76 per cent of those in the same age group living in Rhondda in the same year. There were more older people, far fewer babies and much smaller families in the west-Wales county than in the overcrowded, densely-populated streets of Rhondda, where population was primarily young (in 1881, 40 per cent of the population was under 15 years of age) and extraordinarily prolific. Fertility rates in the mining communities remained high even when, from the end of the nineteenth century onwards, the national trend was towards people having fewer children. As the rural areas stagnated, the balance of power, wealth and resources had shifted, and the majority Welsh experience now lay in the new, dynamic industrial communities of south Wales.

Wealth, Health and Houses

The continuing significance of change and continuity, and of diversity and disparity, as central themes in people's experiences in Wales is reaffirmed when wealth, health and accommodation are considered. Throughout the years between 1870 and 1914 there were massive inequalities in the amount of financial and property resources people had at their disposal and, inevitably, these disparities were also reflected in housing and diet. For some, this period was one of intense wealth creation and accumulation, and, in general, the greater the personal income, the greater the comfort of its possessors and the stronger their shield against the ravages of life. The vast majority of Wales's inhabitants, however, either experienced poverty, or were only one or two steps removed from it. Whether on the land or in the terraces, their living conditions ensured the shared reality that existence remained precarious.

The land of Wales was not owned by the people of Wales – at least not by the overwhelming mass of them. The concentration of landownership in the hands of a very small number of nobility and gentry, like Sir Watkin Williams Wynn or the Earl of Cawdor (the two largest landowners in Wales at the time), had been a perennial feature of the Welsh economic and social structure for centuries. It would remain so right up until the years immediately before the first World War when landowners began to sell off their estates. In the 1870s it was recorded that 60 per cent of the total area of Wales consisted of estates of over 1,000 acres; these were owned by just 571 people, who made up a mere 1 per cent of the total number of landowners in Wales (including small farmers and cottagers). The size of estates and the scale of the monopoly on landownership differed in various parts of Wales but these variations did not affect the basic pattern; here was concentration on a grand scale. In the last quarter of the nineteenth century almost half of Caernarfonshire was owned by five families, whilst over three-quarters of the county was owned by just thirty-five families. At the other end of the spectrum, 94 per cent of households in that county did not own any area of land bigger than a garden. Farms in Wales were generally small, especially in Cardiganshire where, in the early 1900s, a fifth of all holdings were less than five acres in size and 70 per cent of them were under fifty acres. Smallholdings could barely support existence and, as a result, parts of that county, and indeed many other agricultural districts, were crushingly poor.

Fortunately for some of the great landowners, the presence of rich mineral reserves under their estates, and/or the ownership of industrial concerns, greatly enhanced their income and made them even more rich and powerful. The three richest landowners in Wales were the Marquis of Bute and Lord Tredegar, both of whom owned extensive lands in, respectively, the Glamorgan and Monmouthshire valleys as well as docks at Cardiff and Newport, and Lord Penrhyn, who secured immense profits from his landed estates and massive slate quarries at Bethesda. Industrial expansion and entrepreneurship enabled some of more lowly origin to become very wealthy. One example is William Thomas Lewis (1837-1914), later Lord Merthyr of Senghennydd, who skilfully built on his powerful position as the mineral agent of the Bute Estate to become a major coalowner and shareholder in his own right. Such rags-to-riches stories, however, were extremely exceptional.

In broad terms, the ranks of society between the exalted levels of the richest and the mass of the people were occupied by those who can, simplistically, be described as the middle class. They comprise a rather shadowy group in the written history of Wales during this period, and their strength and composition varied depending on region. In the industrial south, in particular, there developed a confident, assertive middle class which took pride in fostering the civic development of urban settlements, building parks, libraries and other public amenities (the magnificent development of Cathays Park in Cardiff is the most obvious example). In north-west Wales the growth of a middle class was restricted by the power monopoly of the Penrhyn interests. Nevertheless, throughout Wales, there was a marked increase in numbers in professional occupations such as doctors and lawyers, and, at a lower level, of what has been described as the 'shopocracy' (smaller businessmen and shopkeepers, for example). In the same way as the gentry and greater industrialists graced the landscape with their country houses and stately homes – like Llanwern House, owned by D.A. Thomas, Lord Rhondda, the driving force who put together the mammoth Cambrian Combine of coal companies after 1908 – the Welsh middle class left its own architectural imprint, notably in the new suburban housing retreats of Cardiff and Swansea.

In late Victorian and Edwardian Wales, then, there were, literally, many mansions – but so too were there many uninhabitable dwellings and, in general, housing was basic and poor. By and large the lines of terraces that scored the sides of the valleys were not constructed by coal companies. Either they were erected by speculative builders or they were financed by building clubs set up by mining families themselves. This was in marked contrast to the earlier, iron-industry phase of industrialization when most housing was built by the ironmasters. A further important feature was the high percentage of home ownership. As many as 60 per cent of the houses were owned by their occupiers, and the rate could be even higher in the anthracite-mining valleys in the western part of the coalfield. Here, a less frenetic rate of expansion, and with it a slower population growth and less inmigration, combined with the topography to enable more leisurely-paced, and indeed -spaced, development.

Housing shortage and overcrowding plagued most areas of Wales (rural as well as industrial), although the situation was most acute in the rapidly and intensively developing colliery settlements in the south-east. Like the world's insatiable appetite for coal, supply of accommodation could not keep up with demand. Large families and large numbers of lodgers and boarders meant some communities counted among the highest densities of population in Britain. Even so, almost literally living on top of each other helped foster solidarities and a strong sense of community. Probably the worst accommodation in Wales, however, was that suffered by agricultural labourers (although one exception to this must have been the husband, wife and three children who, because of either poverty, housing shortage or both, lived between 1885 and 1906 in the lime kilns at the disused Nantyglo Ironworks). The often appalling living conditions in the agricultural areas remained a constant feature of Welsh society throughout the years 1870-1914 as little was done to ameliorate them. Single male agricultural labourers normally lodged in insanitary lofts above stables or outhouses on the farms where they worked. The Commission on the Employment of Children, Young Persons and Women of 1870 found that the majority of cottages for farm workers were in a poor condition and often unfit for human habitation. Particularly bad were those in the counties of south-west Wales which consisted of one room only, a thatched roof, clay walls and a floor of beaten earth. As well as poor conditions, farmers and their labourers alike had to face insecurity of tenure. For labourers, tied cottages were let annually and dismissal from work also meant losing their homes.

The standard of working-class housing in the industrial areas varied, but generally houses lacked bathrooms, and, because of the rapid and unplanned nature of development in many of these new communities, the provision of essential facilities such as water and sewage disposal was derisory. Whether in rural Meirioneth or industrial Monmouthshire, much of Wales's housing was the hotbed of diseases like tuberculosis, cholera, typhus and diphtheria, and the poor living conditions people had to endure can be measured in the high mortality rates, especially those of infants and children. In Rhondda in 1891 55 per cent of all deaths were of children under the age of five; in 1909 in the Newcastle Emlyn district of Carmarthenshire, the infant mortality rate (that is, deaths of children aged under one year) was a chilling 246 per 1,000.

In many parts of Wales during the late nineteenth and early twentieth centuries efforts were made to try to improve this state of affairs. Parliamentary legislation enabled the implementation of major public health schemes which provided fresh water supplies to homes, and refuse and sewage disposal systems. Main sewers came to Rhondda for the first time in 1894 – when its population was nearly 100,000. Under the impact of these works, by the last ten to fifteen years or so of our period there was in motion an appreciable decline in mortality rates in Wales. Even so, in 1911 in Aberdare, the infant mortality rate was 213 per 1,000 births.

A healthy existence was obviously also dependent on good nutrition and diet. These, however, are areas of human experience in late-nineteenth- and early-twentieth century Wales which have hardly been examined by historians. It is clear that there were widespread variations in the quality and nature of the diet in various parts of Wales, though for most people it was basic and food was eaten in lesser quantities than today. The diet of the poorer in society was notoriously monotonous, inadequate and insufficient, leading to a high incidence of malnutrition. However, from the late nineteenth century onwards, common eating habits were emerging. The general growth of mass production, consumerism, standardization and food imports, allied to the existence of a national railway network which could transport goods all over Britain, meant that diet was becoming more uniform, if not necessarily more wholesome. In Britain generally during this period, for example, home baking of bread was being slowly but surely superseded by the purchase of the standard commercial loaf.

Whereas self-sufficiency in food production probably continued to be most common in the predominantly agricultural districts of Wales, in the cash economy of the industrial and urban communities shopping was an essential activity. One of the most striking aspects of the growth of urban centres, and even of smaller colliery villages, was the emergence of a phantasmagoria of shops and stores which catered for a wide range of tastes and demands. In the more populated areas there developed busy and flourishing commercial districts, with chain stores such as Hodges, and Home and Colonial, and by 1900 most shopping centres in the valleys would have a Co-operative store. There was no shortage of establishments where one could buy the necessities of life – and certainly when times were good, a few luxuries as well.

Behind closed doors
If there is much we do not know about matters such as shopping and diet in late-nineteenth and early-twentieth century Wales, then the same can even more forcefully be said about the nature of relationships between men, women and children during the same period.

Historians are only beginning to explore subjects such as family dynamics, how parents 'prepared' their children for life, sexual matters, and domestic violence and abuse within the home, whilst we know nothing at all about homosexuality and lesbianism in what appears to have been a very macho, male society, particularly in the coal-fields.

Recovering these experiences is extremely difficult because they were private and secret, and public discussion of these topics was something of a taboo. Moreover, such experiences no doubt varied considerably, not only throughout Wales but from individual to individual and from family to family. It is impossible, for example, to quantify the number of prostitutes in Wales or the number of women who had to resort to abortions. The former operated in rural and industrial areas, either full time or to provide occasional income when times were tight, whilst newspaper columns tell their own story of the horrific consequences of efforts to get rid of unwanted pregnancies and babies. Penetrating human experiences which many wanted to be securely locked behind the closed doors or closets of late-nineteenth- and early-twentieth century Wales is made all the more difficult by prevailing contemporary beliefs and ideologies. A large body of opinion – mainly, but not exclusively, that of the middle class and of religious leaders – did not regard sex as something to be enjoyed, especially by women. The woman's place was in the home ('the angel in the house'), and she was required to be pure, to be the guardian of society's morals, to look after the home, and to be untarnished by the public, male sphere. It was also asserted that the family was the social institution which fostered Christianity and respectability, and provided a bulwark against the evils of the outside world. These views were common throughout Britain but in Wales they were also central to Nonconformist thinking.

We cannot know how many families lived up to these ideals nor, just as important, how many did not believe it was necessary to do so. Moreover, the emphasis on outward respectability resulted in the cultivation of the so-called eleventh commandment – 'thou shalt not be found out' – as a standard. But it is clear that for many, moral strictures exerted great pressures, particularly on wives and mothers. In this respect the central role of women (unfortunately fatherhood is yet another unstudied topic) in creating a rich family

and communal life in the home – sometimes in the face of overwhelming odds – needs to be emphasized. Studies of Carmarthenshire
and Senghennydd in this period have painted rather a different picture
from traditional Victorian views of family relations, sex and similar
matters. As well as the cradle of morality, purity and religiosity, the
family unit could also be the arena for deep tensions, caused by
repressed emotions, failed promises, drink or, above all, financial
hardship. These frustrations could and did burst out into violence,
whether wife abuse, child abuse or the abuse of older people. Divorce
was a possibility for those who could afford it, but for few others,
although separation and maintenance orders became more common
following legislation in the 1880s and 1890s. That women frequently
decided to tolerate domestic violence indicates their socially and
economically disadvantaged position in society.

Frequent premarital sex seems to have been common, if not the norm,
whether on the understanding that marriage would follow or not, and
couples were not averse to making love on the first or second meeting.
On the other hand, as well as consenting sex, rapes and indecent assaults
were also commonplace. Knowledge and usage of birth control methods
and abortifacients were widespread, aided by copious advertisement in
newspapers. Though frowned upon and severely punished in chapels,
illegitimacy was rife and probably grudgingly accepted, though
historians have disagreed over whether illegitimacy rates were higher in
the industrial areas of Wales or in the rural areas. As Russell Davies has
vividly described it, 'beneath the respectable façade the world of the
senses thrived. Passion flourished among the prudery.'

PASSING THE TIME

When we turn to explore some of the major ways in which people
spent their time between 1870 and 1914, two crucial facts
immediately become apparent. First, work was central to the lives of
most people. Having to labour was an inescapable necessity in order
to maintain existence, and a considerable amount of time was devoted
to it. Second, however harsh living and working conditions were, and
however much survival was a hard struggle, the evidence suggests
that, as far as possible, life was lived to the full. People thrived on

diversion and entertainment. Once again, there were significant changes and differences in ordinary people's experiences when in and when not in work, but there were also important features which were almost universally shared.

In Work

A major continuity in Wales between 1870 and 1914 was the narrowness of its economic base. Apart from some growth in service industries in the largest towns, the Welsh economy did not diversify to any marked extent, and coal, steel, tinplate, slate, transport and agriculture retained their status as the largest – and virtually the only – sources of employment. Between 1881 and 1911 there were significant increases in the number of workers employed in all of these, with the exception of agriculture, in which there was a decline in the size of the workforce. However, the most striking development of all was the tremendous concentration of workers in one industry, coal, and in the south Wales coal industry at that (there were about fifteen times as many employed in the south than in the smaller coal-field in north-east Wales). Such was the scale of the industry's continued expansion throughout these years that, by 1911, nearly one in three of the entire male occupied population of Wales was a miner. This was one of the most obvious areas of Welsh life where clearly an intense 'massing' was occurring. In 1874, 73,328 men were employed in the coal industry in south Wales; in 1913 that figure had risen to 234,134, equivalent to about 10 per cent of the total population of Wales.

The lack of diversification of the Welsh economy, and the dependence on a small number of heavy industries, meant that large numbers of men worked in similar environments – in a quarry, in a mine, in a steelworks or in a tinplate works, in which a significant number of women also worked. Employment opportunities were even more restricted for women, especially in the effectively one-industry coal- and slate-quarrying districts, a situation which usually resulted in early marriage. Officially-recorded figures for female participation in the economy in Wales were lower than those for England and, despite more women being employed in teaching and nursing, participation rates fell between 1871 and 1911. However, the census greatly under-represented the scale of women's paid work and its vital contribution to the Welsh economy. As with men, women were equally concentrated into a narrow range of occupations. In agriculture they often constituted a sizeable regular workforce as well as an army of casual labourers. There were large numbers of female domestic servants – they formed over half the total number of women employed in Wales between 1871 and 1901. Moreover the world of work in Wales included not only the formal economy but also unpaid domestic labour by women at home. The most numerous workplaces of all, then, were the very homes of the people themselves.

Work was not only an experience for men and women but also for children. Childhood was short and punctuated by casual chores or tasks from an early age. By 1899 successive acts of Parliament had made attendance at school compulsory and raised to age 12 the lower age limit at which children could leave school and start work full time. There was significant evasion of the age limit, however, and prolonged absenteeism, especially in the agricultural districts, as families sought extra income. Children were involved mainly in seasonal tasks, like hay and corn harvesting, and on other occasional work such as planting and raising potatoes, weeding, stone-picking and trimming turnips.

Throughout the period ordinary people's work experiences had much in common. Work took up a lot of their time. The vast majority endured long working hours, a long working week and a long working lifetime. Some groups worked inordinately long hours. Shop assistants in Merthyr were working eighty hours a week into the twentieth century. In agriculture the working day in summer was often thirteen hours long, and although working hours varied from place to place, they differed only in their degree of excess. In some areas of employment, hours and days of work had been, or were being, shortened during the period. Yet, though becoming more common, improvements like the granting of the Saturday half-day did not extend to all workers. For women who worked in their own homes – or for that matter agricultural labourers who lived on the farm – there were no fixed hours of work. For the women houseworkers of the valleys, each working day was in part a series of preparations of food and hot water in order to equip their menfolk to produce more coal.

A further shared characteristic was that most people were engaged in manual labour, and for men, women and young adults alike this usually meant hard physical toil, often in unpleasant and dangerous conditions. There could hardly be more strenuous work than the battle to keep away dust and dirt in the mining terraces – washing clothes by hand, keeping the house clean and scrubbing doorsteps. Underground miners worked in cramped, dusty, wet and hot stall and roadways. The fact that miners at Daniel Thomas's Pwllgwaun Colliery (located on the site of what is now Pontypridd Rugby Football Club's ground at Sardis Road) nicknamed their workplace 'Dan's Muck Hole' speaks volumes about how difficult, oppressive and uncomfortable working conditions underground could be. The same was true of other industries, and on the land. One late-nineteenth-century observer of tinplate manufacture likened work in the mill to 'a lot of madmen throwing red hot plates at each other'.

Arduous toil was also accompanied, to a greater or lesser extent, by all-too-real possibilities of premature death or injury through accidents, let alone the longer-term effects for miners and quarrymen of the constant inhaling of dust (causing fatal lung diseases like silicosis). Work-place risks added considerably to the precariousness of life, and had serious economic consequences for dependants. In the heat of the steel or tinplate works, burns and cramps from dehydration were common occurrences. Workers' faces in most industries bore the scars incurred at work. In tinplate manufacture both the men who worked in the mills and the women who sorted and cut the plates suffered from cuts from the sharp plates. Though irritating and painful, such mishaps were nothing when compared to the bigger risks that had to be faced in every working shift. In mining and quarrying, for instance, rock falls or slippages while working at the coal- or rock-face, handling large and heavy slabs of rock, and using explosives were only some of the causes of death and injury. The horrific series of large-scale mining disasters which rocked south Wales during the late nineteenth and early twentieth centuries inevitably grab our attention more than day-to-day occurrences, but it should also be remembered that about four fifths of deaths in coal mining occurred in single, isolated accidents. Fatalities descended on the mining communities of south Wales in constant drips even more than they did in deluges. Moreover, the strain of keeping up with the rhythm of the colliery's work patterns, and of producing, raising and tending large families and the wage-earners of the future, wore out many miners' wives long before their time.

The shared experience of hard labour and harsh conditions was a potent force in forging solidarities between workers and making concerted action possible. Equally, workplace demarcations and craft loyalties could as easily divide them. Workers created their own value systems. The possession of skill was highly prized, and status also played an important part in workplace relationships and hierarchies. Surviving evidence suggests that many workers – and this is just as applicable to the standard of cleanliness of a home as it is to a well-kept stall underground – had great pride in their work. Workers in industry also reserved the right to control their own work – a right which their employers concertedly began to challenge towards the end of the nineteenth century with, as we shall see, profound consequences. The financial rewards for work were almost always meagre, as periods of high wages were easily offset by more lean times. It is difficult to compare wage rates in Wales during these years as methods of payment varied considerably both within particular industries and between regions and, in any event, the standard of living depended on other considerations such as price levels. Generally speaking, wages were considerably higher in the coal-mining districts than in the rural areas. In 1913 the weekly wage of Cardiganshire farm labourers was 16s 4d (about 82p); in Rhondda, underground labourers (who were among the lower-paid grades of workers in the coal industry) could expect to earn twice that amount.

Conditions seem to have changed little during these years. In 1913 about 1 per cent of the coal produced in south Wales was machine-cut; 99 per cent of it was won by human muscle and skill at the coalface. In agriculture there was some introduction of machinery but it was localized and sporadic. Many areas were untouched by mechanization, yet such was its impact in Defynog parish, Breconshire, that in 1906 a local historian could declare that 'almost a revolution' had occurred as a result. There were some improvements as far as the safety of working environments was concerned. New legislation compelled compliance with a larger body of rules and regulations, and sought to ensure the competence of managers and officials in mines and other industrial concerns. Even so, the worst disaster in the history of mining in Britain occurred in October 1913, when 439 underground workers were killed in an explosion at Universal Colliery, Senghennydd. The deceased left over 900 dependants. It has also been estimated that in the years before the first World War the mortality rates of young women who laboured at home were higher than those of their fathers, brothers, husbands and sons who worked in the pit. In more ways than one the shadow of the pithead gear dominated the landscape of work in Wales during these years.

Not in work

Throughout the late nineteenth and early twentieth centuries people made their own entertainments. They continued to enjoy pastimes and activities that had pleasured their predecessors earlier in the nineteenth century. They also partook of the innovations in popular culture that so dominate the story of leisure activity during this period. Popular culture meant amusement and entertainment; it satisfied the yearning for spectacle and excitement and gave people something to look forward to. Perhaps one of the most profound changes of all that occurred between 1870 and 1914 was that significant numbers of people in Wales decided they would spend more on entertainments than on drink, and came to regard spending on leisure as being a far more essential item in the family budget.

As well as a place of work and happiness, and of danger and death for many families, the home was also a focal point of leisure. The study of usage of non-working time in Victorian and Edwardian Wales is of recent origin, and what has been done – understandably, perhaps – has tended to focus on mass participatory forms such as rugby or choral singing. Much less is known about recreation at home, but activities such as reading, playing the piano and playing games with children probably grew in popularity among slightly better-off, and possibly more respectable, working-class families. For the classes above them the first two activities had much longer pedigrees as ways of spending free time. The late nineteenth century, particularly after the 1870 Forster Education Act, saw continued increases in literacy. The demand for reading matter was met by a wide range of newspapers and periodicals, in both Welsh and English, and, to the dismay of promoters of uplifting literature, the new public libraries stocked shelvesful of 'cheap', popular novels. For women who looked after the home full time, houses and the street were also the focal points of the networks of conversation and mutual aid they created.

For children in urban areas the streets and the parks or surrounding hills were the arenas for a myriad of games and pastimes. Reminiscences of late-nineteenth-century childhoods, though often coloured by nostalgia, usually describe an almost endless whirl of iron hoops, spinning tops, marbles, skipping, leap-frog, and catty and doggy – to name but a few – as well as more mischievous exploits. Little is known about the experience of play among children brought up on farms in the more isolated rural areas, though probably similar types of games were enjoyed. The amount of 'playtime' children had at their disposal inevitably varied greatly depending on the prosperity of the family as well as a whole range of attitudinal factors, but there was probably more time than had been the case earlier in the century, when they had to begin work at an earlier age. Even so, it is probable that girls had less time than boys, as they were expected to help out in looking after the home. As they reached adolescence the role of girls in keeping house for the rest of the family became increasingly formalized.

As well as informal recreations, schools and chapels organized a continuous series of events for children, such as tea parties, penny readings, concerts and eisteddfodau, whilst numerous travelling fairs and circuses toured Wales. Of course, these types of entertainments were also for adults, and they demonstrate powerfully the tremendous range and number of organized events held in late Victorian and Edwardian Wales both locally and nationally. Including religious institutions in a discussion of leisure and popular culture is in some respects unwarranted as they were reflections of piety and devotion. Even so, they were also some of the great social centres of nineteenth- and early twentieth-century Wales. Normally, each church or chapel had an extensive calendar of activities, testifying to the energy of their reading groups, choirs, and dramatic and debating societies, as well as more religiously-inspired endeavours such as missionary societies, prayer- and Band of Hope- meetings, and Sunday schools. A Llwynypïa woman recalled that her social life was

> all with the chapel. Because there was something there every night of the week for us. Either little plays, or ther'd be children's operettas. Or the big choir then, we'd have the cantatas. And ther'd be Young People's Society and Prayer Meeting on Monday night. Our social life was all around the church. And it wasn't dull, mind. We had an awful lot of fun.

It is worth emphasizing that women played a full role in the social side of religious life, though not, it should equally be remembered, in the governance of these institutions.

Historians have tended to see the chapel and the public house as the two opposite poles of nineteenth-century Welsh communities, rivalling each other for the hearts and minds – and pennies – of the people. The line between them may have been too starkly drawn and, apart from a hard core in each, there was perhaps much cross-fertilization of clientele between them. In Jack Jones's novel *Black Parade*, on an August Bank Holiday weekend Glyn and Saran manage to frequent pubs, boxing booths, bicycle races and the theatre, and also go to hear a great preacher at Zoar Chapel. At the beginning of the twentieth century in Bethesda, two local characters – 'Deryn Nos' and 'Wil Betsy Bwtsh' – were casually employed to deliver beer 'take-outs' to the houses of some local religious leaders. They wore long coats to hide their cargo of bottles and jugs.

That Bethesda in the late nineteenth century had about forty official public houses and an uncertain number of unlicensed premises selling home-made beer illustrates the significance of drink to much social existence in Wales at the time. Whether imbibed in search of release from the tensions of life, or as a quencher of immense thirst induced by heavy manual labour in often very hot conditions, or as a by-product of being sociable, for many men, at least, drink was one of life's necessities. It is probable that, given alternative amusements and recreation, people were consuming less alcohol in Wales as the years went on. Certainly, landlords and breweries responded to reformers' calls to 'clean up' their establishments by building grand, more 'respectable' public houses. To what extent the public house was a 'masculine republic' is difficult to establish; some women frequented public houses, but this practice was also frowned on by many men and women alike. The same ambiguity regarding female exclusion or inclusion applies to another major institution which established itself in industrial towns and villages during the late nineteenth century, and one which rapidly emerged as a focal point of community life: the working men's institute. Often replete with libraries, billiard rooms, concert halls and, later, cinemas these were effectively maintained by working-class families themselves. Though it appears that some institutes were open to both sexes, the majority of them – or at least their libraries and games rooms – were probably male preserves, and remained so well into the twentieth century.

As the nineteenth century wore on there occurred in Wales what might be described as an explosion of mass popular cultural activity. The number of eisteddfodau, concerts, brass band and choral competitions multiplied, while a host of amateur and professional performers toured the country to entertain the audiences in the stalls. Choral singing, for example, was certainly not new in 1870 but thereafter, aided by widespread tuition in the music notation of sol-fa, it expanded out of its Nonconformist roots and enjoyed a great surge in secular popularity. Right at the beginning of our period, as we have seen, the identification of Wales as 'the land of song' was effectively sealed by the victories of the South Wales Choral Union at the Crystal Palace in 1872 and 1873 and, for generations, the vocal performances of amateur and untrained choirs would thrill audiences within and outside Wales. By the end of the century most towns and villages had a range of choirs – male, female, mixed – some with a hundred or more choristers. Those choirs that entered the numerous regional and national competitions usually enjoyed a fanatical following, even if the rowdy and raucous behaviour of some supporters at such events was an offence to those who promoted music as a moral and elevating activity.

From the 1880s onwards, in particular, there also came on stream a dazzling array of new recreations. Parts of urban and industrial Wales, especially the south, were in the vanguard of the growth of organized commercial leisure and spectator sports: seaside trips and amusements, football, rugby, the building of theatres and skating rinks, the music hall (from the 1890s onwards) and the cinema (from about 1910 onwards) all flourished and permeated to the core of many people's experiences and priorities. What was occurring was a crucial dimension to the much wider process of the creation of a working-class Welshness, and popular culture was one of the key ways in which a sense of Welshness was created and then learned.

Though it remained an essentially middle-class game elsewhere in Britain, in Wales rugby caught the public imagination and was embraced by all classes. From the 1870s onwards large numbers of clubs were founded in south Wales. Initially Liberal-Nonconformist leaders regarded the game with contempt and hostility but their opinions changed with the national team's successes during the 1890s and first decade of the twentieth century. Wales won its first Triple Crown in 1893 and repeated that feat a further six times between 1900 and 1912. But rugby was not the only spectator sport that flourished, or indeed the only one which brought success to Wales: soccer was popular in both north and south Wales; boxers like Freddie Welsh became world champions; and cycling and foot-racing had large followings.

Several crucial factors were in operation in these dramatic developments. In the first place, urbanization and the growth of a transport network were essential prerequisites. Scattered rural villages simply did not possess the population or financial resources needed to nurture and sustain, for example, large choirs, whilst the attendance of people from all over Wales at national gatherings such as the National Eisteddfod would not have been possible without railways. The development of mass popular culture was also made possible by more leisure time and greater disposable income, though in effect this placed it beyond the reach of the poorest in Welsh society. Moreover, in the new industrial settlements (whether Blaenau Ffestiniog, Bargoed, Brymbo or Brynaman), mass recreational activity was one means of building community spirit. Competitions, whether for brass bands or choirs, and derby football matches sharpened the edges of local rivalries and heightened local loyalties. Popular culture not only gave meaning to people's lives; it also gave them new identities.

MULTIPLYING IDENTITIES

Identities are not fixed, singular entities, rather they are constantly changing and are situational, varying according to the time, place and occasion. Under the impact of massive industrial, social, political and cultural changes going on around them, people in Wales changed their perceptions of themselves, and their ideas about who they were. In other words, they subscribed to new beliefs and embraced new identities. Workplace relationships and popular cultural practices, as we have already seen, could foster common identities. During the period 1870-1914 Welsh people also acquired, maintained or spurned allegiances to a whole range of other concerns: Nonconformity, superstitions, political affiliation, consensus policies in industrial relations, class consciousness, the Welsh language and local, national and imperial identities. Not everyone, everywhere in Wales changed dramatically, and patterns of change varied in scale and pace. Few, however, would be unaware of the changes that were occurring, whilst many people undoubtedly saw the world in a very different way compared to their predecessors a generation earlier.

Beliefs, new and old

The late-Victorian and Edwardian period was one which witnessed dramatic scientific and technological advance, or to use the favourite contemporary term, progress. It was only the richer members of Welsh society who could actively acquire some of the spectacular new inventions like the telephone or the motor car, but all urbanites could share benefits accruing from, for example, electric street lighting or the revolution in transport. Moreover, the telegraph and the telephone made the world a much smaller place, enabling people in Wales to learn of global events very soon after they had occurred – news of Jack the Ripper's atrocities in the 1880s, for example, or the sinking of the *Titanic* in 1912.

Innovations such as these, and, more generally, industrialization, urbanization and the triumph of scientific thought and rationality, permeated Wales, perhaps even into its remote areas. People embraced the modern and, in so doing, turned away from 'traditional' beliefs and customs which had existed for centuries. Yet, as some historians have maintained, it would be unwise to regard this as an all-embracing and all-inclusive development. It has been shown that, in rural Carmarthen-shire, a plethora of superstitious beliefs and practices, and an array of traditional folk customs like herbal medicines and healing, remained strong well into the twentieth century, not only among the uneducated. They were not eradicated by increased religiosity during the nineteenth century but coexisted alongside it. In the new coalfield towns and villages, traditional methods of community sanction were adapted but not discarded. This is not to deny that profound change took place, but to suggest that its pace varied greatly and that, for some, a changing world-view did not necessarily mean wholesale rejection of previous certainties.

Religion itself was not exempt from forces of change. For many people in Wales their faith exerted a powerful hold over their lives, giving them hope and comfort, and influencing their world-view and conduct. Moreover, the picture of an overwhelmingly devout and pious Welsh population is one of the most powerful images modern-day Wales has inherited from the nineteenth century. By the 1870s, many in Wales came to see religiosity, and indeed Welshness itself, as being interchangeable with the Nonconformist faith, a belief famously endorsed by the Liberal leader W.E. Gladstone in 1891 when he declared that 'the Nonconformists of Wales are the people of Wales'. Yet two qualifications must be made to emphasize once again the diversity of human experience in Wales. First, approximately half the population were not religious, at least as measured by attendance at religious services. Second, religion was by no means confined to Nonconformity, even if it held sway. There were sizeable numbers of Anglicans and Roman Catholics, for instance; but as Gladstone's remark suggests, Nonconformist leaders did not regard these faiths as 'Welsh'.

Nonconformity maintained its position as the largest religious body throughout the late nineteenth century. As well as its strength in the rural areas, it also successfully put down roots in the new, developing coalfield communities. Chapels were built in the valleys at a remarkable rate – by 1914 it was estimated that there were 200 of them in Rhondda alone. During the same period, Nonconformity, especially in alliance with Liberalism, was a powerful force in Welsh life and was influential in shaping key political, cultural, social and educational agendas. By the turn of century, however, its power and cultural authority were increasingly under challenge: from other religions (for example, a revival in the fortunes of Anglicanism) and from organized labour and socialism. Above all, Nonconformity was being marginalized by new forms of commercialized leisure activity. There were also internal tensions – there is evidence to suggest that some chapel members were alienated by Nonconformity's increasingly institutionalized, plutocratic and hierarchical character.

As with so many other patterns of change in human experience, it is impossible to reach firm conclusions regarding the extent to which a retreat from Nonconformity had occurred by 1914. Nevertheless, from the beginning of the twentieth century, it is clear that Nonconformity's influence was waning in many industrial areas and probably some rural areas as well. Long-term trends towards secularization were making themselves felt. Fewer people felt the need for spiritual comforts than had been the case a generation earlier, and religion was becoming more and more a matter of indifference to more and more people. Such a shift did not manifest itself in a massive fall in chapel membership or attendance, although clearly the foundations for the decline that occurred after 1914 were being laid. Once again, however, bearing in mind the continuing operation of uneven development and regional diversity in Wales, there were major local, regional, gender and generational variations.

Changing political allegiances

Between 1870 and 1914 there was a greater, though still restricted, democratization of Welsh society. In 1872 the secret ballot was introduced and, as a result of a further extension of the franchise in 1884, the Welsh electorate grew to 282,000. By 1910 it had reached 425,000. Yet in 1910 only 18 per cent of the population had the vote. It was the prerogative of certain classes of men only, whilst only men could become members of parliament. Much less is known about the involvement of women in political life, although it was probably becoming less marginal than many commentators have assumed. Some middle-class and working-class women were active in campaigns to win women the vote and some working-class women became involved in the Labour Party (although it remained uninterested in women's issues). Greater scope for female – and, of course, male – involvement came with two further crucial democratic initiatives, the Local Government Act of 1888, which provided for elected county and borough elections, and the inauguration of urban and district councils in 1894.

By the 1880s and 1890s these new democratic structures had become dominated by one political party, the Liberals. Because the story of Welsh politics for most (and some historians would say all) of the period 1870-1914 is in large part the quite remarkable political ascendancy of the Liberal Party, it is worth noting that it was not the only political party. As we shall see, the Labour Party was mounting a challenge from the turn of the century onwards whilst, between 1886 and 1914, the Conservative Party vote in Wales rarely fell below 30 per cent, and was nearly 40 per cent in 1895. The party had a strong constituency of support, and it possessed its own organization and mouthpieces such as *The Western Mail* newspaper.

These alternative political allegiances notwithstanding, the extent of the support the Liberal Party received from the people of Wales is staggering. Although in the 1874 general election the Liberals lost some of the seats they had won in 1868, in the 1880 election they secured twenty-nine out of the thirty-three parliamentary seats in Wales. In the next two decades they frequently enjoyed over 60 per cent of the vote in elections and their dominance was crowned, famously and spectacularly, by their achievement in 1906 when they won all the seats in Wales bar that of Keir Hardie who was returned as Labour member for Merthyr Boroughs. Although some historians have rightly cautioned against exaggerating the extent to which the political control of the landed gentry was broken, nevertheless, at parliamentary and local government level, a fundamental seizure of power had occurred.

The massive support the Liberals came to enjoy reflected the popularity of their policies and what they represented. The Liberal leadership was composed primarily of Nonconformist ministers of religion and members of the professional and commercial middle class. Liberalism also had a working-class dimension and succeeded in securing mass support from ordinary working people. It purported to represent their interests, and its dominant philosophy in this regard was to promote consensus in industrial relations and to insist on mutuality of interests between capital and labour, all for the common good. Apart from educational reform and, as we shall see, the setting up of national institutions, most of the Liberal programme was geared towards redressing the grievances of farmers and tenants in rural Wales, and addressing injustices towards Nonconformists, with whom the Liberals had formed a powerful political alliance. Having to pay tithes to the Established Church of England was especially detestable to Nonconformists, and disestablishment was eventually secured on the eve of the first World War. In both campaigns, Liberal Nonconformity was confronting head-on the anglicized, Tory, landowning class in Wales.

Towards the end of the nineteenth century, and especially during the early years of the twentieth century, major shifts were occurring: industrial relations became increasingly polarized, and there was a growth of class consciousness and of interest in various forms of socialism. These trends were very marked in the case of the coal industry and in the development of the miners' union, the South Wales Miners Federation, formed in 1898. Working men increasingly began to regard the traditional concerns of the Liberal Party as being irrelevant to their needs. For a number of reasons many came to see independent labour parliamentary representation and more militant trade unionism as the best defenders of their interests. The Liberals seemed hostile to workers having their own say in politics, and they were unconcerned about growing social and labour problems like poor working and living conditions and the dramatically uneven distribution of the wealth being accumulated as a result of industrial prosperity. Many prominent industrialists were themselves Liberals – for example Lord Rhondda, 'the Tsar of the coalfield' – whilst, from the 1890s onwards, employers launched an aggressive counter-attack against their workers. This assault took the form of introducing new working practices which undermined traditional independence at the work place, locking out their workers if they did not accept the new arrangements, and resorting to the courts to end the immunity of trade unions. Judgements like that over Taff Vale in 1901, which enabled employers to seek damages when unions called a strike, forced labour organizations to seek parliamentary redress.

From 1898 onwards, and especially in the last few years before the outbreak of the first World War, Wales was rocked by a series of bitter industrial strikes and lockouts: the 1898 coal lockout, the Cambrian Combine stoppage in the collieries of the Rhondda valleys in 1910-11, the seamen's strike of 1911, and the national railway strike of 1911. In north Wales, a series of stoppages in the slate industry culminated in the three-year lockout of the Penrhyn quarrymen between 1900 and 1903, when industrial antagonisms over work practices were infused by social, cultural, political and linguistic tensions between Lord Penrhyn and quarrying families in Bethesda. Industrial disputes were often accompanied by violent confrontations between working families and police, troops or strikebreakers – in a clash in Llanelli during the 1911 railway strike two railway workers were shot and killed by troops – and women often played a prominent role in community action. In parliamentary elections before 1914 the Liberals were able to keep at bay the Labour challenge. Nevertheless, the foundations of the widespread shift in allegiances from Liberal to Labour which occurred after the first World War were laid before the outbreak of hostilities. That shift was rooted in the great upsurge in militant class consciousness and continued growth of aggressive trade unionism that occurred from 1910 to 1914.

A *nation reborn?*

Some historians have maintained that during the late nineteenth and early-twentieth centuries Wales experienced a rebirth as a nation. They have pointed not only to industrial and political development but also to Wales's increased institutional profile, significant advances in education, the renaissance in Welsh-language culture and more rigorous academic study of Wales, its language and its people. These factors, combined with common values and beliefs such as Nonconformity and Liberalism, created a growing sense of national consciousness on the part of the people of Wales, and a powerful sense of unity among them. Others have seen the late nineteenth century, particularly the years immediately before the first World War, as a period of widening, unbridgeable cleavages within Welsh society. To them it was a time when traditional notions of Welshness came increasingly under attack, when economic and social inequalities were undermining common interests, and class loyalties were becoming more important than national ones. Both these interpretations have their truth, partly because the incidence of change varied. Undoubtedly, more and more people came to regard themselves as Welsh during this period. Yet, although some clung to a vision of Welshness which crystallized around their native language, Nonconformity and Liberalism, a greater number adopted a more flexible approach to Welshness, and the idea of what it meant to be Welsh was being constantly reworked. For many, the joys of choral singing and the thrills of a rugby game were the agencies for becoming Welsh.

Increased national consciousness in Wales was partly developed by the fact that, during the late nineteenth and early twentieth centuries, Wales was becoming more clearly identifiable, more of a fixed entity. National institutions were established, complementing the existence of a much-expanded and popular National Eisteddfod, and national football teams; by the end of the century there was also widespread acceptance of '*Hen Wlad fy Nhadau*' as a national anthem. Although

Wales did not gain a capital (that would not come until 1955), the setting up of bodies such as the University of Wales in 1893, the National Museum in 1908 and the National Library in 1909 testified to the embracing of modern nationhood. The passing of the Sunday Closing Act in 1881 established the precedent that Wales merited separate parliamentary legislation. It was followed by the 1889 Welsh Intermediate Education Act which allowed for specific provision of state-aided secondary education in Wales earlier than in England. There was even a modicum of devolution when, in 1907, substantial responsibility for state education in Wales was given to the newly created Welsh Department of the Board of Education. Though it is difficult to evaluate what people outside Wales thought of the country, clearly this institutionalizing of Wales and Welshness made it more tangible to outsiders, and helped nurture wider acceptance of it as a distinct country with its own problems and aspirations which required their own particular solutions. Late-nineteenth and early-twentieth-century governmental commissions and enquiries into matters pertaining to Wales adopted a more sympathetic and measured tone than had spectacularly been the case with, for example, the infamous 1847 Education Commission Report. Yet despite growing recognition all around of Wales's separate and distinctive identity, within Wales itself, throughout the period, there were no overwhelming demands for autonomy or self-government for Wales; *Cymru Fydd* (Young Wales), a movement which after 1892 advocated Welsh Home Rule, was probably more influential in cultural than in political life. The Liberals, responsible for introducing many of the measures referred to, were more concerned with securing parity within Britain, not the break-up of Britain, and in this respect it is likely that they represented the wishes of the majority of their voters.

For many people, changing identities meant speaking English instead of Welsh, though others continued to speak Welsh only. Moreover, it is a measure of the complexities of the situation that many of those who could not – or would not – speak Welsh nevertheless regarded themselves as Welsh. The late-nineteenth and early- twentieth-century period is crucial to the fortunes of the Welsh language. The number of Welsh speakers continued to grow markedly – by the eve of the First World War there were more people in Wales who could speak Welsh than ever before, or since. Yet, during the same period, the percentage of Welsh speakers continued to fall sharply. The 977,366 people who could speak Welsh according to the 1911 census formed about 43 per cent of the population; in 1891 the percentage had been about 54 per cent and had been higher still in the 1870s. By the end of the nineteenth century, therefore, the majority of people living in Wales could not speak the native language.

The national figures, however, concealed massive variations in the location of Welsh speakers. The industrial districts of south Wales (with the exception of the anthracite valleys to the west) continued to register declining numbers of people who could speak the language. Immigration was a key factor here, of course. A significant proportion of the 58 per cent of the population of Glamorgan who could only speak English in 1911 had come from outside Wales and had not been Welsh speakers in the first place. Yet by the beginning of the twentieth century, in the valleys in the eastern part of the south Wales coal-field, a language shift had occurred, although the timing of the change varied. These were now areas where the predominant language of public life was English, whereas Welsh was the language of a narrower range of domains. It was the medium used in Welsh-language chapels, in Welsh-language cultural circles and in some homes. Moreover, younger people in the valleys were not acquiring, or were abandoning, a knowledge of Welsh. Explanations for the changing patterns of language use are immensely intricate and confusing. Historians have disagreed over whether the language shift was primarily a matter of choice or compulsion, and over the relative importance of demographic factors, of state educational policies in enforcing English, and of élite and popular attitudes which were complacent or apathetic regarding the survival of the language. Many people associated Welsh with Nonconformity and what might be termed the 'old world', and saw English as the language of progress and social and economic improvement. Above all, perhaps, in industrial south Wales, people's desire to create a new, secular, cosmopolitan and class-conscious society was greater than their wish to see Welsh as the language of public life. Consequently, they did not pass on a knowledge of Welsh, and adopted English as the new common language. Yet the continued diversity of experience in Wales reminds us that, in most of north-west and south-west Wales, society remained overwhelmingly Welsh-speaking, with Welsh being often the only medium of public and private life. Between 1891 and 1911 the number of Welsh-speakers in Anglesey, Caernarfonshire, Carmarthenshire, Cardiganshire and Meirioneth ranged from 89 to 95 per cent of their populations. In terms of the future of Welsh, however, the excruciating problem was that it was losing its hold in the most rapidly expanding areas of Wales.

If more people came to regard themselves as Welsh, this did not necessarily mean a breaking down or abandonment of more local identities. These remained important, although their intensity varied from individual to individual and from area to area. Moreover, their public expression was influenced by the immediate context – a local celebration or event, for example. Several developments during the period helped to nurture and sustain local loyalties. As we have seen, establishing local football teams, choirs and brass bands fostered local identities, especially when one team or band came to represent a town or village's interests and when the competitive element heightened passions. One of the primary concerns of Wales's urban middle class was to develop the civic profile of the particular town whose interests they purported to represent, and to instil pride in its achievements on a collective and an individual level. Local newspapers were often crucial vehicles in furthering this process. It was expected that a 'home town' would celebrate the achievements of its local heroes, while it was a convention at local public events that speeches should assert the excellences of a particular locality and even its superiority over others.

At a yet more pronounced micro-level, loyalties and identities could focus on a particular district or a certain street. But so too could they embrace territories much larger than Wales itself. It is a defining development of the years between 1870 and 1914 that Wales became more politically, economically and socially tied to, and integrated into, Great Britain (some would say England). To what extent the people of Wales came to regard themselves as British is a difficult question, but clearly many did, especially in the mining valleys and the ports of south Wales. For some in Wales it was a case of being British only; others, a small minority perhaps, did not regard themselves as British at all. For most, a sense of their own Britishness and a pride in Empire co-existed more or less comfortably alongside their identification of themselves as Welsh.

People can possess a multiplicity of identities. As Linda Colley has perceptively written, 'Identities are not like hats. Human beings can and do put several on at a time.' The relevance of class, religious, workplace, gender, popular-cultural, local, Welsh, British and imperial identities to each individual varied according to age, time and place. Nevertheless, for more and more people, living in Wales between 1870 and 1914 meant access to a widening range of identities which helped them understand themselves and their world and shaped their thoughts and actions. As far as a national identity for Wales is concerned, there were many who still subscribed to a specific idea of what Welshness was. For some, that concept of Welshness was elastic enough to incorporate beliefs that the Welsh possessed innate excellence in singing and at rugby. Rugby, especially after that key defining moment of Wales's victory over the New Zealand All Blacks on 16 December 1905, became a signifier of Welsh national identity, and was seen by contemporaries as something around which the whole nation could unite in celebration of something which was 'Welsh'. For others, Welshness was firmly and unexceptionally rooted in the rural and agricultural districts and embodied in the *gwerin*, the classless, religious, Welsh-speaking, loyal, hardworking common people. For more and more people in Wales during this period, though, Welshness was a moveable feast and they banqueted at it eagerly.

Conclusion: Gazing back

It is easy to identify ways in which Wales was a very different place in 1914 compared with what it had been forty-four years earlier, and how the lives of large numbers of its people had been remoulded and reshaped by the driving forces of profound change, of concentration of experience and of 'massing'. Yet human experience in Wales during these years was also diverse, whilst the momentous transformations varied in their completeness and coverage. At the same time, many of the brute facts of life, many of the basic struggles for existence, remained essentially the same. Again, throughout the late nineteenth and early twentieth centuries, many people in rural as well as industrial Wales felt they were living through a time of rapid and extensive change in their daily lives, changes which left many of them bewildered, yet no less excited. Between 1870 and 1914 Wales was, to use Dai Smith's unforgettable phrase, 'a singular noun but a plural experience'.

It is no less easy to see these years as being particularly important ones in the history of Wales and its people, though of course this could be said of most, if not all, of the periods into which we divide our history. Nevertheless, the period can be justifiably regarded as formative because, quite simply, so much of what is familiar to us in Wales today was either created or acquired mass significance during these years. Out of the flux of late-Victorian and Edwardian Wales there solidified some of the most formidable symbols and icons of Welshness its people have possessed: coal, choirs, rugby, the 'Welsh mam', the 'Valleys'.

Yet perhaps the real resonance of these years lies in the triumphs and tragedies of individual experience. The Wales of 1914 was on the verge of more unimaginable challenges which would erode many of the central elements of its buoyancy and dynamism. In retrospect we can, perhaps, identify the people who lived in Wales between 1870 and the first firing of the guns of international conflict in August 1914 as one of the few generations of the twentieth century who were able to look forward to the future with any measure of hope and confidence. Our hindsight, though, adds an eerie, even macabre, tone to the words of *Baner ac Amserau Cymru* ('The Banner and Times of Wales') in its first issue in 1914 (10 January) when, after its customary review of the passing year, it contemplated what the coming one might have in store for the people of Wales. The paper was confident that 1914 would bring them 'unlimited comforts and merciful gifts' but it also wondered how much division and agony would there be, 'how many graves are today hidden in its [i.e. the new year's] deep and dark shadows' and 'how many rivers of tears flow through its heart'. The paper concluded that it was a good thing they did not know what awaited them – and gazing back to 1914 over a twentieth century dominated by the carnage of two World Wars and the Depression, we should perhaps be glad that they did not.

CHAPTER 6

'IN THE WARS': WALES 1914–1945

MARI A. WILLIAMS

The period 1914–45 was one of the most tumultous in the history of modern Wales. It began with a war which claimed the lives of over 40,000 Welshmen; it ended with a conflict which placed both civilians and members of the armed forces in the front line, as war raged on the sea, the land and in the skies across Europe and Asia. The inter-war years, meanwhile, provided little respite for the people of Wales. Communities across Wales suffered acutely as a result of the economic Depression which started in the mid-1920s, and endured a crippling period of mass unemployment, poverty and ill-health. In essence, the social and economic turmoil which characterized this period was in stark contrast to the optimism and assertiveness of Edwardian Wales.

The period also witnessed sweeping changes in Welsh politics. After the first World War, the Liberal Party was sidelined by a substantial section of the Welsh electorate, particularly in the industrial districts where class conflict and social discontent were heightened. Allegiance was transferred to the newly-organized Labour Party, whose grip on Welsh political life was tightened during the 1930s and culminated in the landslide victory of the 1945 General Election. Despite the apparent political unity of Wales, significant social and cultural divisions remained and became increasingly problematic. Indeed, far from serving to unite Wales, the economic crisis of the inter-war period merely perpetuated the divide between Welsh-speaking and non-Welsh-speaking Wales, and between rural and industrial Wales. From 1914 to 1945, the people of Wales were truly 'in the wars'.

WALES AND THE GREAT WAR, 1914–18

On 4 August 1914, the people of Wales became embroiled in one of the most horrific conflicts of the modern age, when Britain joined France and Russia in war against Germany and its allies. By the time the Armistice came on 11 November 1918, at least 40,000 Welsh servicemen and personnel had lost their lives, while thousands more had suffered serious physical injuries. Few could have foreseen that the war would have such a devastating impact on Welsh life. Initially, most Welsh people appeared somewhat bemused, if not confused, by the sudden declaration of war in a far-away country, and few believed it would last long. Describing the reaction of the slate-quarrying communities of north Wales to the news, Kate Roberts wrote in her novel, *Traed Mewn Cyffion* (1936), that, 'When war broke out, nobody . . . knew what to make of it.' Such uncertainty was soon swept to one side, however, as news of the 'military despotism' of the Kaiser, and the suffering inflicted on small nations such as Belgium and Serbia, reached Welsh ears. Among the Welsh social, political and religious leaders, support for the government's decision to enter into hostilities was overwhelming right from the start. Politicians and preachers whose beliefs were firmly rooted in a Welsh radical and anti-militaristic tradition, were among the first to rally to the cause and condemn the atrocities committed by the evil 'Hun'. In October 1914, twenty leading Welsh Nonconformist ministers issued *A War Manifesto*, urging members of their churches to join the colours. Prominent Welsh scholars, politicians and trade union leaders, such as Sir John Morris-Jones, professor of Welsh at the University College of North Wales, Bangor, W. Llewelyn Williams, Liberal MP for Carmarthenshire, and the representatives of the south Wales miners', William Abraham (Mabon) MP, and T. I. Mardy Jones MP, also pledged their support for the stance taken by the British government.

Championed as 'the war to end wars', the conflict was regarded by many such individuals as a crusade against injustice and oppression in defence of the liberal values which they held dear. It was an opinion shared by the vast majority of the Welsh people, and those who ventured to express their opposition to the war faced a hostile reception. Individuals such as Rev Puleston Jones, the blind Methodist preacher from Pwllheli, and Thomas Rees, principal of the

Bala-Bangor Independent College, were persecuted for their anti-war stand, while the socialist pacifists, Keir Hardie and T. E. Nicholas (Niclas y Glais), who voiced their objections to the war in public, were jeered and jostled by angry crowds. Welsh conscientious objectors, who numbered some 1,000, met with even shorter shrift from the authorities and the general public.

The great mass of the Welsh people placed their support firmly behind the war effort. By December 1915, 122,995 men from Wales had volunteered for the army and, following the passing of the Conscription Act in January 1916, a further 149,988 men enlisted. In total, therefore, some 280,000 men, comprising 21.5 per cent of the Welsh male population, served in the armed forces during the first World War. The majority of these joined the battalions of the Royal Welsh Fusiliers, the Welsh Guards, the Comrades or 'Pals' brigades, and the newly-formed Welsh Division. Led by General Sir Ivor Phillips, the 'Welsh Army Corps' was largely the brainchild of Lloyd George, whose support for the war effort not only secured him the influential positions of Minister of Munitions in May 1915 and Secretary of State for War in July 1916 before he became Prime Minister in December 1916, but was also a crucial factor in inspiring thousands of Welshmen to join the colours. In the Welsh-speaking communities of north Wales, the task of recruiting men for the Welsh Division fell to two natives of Anglesey, namely, Brigadier-General Sir Owen Thomas and Rev John Williams, Brynsiencyn, a Methodist minister who was made honorary chaplain of the Division, and gained considerable notoriety for delivering stirring pro-war addresses from the pulpit in full military dress. In the south Wales coal-field, miners' leaders such as C. B. Stanton, Ted Gill and Noah Rees played an equally active and highly successful role in local recruitment campaigns. By December 1914, 40,000 south Wales miners had joined up; four battalions for the Welsh Division were recruited from the Rhondda valleys alone. The miners' enthusiasm for the war was further endorsed in November 1915 when C. B. Stanton, the jingoistic miners' agent, achieved a resounding victory in the Merthyr Boroughs by-election, defeating James Winstone, president of the South Wales Miners' Federation, by 4,206 votes. The contrast between the pro-war rhetoric of the new member and the pacifist ideals espoused by his predecessor, Keir Hardie, was striking and spoke volumes for the scale of support for the war among the electorate.

While many of those who volunteered for the army during the early months may have viewed the conflict as a great adventure, providing them with an opportunity to see the world and fight for 'King and Country', growing public awareness of the grim reality of modern warfare soon put paid to such romantic notions. As the months passed and news of continued heavy losses at the battles of Neuve Chappelle, Ypres, Aubers Ridge and Loos reached home, the scale and horrific nature of the deaths and injuries sustained by British forces cast a long shadow over many Welsh homes. The years 1916–17 proved disastrous. The Battle of the Somme, which lasted from July to November 1916, claimed the lives of 450,000 British soldiers, 19,000 of whom were killed on the first day of fighting. The following summer, 270,000 British soldiers fell at Passchendaele ('the Third Ypres'). Welsh regiments played a prominent role in both military campaigns and suffered heavy casualties. Glyn Roberts, a native of Blaenau Ffestiniog, was among the victims of the carnage on the Somme. In one of his last surviving letters to his brother in October 1915, he provided a moving account of the brutality and suffering which he had witnessed in France as an officer with the 9th Royal Welsh Fusiliers:

> As I led them up to the firing line there lay in the trench on his face a man of whom half his back had been torn away. You could see distinctly, as I have never seen before, the fibres as it were of his flesh with blood everywhere. I had never seen a *dead man* before, yet somehow I was able without turning a hair to walk right over him, as all the men had to do who were following me. You may find what I have just related rather gruesome and what I am going to tell still more so, but I do it in order to put on record the grim hideousness of war in all its reality, showing you at the same time what heroes our men are.
>
> (*Witness These Letters: Letters from the Western Front, 1915–18*)

It was several years later before Ll. Wyn Griffith and David Jones, two Welshmen who also served on the Western Front, could bring themselves to write about their traumatic experiences in their moving accounts, *Up to Mametz* (1931) and *In Parenthesis* (1937). Indeed, in comparison with the body of war literature which emerged in England, it is striking that only a handful of literary works were produced by Welsh writers and poets as a direct result of the war.

Ironically, the most famous Welsh 'war poet' – Hedd Wyn (Ellis Humphrey Evans) of Trawsfynydd, Merioneth – was himself a victim of the war and, like so many of those who died alongside him, was denied the opportunity to fulfil his potential. Just over a month after his death at Pilkem Ridge in July 1917, Hedd Wyn was posthumously awarded the Chair – the highest accolade for any Welsh poet – at the Birkenhead National Eisteddfod, for his poem 'Yr Arwr' (The Hero). The chairing ceremony was a highly emotional event and became the occasion for a remarkable outpouring of national grief. Draped in black cloth in honour of the bard, the 'black chair of Birkenhead' came to represent the thousands of chairs which stood empty in war-torn homes throughout Wales.

It is difficult to comprehend the devastating impact which the war had on Welsh home and family life. As the long casualty lists which appear on war memorials in towns and villages across the country testify, almost every Welsh family was touched by the conflict. Between 1914 and 1918, thousands of women were either widowed or deprived of the chance to marry, while a generation of children were left to grow up without their fathers. The sense of despair and emotional trauma experienced by so many bereaved families was exacerbated by the practical difficulties of struggling to make ends meet on the meagre pensions and allowances granted to the dependants of fallen soldiers. Those wives and mothers who were fortunate enough to be reunited with their loved ones also faced testing times. The men who returned from the Front had been profoundly affected by their experiences and the process of adjusting to 'normal' home life did not prove easy. Thousands returned home with severe physical injuries and, unable to work and support their families, faced a future of dependency. Many more struggled to come to terms with the emotional and mental blows struck by the horror and suffering which they had witnessed. Unable to share their experiences with members of their family, the painful wartime memories proved difficult to erase. Alcohol provided solace and temporary relief for many ex-servicemen, but there were some individuals who found it impossible to forget and continually revisited the battlefields in their minds. The psychological impact of the war manifested itself in severe depression and melancholy and, in the period immediately following the war, a large increase was recorded in the number of males admitted to the county asylums of Wales. At the Glamorgan County Asylum in Bridgend, shell-shocked and traumatized ex-soldiers, many of whom were said to be suffering from acute suicidal tendencies, comprised the vast majority of the new influx of male patients. Four men who were being treated at the Asylum in 1920 were found to have self-inflicted throat wounds on admission.

Away from the front line, the pressures of wartime life had also exerted considerable emotional strain on the friends and relatives of those who were involved in the fighting. Female relatives who had been left to take charge of households and families on their own, lived in dread of the arrival of the War Office telegram and its official notification of their worst nightmare. Some found the strain too much to bear. Ann Williams of Llanelli, who was said to have worried very much over her two sons in the trenches in France, cut her throat with a razor in July 1916. The majority of Welsh women battled on, however, and kept themselves busy by undertaking voluntary relief work, ensuring that a steady supply of parcels filled with food, clothing and cigarettes reached the troops at the Front. Welsh women also found themselves being called upon to fill some of the jobs which had been left empty by the men who had joined up. In the offices of the expanding civil service, female clerks performed tasks previously reserved for men, while transport companies employed women as conductors and drivers on their buses and trams. In the rural districts, farmers were assisted by members of the Women's Land Army, established in 1917. Over 200 young women were employed on the land in the three counties of Anglesey, Caernarfon and Merioneth, while some 150 found work on various farms in Cardiganshire. Some Welsh women were more directly involved in the wartime campaign. Women who served with the newly formed women's services – the Women's Army Auxiliary Corps (WAACS), the Women's Royal Naval Service (WRNS) and the Women's Royal Air Force (WRAF) – undertook administrative, clerical and canteen jobs behind the lines. Members of the nursing profession, especially those who had enlisted as Voluntary Aid Detachment (VAD) nurses, experienced the horrors of war at first hand as they attended to sick and wounded soldiers. Meanwhile, the thousands of Welsh women who entered wartime industries to manufacture shells, bullets and explosives – the basic tools of the military campaign – contributed to the war effort in a manner which was in stark contrast to the traditional wartime role of women as carers and healers. At the National Shell Factories at Llanelli, Swansea and Newport, women featured prominently among the ranks of the thousands of employees who made casings, heads and noses for shells. Women also comprised the majority of the workforce employed at the Nobel's Explosive Works, Pen-bre, and the explosives factory at Queensferry in Flintshire, where TNT and gun-cotton were produced. Such work was not only unpleasant and unhealthy but also extremely dangerous. An explosion at the Pen-bre factory in November 1918, killed three Swansea women, one of whom was a 36-year-old mother of seven, and left two others seriously injured.

As war-weariness set in and the casualty lists grew, it became evident that the patriotic fervour and enthusiasm displayed during the early months of the war were fading somewhat. Public attitudes were slowly changing and recruiting rates fell sharply. At Wrexham, the recruiting headquarters of the six north-Wales counties, the monthly rates had fallen from 2,569 in August 1914 to 1,332 in January 1915, and to 634 by December of that year. Efforts to raise men from the slate-quarrying communities of Dyffryn Ogwen during the winter of 1915 were impeded by the refusal of the local authorities to organize recruiting meetings in the area. Although extreme anti-war views remained abhorrent to the majority, sections of the Welsh public, among them members of the Welsh Liberal and Nonconformist élite, became increasingly uneasy about the British government's war policy. The decision to introduce compulsory military service for all males aged between 18 and 45 in January 1916 proved highly contentious, and was the cause of considerable disagreement and bitterness within the ranks of the Welsh Liberal establishment. The Liberal MPs, W. Llewelyn Williams, E. T. John, and G. Caradog Rees, voted against the measure in parliament, while five others abstained. Although all were deeply committed to the war effort, they regarded the introduction of compulsory military service as a serious infringement of the basic principle of individual freedom.

Growing disaffection with the tactics employed by the wartime government was also apparent in the mining communities of south Wales. Although the miners had been enthusiastic supporters of the war, a new climate of wartime industrial relations now threatened to undermine their commitment to the military campaign. The declaration of war had provided a considerable boost to the coal industry as a result of the demand for steam coal for the British Admiralty. Yet, despite the increase in output which reaped great profits for the coalowners, the miners' demands for a wage increase continued to fall on deaf ears. Angered by what they regarded as the coalowners' exploitation of their efforts, the south Wales miners took matters into their own hands. In July 1915 the miners defied the wartime prohibition on strikes to demand a new standard wage rate, and after a seven-day stoppage they returned to work triumphant. The 1915 strike marked a turning-point in the history of social and industrial relations in the coalfield. From then on, the south Wales miners, under the leadership of a new generation of radical trade unionists, took on an increasingly powerful role in Welsh politics. The new spirit of industrial militancy became more evident during 1916–17 as workers across Wales voiced their demands for improved working conditions and expressed a growing dissatisfaction with the policies of the wartime government. At the same time, events in Ireland and Russia attracted great interest among Welsh workers and gave a new impetus to their struggles against capitalist ownership and control. Such was the concern for the spate of strikes and disturbances which took place in south Wales and elsewhere across Britain during this period that the government appointed a Royal Commission to investigate the causes of industrial unrest.

Changes in the social and political fabric of Welsh life were not confined to the industrial communities of the south. Relations between the North Wales Quarrymen's Union and the employers were decidedly less harmonious than they had been in the past. Meanwhile, in the rural districts, tensions between farm labourers and farmers became increasingly strained. At the same time, the pattern of landownership in the Welsh countryside was undergoing massive changes as the high inflation rates of the war years forced the sale of thousands of acres of land. Major landed estates, such as those of Beaufort in Breconshire, the Bodelwyddan estates in Denbighshire, Aberhafesp in Montgomeryshire and Sunny Hill in Cardiganshire, were sold off during the war, the majority of the land being bought up by the tenants.

This fundamental shift in social authority and control provided further evidence of the changing character of Welsh life. By 1919, Liberal causes such as land reform, temperance and disestablishment of the Church had effectively been won and appeared increasingly irrelevant and outmoded to the people and politics of post-war Wales. The passing of the People's Representation Act in June 1918, which granted the vote to all males over twenty-one years of age (apart from conscientious objectors, who were disenfranchised for five years), and enfranchised females over the age of thirty (if they passed a property qualification), expanded the Welsh electorate by 50 per cent to 1,170,974. In the county of Glamorgan the electorate became more than twice as large, while the number of constituencies in the south Wales coal-field doubled. The implications for the future of Welsh politics were immense and soon became apparent. Although the Welsh Liberal Party retained its dominant position in the 'coupon' election of December 1918, winning twenty-five of the thirty-six Welsh seats, the Labour Party emerged as a formidable political opponent, winning ten seats and securing 30.8 per cent of votes. Future parliamentary and local election contests would bring even greater success for the Labour Party in Wales, particularly in urban and industrial districts. Confirmation that the golden age of Welsh Liberalism was over came in October 1922, following the collapse of the coalition government and the resignation of Lloyd George as Prime Minister. In the general election held the following month, Labour secured 41 per cent of Welsh votes and won eighteen Welsh seats, six of which were captured from the Liberals in the south Wales coal-field.

The Great War has long been regarded as a watershed in the history of Wales. Certainly, the social and political mood of post-war Wales was very different from that of the pre-war era and there was very little sign of the self-confidence, prosperity and dynamism which had so characterized old Liberal Wales. At a personal level, the experiences of the war years had a profound cultural and psychological impact on the attitudes and outlook of the Welsh people. Men whose social and working lives had previously been limited to their immediate localities had not only been immersed in a culturally alien environment but also had witnessed scenes which forced them to question previously-held moral and religious values. Small wonder that, on their return, a growing number rejected traditional expressions of Welsh social, political and cultural life, adopting alternative beliefs and patterns of behaviour. Although there were continuities, it is clear that the Great War brought about dramatic changes in Welsh society. This fracture between the old pre-war social order and the values of post-war life was to be illustrated dramatically in the 1920s and 1930s in the manner in which the people of Wales responded to one of the most turbulent and testing periods in their history.

LIVING IN 'A SOCIAL HELL': WALES BETWEEN THE WARS

In June 1928, the Prince of Wales visited Cardiff to unveil the Welsh National War Memorial in Cathays Park. Although almost a decade had passed since the declaration of the armistice, the pain inflicted by the events of the Great War was all too evident as relatives, friends and ex-servicemen gathered to commemorate those who had lost their lives on distant battlefields. The sense of loss was compounded by the despair and hopelessness of their present-day struggles. At the same time as plans for the unveiling ceremony in Cardiff were being finalized, government ministers in Whitehall approved a scheme which was designed to encourage a new generation of Welsh men and women to leave their homes and families. The Industrial Transference Scheme, introduced by the Ministry of Labour in 1928, was a feeble attempt to deal with the problem of mass unemployment, that running sore which had disfigured the industrial communities of Britain since the mid-1920s and would remain a stubborn problem until the outbreak of the second World War.

The Welsh economy, which relied so heavily on the exportation of coal, steel and tinplate, was hit particularly hard by the world-wide Depression of the 1920s, and Wales was to suffer acutely from high unemployment rates throughout the inter-war period. By 1928, 21.9 per cent of the insured population of Wales were unemployed, compared with 9.8 per cent in England. The situation worsened considerably in the years which followed. Between 1931 and 1935, over a third of the Welsh insured population were out of work. Very few areas of Wales escaped unscathed. The full brunt of the slump was felt in the south Wales coal-field, where 241 coal-mines were closed between 1921 and 1936, and the associated male work-force of over 270,000 miners was almost halved. Elsewhere, the scale of the decline may have been less dramatic but the social consequences were no less calamitous. In north-east Wales, the collapse of the coal industry and the closure of the steel works at Brymbo, near Wrexham, had a devastating impact on the local economy, while the decline in the agricultural and slate-quarrying industries left many communities struggling to survive. Mass unemployment wrought havoc on all aspects of community life and brought misery, poverty and despair to thousands of Welsh homes.

It would be wrong, however, to suggest that all parts of Wales and all sections of Welsh society endured a period of unremitting hardship during the inter-war years. Flintshire benefited from several new industrial developments and showed clear signs of economic recovery in the 1930s. With a workforce of over 2,000 the Courtaulds rayon factories, which were established near the town of Flint, became the second largest employer in the county. Those who were fortunate enough to be in work could also afford to buy into the new consumer economy of the 1930s. By 1938, 55,000 private cars had been licensed in south Wales, with the highest concentrations recorded in Cardiff and Swansea, while 21,000 licences were held in north Wales. Thousands of Welsh middle-class homes subscribed to the telephone service, while half the households in Wales had wireless licences by 1935. Outside their homes, more and more people were spending their spare time and money on commercialized forms of entertainment. In the urban areas, film-going became by far the most popular form of leisure activity, with cinemas established in almost every Welsh town by the 1930s. Improvements in both public and private means of transport also had an impact on leisure patterns. As travelling became easier, the number of tourists and day-trippers who visited Welsh seaside resorts swelled. During the summer months, places such as Rhyl, Prestatyn and Llandudno attracted thousands of visitors from the industrial towns of north-west England, while Barry Island and Porthcawl became the mecca for the working classes of south Wales. Some 100,000 trippers, the majority of whom had travelled from the distressed mining valleys, visited Barry Island on August Bank Holiday Monday in 1927. Spectator sports, particularly rugby, soccer and boxing, offered the working classes another form of

release from the grim reality of daily life and, on occasion, served to
unite Wales. The prize-fight held in New York in 1937 between
Tommy Farr of the Rhondda and Joe Louis, was relayed across Wales
in a live radio broadcast, and audiences in places as far removed as
Llanymawddwy and Llwynypïa listened in with bated breath.

The fact remains, however, that for the overwhelming majority of
the people of Wales, the inter-war years stood out as a period when
they found themselves living in what one commentator described as 'a
social hell'. The depth of the economic crisis which faced so many
Welsh communities was dramatically illustrated by the number of
people who were forced to leave their homes during the inter-war
period. Between 1925 and 1939, over 380,000 people left Wales in an
exodus which was described by Gwyn Thomas, the Rhondda-born
writer, as 'a Black Death on wheels'. Several thousand Welshmen and
women ventured as far as America, South Africa and Australia in their
search for a better life, but the vast majority of Welsh migrants headed
for England. With no sign of economic recovery, the Industrial
Transference Scheme was executed with even greater vigour during
the 1930s. Between 1932 and 1936, over 17,000 men and women were
transferred from the depressed areas of Wales to more prosperous
English regions. In addition to those whom the Ministry of Labour
coerced into leaving, thousands more abandoned all hope and set out
independently from their homes to search for employment in places
such as Oxford, Slough, Coventry and Birmingham. Although all the
Welsh counties, apart from Flintshire, experienced a decline in their
populations during the 1930s, by far the greatest losses were suffered
by the industrial communities of Glamorgan and Monmouthshire.
Some 50,000 moved from the Rhondda alone, the vast majority of
whom were young people aged between fifteen and twenty-nine.
Merthyr Tydfil, which experienced acute unemployment following the
closure of the Cyfarthfa and Dowlais steel works, lost some 27,000
people. Young women taking up lowly positions as domestic servants
were prominent among the migrants. 'It all makes me feel there's a
sinking ship out there,' remarked one Rhondda headmistress in the
1930s, 'a ship of old people. I seem to be always writing character
references for girls taking jobs as servants in England.'

In social and cultural terms, the consequences of this Welsh
diaspora were devastating. Particularly disturbing was the noticeable

decrease in the ranks of the younger population. In the Rhondda, a
'dearth of suitable mates' for local men was reported in 1935 due to
'the great exodus of young women'. One local commentator feared
that the valleys would soon become 'the dwelling place of old people
in childless homes'. Almost all aspects of community life were
affected by this outmigration. Between 1925 and 1936, the
Nonconformist chapels of the Rhondda lost over 8,800 of their
members, while the number of children attending the elementary
schools of the district fell by 11,000 during the inter-war period. In
addition to the cost in human terms, this mass exodus posed a serious
threat to the already precarious state of the Welsh language and
culture.

The downward trend in the fortunes of the Welsh language had
been clearly evinced in the 1921 census tables. Between 1911 and
1921, the proportion of the Welsh population able to speak Welsh had
fallen from 43.5 per cent to 37.1 per cent, and significant losses were
recorded in the number of monoglot Welsh. Although the language
remained strong in the counties of north and west Wales, its greatly-
weakened position in the densely-populated county of Glamorgan,
where two-thirds of the population spoke English only by 1921, gave
much cause for concern. Supporters of the Welsh language responded
swiftly to the decline. In 1922, Ifan ab Owen Edwards founded the
Welsh-language youth movement, *Urdd Gobaith Cymru*, while three
years later, at a meeting held during the National Eisteddfod in
Pwllheli, a group of prominent Welsh nationalists established *Plaid
Genedlaethol Cymru* (The National Party of Wales), a movement
which was primarily concerned with cultural issues and made very
little headway as a political party until after 1945.

Despite such initiatives, the Anglicization of Welsh society
continued unabated during the inter-war years. The strains of the
economic crisis, coupled with the growing influence and popularity of
the English-language mass media, exerted considerable pressure on
the indigenous language and culture. The numbers and percentages of
Welsh-speakers were sent spiralling downwards and the cultural
divide between Welsh-speaking and non-Welsh-speaking Wales grew
wider. By 1931, only 36.8 per cent of the Welsh population was able
to speak Welsh; in the county of Glamorgan, the proportion had fallen
to 30.5 per cent. It was evident that many Welsh-speaking families

were choosing not to transmit the language to the younger generation. In 1931, over 60 per cent of the population of the Rhondda who were over the age of 45 were Welsh-speaking, but the proportions of Welsh speakers fell to 34.6 per cent among those under the age of 25, and to 27.7 per cent among children under the age of nine.

Given their economic circumstances, it was perhaps not surprising that the concerns of the majority of the residents of the industrial communities of south Wales rested not with language but with their daily struggle to hold their families together and to make ends meet. For a substantial section of the population, life during the inter-war years was extremely bleak, and prolonged periods of unemployment and extreme deprivation left whole communities feeling utterly demoralized and neglected. In the old iron town of Bryn-mawr, one of many unemployment 'black spots' in the region, the insidious effects of 'life on the dole' were documented by the sociologist Hilda Jennings:

> Visits to the Exchange at most take up part of two half-days in the week. For the rest, some men stand aimlessly on the Market Square or at the street corners, content apparently with a passive animal existence, or with the hour-long observation of passers-by, varied by an occasional whiff at a cigarette. Others work on allotment or garden, tend fowls or pigs, or do carpentry in their backyard or kitchen. Others again 'stroll down the valley' or sit on the banks when the sun is warm. On wet days the Miners' Institute offers papers and a shelter, although shop doors and street corners satisfy many. At night, there are the pictures, and the long queues outside the 'Picture House' probably account for more of the pocket-money of the unemployed than do the public-house.
>
> In these and other ways the unemployed man drags out his time and, whether he expresses it lucidly or not, in almost every individual there is an abiding sense of waste of life.
>
> (*Brynmawr: A Study of a Distressed Area*)

Of greater concern was the detrimental impact which unemployment had on the health and general physical well-being of the population. Although some notable improvements were recorded in standards of health in Wales during the inter-war years, it was also apparent that, among certain sections of the Welsh population, health conditions were deteriorating rapidly. Women and children were among the worst affected. Wives and mothers who 'went without' in order to ensure that other members of the household were fed and clothed, paid a high price for their acts of self-sacrifice. Writing in 1938, the authors of an inquiry conducted in Rhondda noted that 'it was a matter of daily experience to observe the obvious signs of malnutrition in the appearance of the wives of the unemployed men with families. They obviously did without things for the sake of their husbands and children.' Pregnancy and childbirth placed an additional strain on the resources of undernourished and debilitated women, and maternal mortality rates in parts of the south Wales coal-field rose sharply during the early 1930s. The poor physical condition of the female population took its toll on future generations. Infants born in Wales were less likely to survive the first year of their lives than their counterparts in some of the more affluent areas of England. In 1928, when the infant mortality rate was 65.1 per 1,000 live births in England and Wales, a rate of 95.9 per 1,000 was recorded in Wrexham, 91.0 per 1,000 in Aberdare and 80.0 in the Ogmore and Garw Urban District. Commenting on the high infant mortality rate in Mountain Ash in 1936, the local Medical Officer of Health drew attention to the fact that a number of mothers were unable to breast-feed their children owing to malnourishment. The Medical Officer of Caerphilly similarly reported in 1938 that a low standard of nutrition among expectant mothers was largely responsible for the high incidence of infant deaths in the district.

Life in the rural districts of Wales proved equally harsh during this period of economic decline. The tenant farmers who had bought up much of the land which changed hands in Wales from 1914 onwards were crippled by high interest rates and rising costs, while many of the old rural industries, including the woollen mills of west Wales, collapsed. Rural depopulation continued at a swift pace, leaving behind an aged and ailing population, poorly equipped to respond to the desperate social needs of their depleted communities. By the late 1930s, the dire consequences of the failure of the Welsh rural authorities and their rates-conscious members to address issues such as public health, welfare and housing had become all too apparent. The Ministry of Health's report of 1939 into the anti-tuberculosis service in Wales exposed a shocking picture of rural poverty, ill health and scandalous housing conditions. According to Clement Davies, the

Montgomeryshire MP who chaired the inquiry, the appalling conditions of some of the houses which he visited in the slate-quarrying district of Gwyrfai, Caernarfonshire, 'beggar description. They have to be seen to be believed.' Witnesses who visited a particularly squalid home elsewhere in Caernarfonshire proclaimed that 'there was nothing to equal it in the industrial areas of South Wales'. Provision of public health services was also found wanting. Few of the rural authorities had initiated schemes to feed needy children, while hardly any had established maternity and child welfare clinics. The shortcomings of this inactivity and 'dereliction of duty' were borne out by the poor health rates of the rural population, particularly in the excessive incidence of tuberculosis. Indeed, the county of Caernarfon, closely followed by those of Merioneth, Anglesey and Cardigan, returned the highest average death rates from tuberculosis in England and Wales throughout the period 1930–6.

The indolent response of the elected representatives of rural Wales to the social crises of the inter-war years contrasted sharply with that of the ruling groups in the south Wales coal-field. Despite severe financial constraints, the Labour-dominated local authorities showed great sympathy with the problems facing their constituents. They made concerted efforts to improve housing conditions, and to provide essential health services and feeding schemes for those who were most in need. During the seven-month lockout which followed the General Strike of 1926, Rhondda Urban District Council spent over £57,000 on relieving hardship. Some Boards of Guardians, most famously the Bedwellte Guardians in Monmouthshire, even exceeded their legal spending powers and ran up huge debts in order to pay out poor relief to the dependants of striking miners. Such administration was swiftly brought to a halt, however, following the intervention of the Conservative government and the imposition of severe cuts in relief scales.

Surviving on the meagre weekly allowance of 12s for a wife and 4s for every child proved almost impossible, so that unemployed families relied heavily on the financial and practical support provided by the South Wales Miners' Federation (SWMF) and various philanthropic, religious and voluntary societies. In 1926, many mining families were still paying off the debts incurred during the three-month lockout of 1921 – a dispute which followed the 'betrayal' by the Sankey

Commission and the return of the coal industry from public to private ownership. Poverty and distress were widespread, and most of the money raised during the 1926 lockout was used for the running of communal kitchens, centres which not only provided free meals for those in need but were also a vital source of emotional sustenance. The colourful jazz bands which marched defiantly throughout the coal-field during the long 'angry summer of 1926' performed an equally important role in maintaining morale, while at the same time raising funds to support relief work. Such expressions of collective and communal solidarity were severely tested, however, as the cold winter months set in and many families faced extreme hardship. The growing importance of the boot-repair shops bore witness to the severity of the economic situation in many households. In parts of Rhondda, it was reported that many children were unable to avail themselves of the free meals provided in local schools because they had no clothes or shoes to wear. In some instances, determined mothers took to carrying their children to and from the school canteens. Surrender became inevitable as the suffering grew unbearable and growing numbers of miners drifted back to work. On 1 December the stoppage was brought to an end.

The defeat of 1926 dealt a heavy blow to the south Wales coal industry and its society. Membership of the SWMF – one of the most powerful and militant trade unions of the early 1920s – plummeted, falling from 124,000 in 1924 to 60,000 by 1932. The establishment of a new, rival union in December 1926, the South Wales Miners' Industrial Union (SWMIU) – also known as the 'Spencer', the 'company' or 'scab' union – served further to weaken and divide the mining community. Colliery companies such as the Ocean Coal Company exploited this disunity to great effect during the disputes of the late 1920s and early 1930s, by employing members of the company union in their pits. At the same time, activists and prominent members of the SWMF were victimized for their role in the 1926 lockout and found it impossible to find work underground.

Ironically, however, it was the successful campaign to drive out the company union which enabled the SWMF to rebuild and reassert its role as the chief social and political institution of the coal-field. Some of the most bitter struggles against non-unionism took place at the Taff-Merthyr pit near Trelewis, where the shaming rituals employed by the women of the area to intimidate 'scab' labour combined effectively with official industrial action. Considerable success was also achieved with a series of stay-down strikes, the first of which took place in October 1935 at Nine Mile Point Colliery, near Cwmfelin-fach in Monmouthshire, where some seventy miners refused to leave pit bottom and remained underground for over a week. By 1936, the company union had been driven out of the south Wales coal-field and, under the leadership of James Griffiths (1934–6) and Arthur Horner (1936–46), the SWMF emerged as a powerful, efficient and unified organisation, far better equipped to lead the fight-back against unemployment, poverty and inequality. At the same time, the identification of the Welsh mining electorate with the Labour Party was confirmed. In the general election of 1935, the threat posed by the Communist Party was staved off and ten of the thirteen seats won by Labour in the south Wales coal-field were held by prominent SWMF officials. In Wales as a whole, Labour won eighteen of the thirty-six seats and, in addition to regaining seats in Carmarthenshire and Wrexham, made considerable headway in the Liberal strongholds of Anglesey, Caernarfonshire, Merioneth and Cardiganshire. In contrast, political success continued to elude *Plaid Genedlaethol Cymru*. Indeed, it was the unconstitutional events of September 1936 which earned that Party its place in the history books and in the hearts of many Welsh patriots. In protest at the use of Welsh land for 'English' military purposes, three prominent party members, Saunders Lewis, Lewis Valentine and D. J. Williams, set fire to outbuildings of the RAF 'bombing school' at Penyberth in the Llŷn peninsula and, after being tried at the Old Bailey, served time at Wormwood Scrubs prison.

In the south Wales coal-field, the struggles associated with the rebuilding of the SWMF provided the impetus for a new wave of collective action and protest. In the face of continuing attacks on their psychological and practical resources, the grievances of the unemployed of south Wales were voiced in a series of public protests and marches held throughout the early 1930s. Most spectacular of all were the mass demonstrations held during 1935 against part II of the Unemployment Act of 1934. On successive weekends during the cold months of January and February 1935, up to 300,000 people marched together, united in their opposition to the Means Test and to the establishment of a nationally-uniform system of assistance administered by the unemployment assistance boards. Lewis Jones, the Rhondda-born Communist and writer, was a veteran of unemployment and hunger marches and played an active role in the organization of such meetings. In 1936, he volunteered to go to Spain to serve alongside the 174 Welshmen who had joined the International Brigades in the Spanish Civil War against Franco, but later decided to stay at home to lead the campaign against Fascism from Wales. Lewis Jones died in January 1939 and did not see the publication of his second novel *We Live* (1939) in which he recounted many of his own experiences as a political activist in south Wales during the 1930s, including that of participating in one of the monster demonstrations of 1935:

> When the front of the demonstration was two miles advanced, and on the summit of the hill to the east of Cwmardy, people were still pouring from the assembling field. Len lifted his head sharply into the air when he fancied he heard the distant strains of music in the direction of the left of the demonstration. He turned to Mary and the workman next to her.
>
> 'Can you hear anything?', he asked.
>
> They both looked simultaneously past Len, and he, seeing their amazement, turned his head to look in the same direction. He drew his breath sharply and his perspiring face went a shade whiter. The mountain which separated Cwmardy from the other valleys looked like a giant ant-hill, covered with a mass of black, waving bodies.
>
> 'Good God', the man next to Mary whispered, 'the whole world is on the move.'

Although such protests brought few real gains to the unemployed of south Wales, their impact in terms of focusing public attention on the plight of the industrial communities was significant. The area provided the subject-matter for scores of industrial surveys and documentary reports, and inspiration for dozens of artists, film-makers and writers. Eventually, government officials also took note and, with the passing of the Special Areas Acts of 1934, 1936 and 1937, a programme of initiatives which aimed to revitalize the economies of the depressed regions was put forward. The enormity of the problems facing the Welsh industrial communities called for radical action, but apart from the establishment of government-assisted trading estates, the first of which was opened in Trefforest in 1938, the proposals of the commissioners of the Special Areas provided only patchwork solutions to the 'problem of South Wales'. Other parts of Wales whose need was equally great, such as the industrial areas of the north and west, and all the rural districts, were not even included in the Special Areas schemes. In the event, it took another World War and a journey into a different kind of 'social hell', to set the country back on the road to recovery.

WALES AND THE SECOND WORLD WAR, 1939–45

The outbreak of the second World War, on 3 September 1939, did not come as a great shock to the people of Wales. With the rise of Fascism in Germany, Italy and Spain, war clouds had been gathering over Europe since the mid-1930s. Although Welsh pacifists, such as George M. Ll. Davies, continued to campaign tirelessly for their cause throughout the 1930s, conflict seemed inevitable as the ineffectiveness of the government's policy of appeasement became apparent against the growing signs of menace from Hitler. Matters came to a head in September 1938 when Germany invaded Czechoslovakia. Twenty Welsh MPs, many of whom felt torn between their strongly anti-war sentiments and their desire to quash Fascism, wrestled with their consciences and voted against the agreement struck by Chamberlain in Munich, regarding it as a betrayal of the Czech people. From then on, the threat of war was imminent. The government's rearmament programme got under way in earnest, while evacuation schemes, air raid precautions and plans for military conscription were drawn up. By the summer of 1939, the country was poised for war. The Emergency Powers (Defence) Act, passed on 24 August, empowered the government to take whatever action it deemed necessary without referring to Parliament. On 1 September, Hitler invaded Poland and, two days later, Britain entered into hostilities against Germany.

In contrast with the situation during the Great War, the vast majority of the people of Wales supported the aims of this conflict and remained firmly committed to the war effort throughout its duration. For many, the second World War was a crusade against tyranny and oppression and, as such, was wholly justified. Thousands of Welshmen had volunteered for civil defence duties even before war had been declared, and there was very little opposition to the introduction of military conscription from April 1939 onwards. Even Communists and some of the more left-wing representatives of the Welsh working class, who initially denounced the conflict as yet another imperialist war, came to view the struggle in a different light. From the outset, Arthur Horner, the Communist president of the SWMF, had been unwilling to adopt a firm anti-war stance, but following Germany's invasion of the Soviet Union in June 1941, he was able to commit himself fully to supporting this 'people's war'.

Nonetheless, some dissenting voices were raised. Almost 3,000 people registered as conscientious objectors in Wales during the second World War, a greater number than during the conflict of 1914–18. On the whole, they received much fairer treatment at the hands of the local tribunals but public opinion remained hostile towards those who refused to fight. Members of the Peace Pledge Union who met at Porthmadog in May 1940 were attacked in the street by an angry crowd, while many of those who registered as conscientious objectors were persecuted for their beliefs. The writer and scholar Iorwerth C. Peate was dismissed from his position as keeper of the Folk Life department by the National Museum of Wales, while local authorities in Cardiff and Swansea terminated the employment of workers who refused to sign declarations of support for the war. In addition to the small group of individuals who steadfastly refused to take up arms on pacifist grounds, a number of Welsh men and women opposed the war for political reasons. Under the leadership of Saunders Lewis, *Plaid Genedlaethol Cymru* adopted a neutral wartime policy and refused to participate in what it regarded as 'an English war'. Although Welsh nationalism was formally adjudged to be a valid basis for conscientious objection, the tribunals which were held in Wales failed to recognize this ruling and, of the two dozen or so who refused to undertake military service on nationalist grounds, a dozen were imprisoned. One of those who spent a period in jail was A. O. H. Jarman, editor of *Y Ddraig Goch*, the monthly journal of *Plaid Genedlaethol Cymru*.

Opponents of the war may have attracted considerable attention as individuals, but the fact remains that the overwhelming majority of the

Welsh public pledged their full support and played an active role in the war effort. Some 300,000 members of the British armed forces lost their lives during the fighting, 15,000 of whom hailed from Wales. Upon the outbreak of the war, the National Service (Armed Forces) Act came into operation, making all males aged between eighteen and forty liable for military service. By December 1941, not only had the male call-up age been raised to fifty-one, but single women aged between twenty and thirty had also become liable to be conscripted for the Women's Auxiliary Services, the Civil Defence Forces or industrial employment. Considerable powers to control and direct all available labour to 'essential' wartime work had also been vested in the Ministry of Labour and National Service by this time. Increased wartime production and labour demands proved particularly beneficial to the Welsh economy and virtually eliminated unem-ployment. Agriculture, a key industry during war time, entered a period of relative prosperity, with thousands of acres of Welsh land being turned over to arable farming in order to fulfil the demand for food. In the old industrial districts, wartime conditions had a marked impact on the local economy. From 1938 onwards, the government assumed powers to direct industries to manufacture 'essential' goods and many Welsh firms won substantial war-time contracts. At the Trefforest Trading Estate, some twenty-four factories were requisitioned by the Ministry of Aircraft Production, while production at the steel works at Shotton and Brymbo in the north-east received a considerable boost. New industrial establishments, such as the Royal Ordnance Factories (ROFs) built at Marchwiel near Wrexham, and Bridgend, Glascoed (near Pontypool) and Hirwaun in south Wales, turned out explosives and shells for the armed forces and provided employment for thousands of local people. Bridgend ROF, the largest shell-filling factory in Britain, employed some 35,000 people at its peak, most of whom were females who travelled daily from the surrounding industrial communities. To such women, wartime employment not only provided a unique opportunity to undertake full-time work in their locality but also brought many financial benefits. As W. H. Mainwaring, MP for Rhondda East, pointed out in 1946, 'one reason why the women of Wales became available for work in their thousands is because they had lived on such a narrow economic base that they were glad to welcome an added shilling'.

In contrast, some of the traditional heavy industries of Wales struggled as a result of wartime conditions. Both the tin-plate and slate industries lost thousands of their male employees to the armed forces and the war industries, while over 25,000 miners left the pits of south Wales between 1938 and 1941. Since coal supplies were in great demand, action was required to put a stop to this drift away from the industry. The Essential Work Order of 1941 tied miners to their 'reserved occupation', preventing them not only from enlisting for active service but also from entering local munitions factories, where both working conditions and wages were deemed to be far superior. In July 1943, Ernest Bevin, the Minister of Labour, took further steps to boost manpower in the mines when he ordered that one in ten of the eighteen-year-olds who were called up, should be directed to work as 'Bevin boys' in the coal industry. Such measures merely served to heighten the grievances of the miners, who vented their anger in a series of unofficial wartime strikes. The most serious stoppage took place in March 1944, following the Porter Award, when some 100,000 south Wales miners went on strike to demand a new wage structure. Eager to bring the strike to a halt and resume coal supplies, the government (which had taken control of the industry in 1942) stepped in and negotiated a settlement. In April 1944 a new wage agreement was signed and the miners returned to work victorious, having won higher rates of pay and a national minimum wage. More important, perhaps, the 1944 victory marked a significant step forward in the miners' campaign to take the coal industry out of private ownership.

Some of the hardest struggles of the war years were fought by civilians on the 'home front'. The waging of this 'total war' had an unprecedented impact on the daily lives of British civilians. As one commentator remarked in December 1939, the war 'upset every single institution and practically every habit from smoking to dreaming, from washing to wishing'. The total blackout which was imposed across the country from sunset until sunrise caused widespread disruption and, coupled with the introduction of petrol rationing, made 'non-essential' travel almost impossible. Shortages of both 'essential' and 'non-essential' commodities became commonplace, and by February 1942, 'points' and coupon rationing had been introduced to cover many food and clothing items. Shopping for a family became a major operation and many hours were spent standing in queues only to find that items had already sold out. A journalist who visited the Rhondda in 1941 noticed how local women had to 'scout around' the shops of the area in their never-ending search for 'some titbit for their men'. Considerable ingenuity was required on the part of the housewife to feed and clothe her family with the narrow range of foods and materials which were available to her. A miner's wife from Blaenafon recalled that when she made her invariable reply, 'Wait and see', when her husband asked what was for supper, he would retort, 'Oh, I know, dried egg!' Significantly, however, in some parts of Wales it was apparent that conditions were not much worse than those which had prevailed before the war. 'We've been rationed here for years, so it's nothing new to us,' remarked a housewife from Blaina in Monmouthshire in 1942. Indeed, in some south Wales districts, standards of health actually improved as a result of wartime rationing and the receipt of regular wages.

The second World War was an ordeal which placed every member of Welsh society in the front line, and the sharing of such hardships and sacrifices fostered a strong community spirit which helped maintain morale throughout the darkest hours of the crisis. During the early years of the war, enemy invasion of the British mainland was feared as a real possibility. In preparation for any sea or air landings, trenches were dug, roadblocks set up and fortifications put in place near the coastline. In May 1940, a force of Local Defence Volunteers, soon rechristened the Home Guard, was established and its elderly members patrolled Welsh towns and countryside, keeping watch for any sign of the enemy. Such was the feeling of distrust and alarm which swept through the country that 'enemy aliens' who resided in Britain were rounded up and either interned or placed under curfew for the duration of the war. In June 1940, following Italy's declaration of war against Britain, members of the small but long-established Welsh-Italian community suddenly found themselves subject to such treatment. In the county of Glamorgan alone, some 160 Italian men, the majority of whom were owners of 'Bracchi' shops or cafés, were arrested almost overnight.

A far more realistic risk of enemy attack was posed by the threat of aerial bombardment. Some 60,000 British civilians were killed as a result of enemy air strikes during the second World War but it is probable that the death toll would have been far higher had the government not acted in advance to limit the damage which might be inflicted on the populous areas. By October 1938, gas masks had already been issued to most adults and children and, although gas was never used in an enemy attack, the very existence of these rubber-snouted contraptions served to heighten fears of the dangers which lay ahead. Barrage balloons appeared in the skies above towns and cities, while air raid shelters were hastily dug out and erected. In built-up areas, air raid wardens kept a watchful eye on blacking-out procedures, and reported those who neglected to ensure complete darkness after sunset. Anticipating the panic which could ensue if residents of the towns and cities fled their homes at the outbreak of war, the government had also prepared an elaborate evacuation scheme. On 1 September 1939 the scheme was put into action. Three days later, almost one and half a million mothers and children had been evacuated from English towns and cities. Since Wales was not thought to be a prime target for air attacks, most of the country was designated a 'reception area' for the official evacuees. Thousands of 'unofficial' evacuees also made private arrangements to come to Wales. During the first two years of the war alone, 200,000 or so people had migrated there, among them many exiled Welsh men and women returning home to seek refuge and employment. Those parts of the country which had witnessed considerable outmigration during the inter-war years experienced a sudden reversal of fortunes. Writing in October 1941, Thomas Jones C.H. penned a vivid description of the social and economic changes which war had brought about in the mining valleys:

> The waging of war had filled the valleys with work and wages. Boys swagger in the streets with pocketfuls of money. Omnibuses crowded with women and girls rumble to and fro between the scattered mining villages and the concentrated munition factories. The tide of migration has turned. The little houses of the hospitable miners are filled with English children from the 'blitzed' towns over the Border. The expulsive power of a new experience has dimmed the memories of the nineteen-thirties. The sufferings of enforced idleness have given place to the horrors of bombing and burning.
>
> ('Foreword' in Eli Ginzberg, *A World Without Work: The Story of the Welsh Miners*, 1991)

In the event, however, the belief that Wales would provide a haven during the war proved unfounded. During June 1940, Cardiff suffered the first of several air raids, while two months later, three German aircraft attacked the oil storage depot at Pembroke Dock. Cardiff was to endure further air strikes during 1941. The raid, which took place during the night of 2 January, killed 150 people and inflicted terrible damage on hundreds of buildings, including Llandaff Cathedral. Worse was to follow in the months that followed. This time, however, it was the town of Swansea which suffered from the German bombers. Between 1940 and 1943, a total of 369 people were killed as a result of 44 air attacks on the town. The raids which took place during 19, 20 and 21 February 1941, when Swansea endured 'three nights of hell', claimed 230 victims, injured over 400 people, and destroyed not only a substantial section of the town centre, but parts of Townhill, Manselton and Brynhyfryd. Surveying the scene of devastation a few days after the bombings, one observer remarked that 'Swansea, like Coventry, is now a monument to the beastliness of war'. As if to reaffirm the fact that parts of Wales were just as vulnerable to air strikes as some of the large urban districts of England, two evacuated children were among the twenty-eight people killed in April 1941 when high explosive and parachute mines were dropped on the small mining village of Cwm-parc in the Rhondda.

Although the failure of the government to take steps to protect Welsh mothers and children from enemy attacks provoked an angry response from some Welsh patriots, for others the experience of the blitz merely encouraged a spirit of collective endeavour and served to strengthen the sense of Britishness which pervaded Welsh wartime society. Enemy bombs had exposed Welsh householders to the same horrors as their counterparts in England and, as such, their sacrifices to the British wartime effort had been equal. The powerful administrative machinery of wartime government played an important role in promoting this united British front. For example, the outbreak of the war brought an end to Welsh regional radio broadcasting as the BBC 'Home Service' took over the air waves. Maintaining a distinct Welsh social and cultural identity proved extremely difficult under such centralizing pressures. Wartime conditions affected all aspects of Welsh life and severely disrupted the activities of religious and cultural societies. Attendance at Welsh chapels and churches suffered acutely. The officials of one Nonconformist cause in the Rhondda remarked in 1940 that the war had 'breached and weakened' almost every aspect of the work of the chapel.

It was also apparent that the increased mobility of the population was leading to the adoption of new social mores. The pressure which was put on local authorities across Wales to lift their restrictions on Sunday entertainments gave some indication of the changing nature of Welsh society. A marked increase in the incidence of female drinking was also reported, attributed to the influence of female evacuees and war workers from England: 'They are teaching local women to drink!' proclaimed one senior police officer from Carmarthen in 1941. One issue which caused particular concern to Welsh patriots was the detrimental impact which the influx of thousands of English evacuees could have on the Welsh language. Such were the fears for the havoc which might be wrought in the predominantly Welsh-speaking areas, that a group of prominent nationalists convened an urgent meeting in December 1939 to discuss ways and means of safeguarding Welsh culture. By August 1941 members of *Pwyllgor Diogelu Diwylliant Cymru* (The Committee for the Defence of the Culture of Wales) had joined ranks with *Undeb Cenedlaethol y Cymdeithasau Cymraeg* (The National Union of Welsh Societies) to form *Undeb Cymru Fydd* (The New Wales Union), a society which was to wage a high-profile campaign to protect the social and cultural interests of Wales and her people throughout the war years.

Despite such efforts, the war dealt a severe blow to the 'Welshness' of the nation so that, by 1945, the Welsh people were more divided than ever by language and culture. In many other ways, however, the country emerged from the Allied victory of 1945 with a new spirit of unity and optimism. Economically and politically, the Wales of 1945 was a very different society from the industrially-ravaged, despairing nation which had entered the war in 1939. The exigencies of war had provided the necessary stimulus to restructure the Welsh economy. Not only had new factories been built, but a new workforce had been created, one which had grown familiar with 'working to the hooter' and with commuting to and from the workplace. The egalitarianism of the war experience had also focused public attention on the inequalities and indignities endured during the inter-war years and served to deepen the conviction that Wales should never be exposed to such a betrayal in the future. As the results of the General Election of 1945 confirmed, the ending of the war marked a new beginning in the history of the people of Wales. Labour captured twenty-five of the thirty-six Welsh seats, winning 58.5 per cent of votes, compared with 48 per cent in the United Kingdom as a whole. Constituencies in industrial Wales secured some of the largest Labour majorities in the country. In Llanelli, James Griffiths succeeded in placing 34,000 votes between himself and the runner-up. Labour even came close to winning the Liberal territories of Anglesey and Merioneth in the north. Central to the achievement of the Labour party in Wales was its commitment to a comprehensive programme of social and economic reforms. The 1942 Beveridge Report laid the foundation for a series of radical post-war welfare schemes which were to have an immense impact on the lives of the people of Wales. Welsh MPs, such as James Griffiths and Aneurin Bevan, played a key role in the creation of the new welfare state. Informed by their experiences of life in the 'social hell' of inter-war Wales, these architects of the National Insurance and National Health Service were driven by their determination to lead the people of Wales to a new and fairer post-war society. Writing in the *Aberdare Leader* in January 1946, the columnist 'Aberdarian' captured the mood of expectancy in the town:

> Coming soon are a great social insurance scheme to banish want, coupled with family allowances and higher compensation for injured workers, long-looked-for nationalisation of the mining industry, a broader and better education system, a comprehensive national health service, more houses . . . The horizon looks bright; we walk into this New Year full of hope of better times to come.

After being condemned to two decades of social and economic deprivation, the people of Wales emerged from the second World War charged with a new spirit of renewal and optimism.

CHAPTER 7

ON A BORDER IN HISTORY?
WALES, 1945-85

CHRIS WILLIAMS

Where they were standing, looking out, was on a border in the earth
and in history: to north and west the great expanses of a pastoral
country; to south and east, where the iron and coal had been worked,
the crowded valleys, the new industries, now in their turn becoming
old. There had been a contrast, once, clearly seen on this border,
between an old way of life and a new, as between a father living in his
old and known ways and a son living differently, in a new occupation
and with a new cast of mind. But what was visible now was that both
were old. The pressure for renewal, inside them, had to make its way
through a land and through lives that had been deeply shaped, deeply
committed, by a present that was always moving, inexorably, into the
past. And those moments of the present that could connect to a future
were then hard to grasp, hard to hold to, hard to bring together to a
rhythm, to a movement, to the necessary shape of a quite different life.
What could now be heard, momentarily, as this actual movement, had
conditions of time, of growth, quite different from the conditions of
any single life, or of any father and son.

At the end of Raymond Williams's novel *The Fight For Manod* (1979),
Matthew and Susan Price contemplate a landscape that is, in itself, a
guide to centuries of Welsh history. Yet, as Williams suggested, neither
the landscape, nor the lived meaning of that past, are static. The fight for
the new town of Manod represents an attempt to move forward from the
'dislocation' of the divisive ravages of the past, to find 'a different future
... that settles people'. It symbolizes a bold design to bring under
democratic control 'the storms' that have blown through Wales, storms
'with their origin elsewhere'. Only by willing the connection of present
and past, can this liberating vision become tangible.

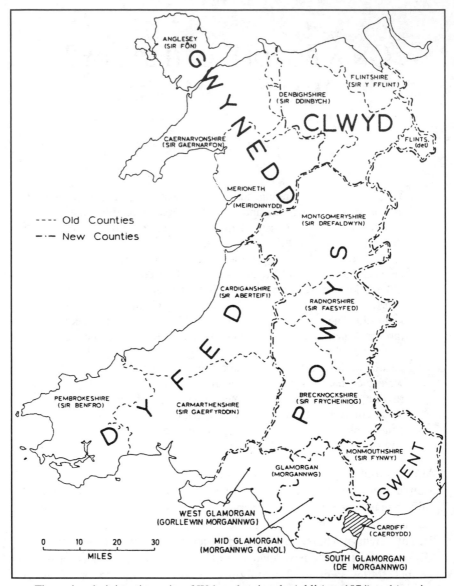

ANGLESEY
(SIR FÔN)

GWYNEDD

FLINTSHIRE
(SIR Y FFLINT)

DENBIGHSHIRE
(SIR DDINBYCH)

CLWYD

CAERNARVONSHIRE
(SIR GAERNARFON)

FLINTS.
(deu)

MERIONETH
(MEIRIONNYDD)

MONTGOMERYSHIRE
(SIR DREFALDWYN)

---- Old Counties
-·- New Counties

POWYS

CARDIGANSHIRE
(SIR ABERTEIFI)

RADNORSHIRE
(SIR FAESYFED)

DYFED

PEMBROKESHIRE
(SIR BENFRO)

CARMARTHENSHIRE
(SIR GAERFYRDDIN)

BRECKNOCKSHIRE
(SIR FRYCHEINIOG)

MONMOUTHSHIRE
(SIR FYNWY)

GLAMORGAN
(MORGANNWG)

GWENT

WEST GLAMORGAN
(GORLLEWIN MORGANNWG)

0   10   20   30
MILES

MID GLAMORGAN
(MORGANNWG GANOL)

CARDIFF
(CAERDYDD)

SOUTH GLAMORGAN
(DE MORGANNWG)

The main administrative units of Wales, showing the 'old' (pre-1974) and 'new'
(1974-1996) county boundaries.

On VJ Day, 15 August 1945, Wales was, recognizably, a country steeped in its recent past. The exigencies of the wartime economy may have generated some new opportunities for industrial growth and employment, but across large swathes of the land the centrality of the old staples – agriculture, coal, steel – was set to resume: there was no alternative, at least not immediately. People were full of fear and hope: fearful that the unemployment and the poverty that had followed the first World War might soon return; hopeful that the votes they had recently cast for a Labour government, for once in line with the electorate in Britain as a whole, might lead to a new social order in which those particular demons could be banished. Culturally, Wales remained deeply marked by the twin identification of Nonconformity and the Welsh language. Religion might attract only a minority of the Welsh people to its services, but it continued to articulate a set of behavioural standards and moral expectations that were widely recognized, albeit sometimes only in the breach. The Welsh language, spoken perhaps by a third of the population overall, dominated much of the north and west of the country, and, in private life at the very least, could make its presence felt in many of the industrial valleys of Glamorgan. Welsh society was publicly controlled by men – only one Welsh MP (Megan Lloyd George) was female – and men out-numbered women at the workplace by more than three to one, a characteristic of a heavy-industry economy.

On 5 March 1985, the miners' strike that had begun a year earlier ended in defeat. Wales in 1985 was neither a perfect, nor an inverted, image of the country that had welcomed peace four decades before. The 1985 that turned a puzzled gaze upon its predecessor, was one bent into a *mélange* of different shapes: some more attractive, and pleasing to the eye, others grotesquely distorted caricatures. Wales had passed, by means of historical changes akin to a fairground hall of mirrors, from realism to cubism in forty years. The classic industrial and employment structures with which the country had entered the post-war era were more likely, henceforth, to be experienced in the form of industrial museums and heritage sites than in the lived patterns of work or in everyday sights and sounds. Of fear and hope, only one was present in the Wales of the mid 1980s. Hope, in its many forms, had been largely obliterated by the referendum and election polls in 1979 and 1983, but it was the callous crushing of the miners by a ruthless and vindictive state that effectively drew a line under two centuries of economic, social, and political history. The message was clear: Wales was now post-industrial, and perhaps, like much of the rest of Britain, it should consider becoming post-socialist as well. There was little compensation to be found in improvements elsewhere: the economy was stagnant, unemployment was at a post-war high, and the welfare state, which had represented both the spiritual achievement and the historical affirmation of the British working class (with the Welsh very much in the vanguard) was under siege. In cultural terms, Wales was undeniably secular, and the Welsh language, now spoken by less than a fifth of the population, was a more marginal presence than ever before in many parts of the country, and, for Welsh speakers, a more compartmentalized, forcibly self-conscious, aspect of their lives. Only in the area of gender relations, with women approaching parity of numbers with men in the workforce, and articulating a more egalitarian ethos in both public and private, could unambiguously positive (if incomplete) changes be identified (although there was still only one female MP – Ann Clwyd).

In 1945, Wales had a past that could be expected to resonate into the future. In 1985, many of the people of Wales could be forgiven for believing that all they, and their country, had was a past. Storms, with their origin elsewhere, were blowing through Wales at gale force. To envisage a future that had any significant connection with the country Wales had become in the course of industrial and urban growth, was indeed to be an optimist of the will. In 1985, Raymond Williams published another novel, *Loyalties*. Loyalty was, perhaps, all that could remain.

LIFE AND DEATH

In 1945, approximately 2,422,300 people lived within the boundaries of the thirteen counties of Wales (including Monmouthshire). Whether or not they necessarily thought of themselves, or were thought by others, as being *Welsh people*, they were the people of Wales. During the post-war decades, Wales made a demographic recovery from the battering it had taken in the 1920s and 1930s. By

1985, its population had risen to 2,810,300, with marked growth in the 1960s and 1970s. During the 1950s and 1960s population growth was due to an excess of births over deaths rather than to Wales being able to attract new residents from outside its borders: these were decades of net out-migration, although on a much smaller scale (62,000) than that of the period 1921-51 (450,000). This pattern changed in the 1970s and early 1980s, as natural growth slowed and net in-migration returned (124,000 between 1971 and 1991).

In common with other Western societies, Wales's natural rates of birth and death continued to fall in the second half of the twentieth century to historically low levels. Death rates dropped by 28 per cent between the early 1950s and 1985. The infant mortality rate fell more dramatically: whereas it had stood at fifty-four deaths of children under one year of age per thousand live births in 1945, it stood at only ten per thousand by the end of the period. These developments meant that, for men, life expectancy had increased to seventy-one years by 1981, and for women the gains had been even greater, so that they could expect to live to seventy-seven. Although all these rates remained below British averages, they nevertheless represented a considerable improvement in health and living standards since the end of the second World War.

In part, longer lives were possible because the threat of certain diseases was reduced to negligible levels during the post-war era. Tuberculosis of all sorts killed 1086 people in Wales in 1951, but only 54 in 1985. Influenza was responsible for 1308 deaths in 1951, but only 37 three decades later. Less than a tenth of the number of women dying in pregnancy or as the result of a botched abortion at the beginning of this period were found at its end. Higher standards of living and, for many, a more sedentary lifestyle, were reflected in changed patterns of death. Heart disease and cancer became proportionately more significant and accounted for over half of total deaths by the 1980s.

The fact that people lived longer inevitably changed the age structure of the Welsh population. In 1951, 11 per cent had been aged sixty-five or over: by 1981 that proportion had risen to 16 per cent. The universal availability of a state pension gave older people greater freedom from the worst extremes of poverty and dependence on their relatives. However, although people enjoyed longer lives, they did not necessarily exhibit what would be considered 'healthy' lifestyles. In 1985 two-fifths of men and a third of women were smokers, two-fifths of the Welsh population were overweight or obese, (the Welsh diet being relatively high in carbohydrates and fats) and a quarter consumed far too much sugar in the form of biscuits, sweets or chocolates, leading to high levels of tooth decay. A third of men admitted to an excessive level of alcohol consumption and only one third of men and one eighth of women took regular exercise. Wales remained one of the areas of Britain with the highest take-up of prescription items per head.

At the other end of the scale of human existence, birth rates fell by about a quarter between 1948 and 1985, although they did not do so gradually. In fact, after a slow decline to the mid 1950s they picked up to peak in 1964 at ninety-one births per thousand women aged between fifteen and forty-four. Thereafter their fall was relatively steady to a low of sixty-one births per thousand in 1983. Extra-marital births averaged around 4 per cent of the total from the late 1940s to the early 1960s, but then began to rise almost every year to reach 19 per cent by 1985. This development was linked to the declining popularity of marriage, with 1985 rates being only two-thirds those of the late 1940s. A parallel trend was the considerable rise in divorce rates, which more than doubled between the early 1970s and the mid 1980s. Nevertheless, many who divorced were, by the end of the period, going on to remarry (and accounting for over a fifth of all those marrying, both men and women). The most popular age at which to marry, usually for the first time, remained the early twenties throughout the post-war era but, by the 1980s, significant numbers of men and women were marrying in their thirties and late twenties respectively. By the end of that decade, the average age of marriage was thirty for men and twenty-seven for women, and more births were occurring later, when mothers were in their late twenties and thirties.

Relatively little is known about the attitudes of Welsh people to love and sex over the period. What evidence there is suggests a variety of customs and practices structured along regional and class lines. To begin with, there are indications that, even in the immediate post-war years, Nonconformist attitudes towards premarital chastity were not widely upheld, with sexual intercourse viewed by many couples as a natural, if covert, stage of serious courtship. As formal contraceptive devices were often not used, whether for reasons of expense, limited accessibility, or ignorance, any resultant pregnancy might be the occasion for a hasty (but still 'respectable') wedding. A study of Llanfrothen in the county of Merioneth, undertaken in the late 1950s and early 1960s, calculated that over two-fifths of marriages were followed within eight months or fewer by the birth of a child, and pointed to the fact that the counties of rural mid and north Wales had the highest such rate in England and Wales. Early marriage, in any case, legitimized sexual contact for young adults. During the 1960s the growing availability of the contraceptive pill, allied to a change in social attitudes over questions of sexual expression and personal freedom, led to a shift in the status of sexual intercourse within relationships. No longer was it necessarily seen as part of a commitment that was expected (often by the woman if not by the man) to end in marriage vows. Rather, it was something that might be enjoyed for its own sake, with no further implications, as well as being an important (perhaps the most important) element in loving relationships. Although the permissive society was rarely fully swinging in Wales, even in the urban south, this transformation in sexual behaviour was amongst the most dramatic, if least studied, of all social changes in post-war Wales. As for homosexuality in Wales, it was Pontypool's Labour MP Leo Abse who inspired a relaxation of the laws in 1967 but, as with so much else of an intimate nature in private life, this is another subject that remains 'hidden from history'.

The factors that governed the choice of a marriage partner are little clearer than those of sexual activity. A study of Swansea undertaken in the 1960s showed that, of over 600 people marrying between 1940 and 1960, virtually nine-tenths married someone from within twelve miles of the town centre, with middle-class individuals being more likely to find a partner further afield than those in the working class. In rural areas, choice was infinitely more limited and more rigorously conditioned by class, occupation and status. Yet, by the end of the period, any control that parents had once sought to operate over the life decisions of their children had largely been relinquished, and questions of personal compatibility and sexual attraction (increasingly put to the test in cohabitation) were dominant.

Once married, the husbands and wives of the 1940s, 1950s and 1960s usually settled into life in a single-family, 'nuclear' household.

This had been the pattern in Wales for more than a century. However, by the mid 1980s, although this type of household remained the experience of the majority, it was accompanied by a greater diversity of household and family forms. Over half of Welsh households contained married couples, with or without children: cohabiting couples accounted for a further 5 per cent of households (a majority of them without children), and single parents 9 per cent. About a quarter of households contained just one person (often older women, although, increasingly, younger people as well), and less than 2 per cent an 'extended family' of any description. Welsh households continued to be larger than the British average, but still declined in size: from 3.05 persons at the start of the 1960s to 2.5 persons by the mid 1980s. The nature of family and kinship bonds varied greatly: for those who continued to live in the area of their birth, often they remained strong, even conditioning social behaviour, but for those who moved away, or who sought other social networks in the towns and cities, connections could easily become tenuous and fitful. Maintaining one's identity as part of a family became, sometimes with good reason, a matter of choice.

Within the context of the nuclear family, changing patterns of work, involving the entry into the workforce of many married women, along with the adoption of more egalitarian ideals, had some impact on gender relations in the home. Women born in the late 1960s have been shown to have much greater expectations that their male partners would share in the responsibility of running a home, than women born in the 1940s or earlier. Nevertheless, most of the responsibility for housework and domestic management remained with women. Men might wash dishes, but they were usually reluctant to wash nappies. With changing patterns of paid work for women this continued imbalance in the sharing of domestic tasks often resulted in women shouldering a double burden of, in effect, two jobs. Feminist views triumphed in theory, but translating them into practice was more a war of attrition than a *blitzkrieg*.

The burdens of domestic labour for men and women were eased by improvements in the houses in which they lived. The Conservative governments of the 1950s continued the programme of council house building begun by Aneurin Bevan in the late 1940s, and the numbers built towered above smaller increases in private-sector stock.

Between 1945 and 1959 the public sector was responsible for four-fifths of all house-building in Wales, much of it located in the south Wales coastal strip and in the north-east around Wrexham. Although levels of owner occupation had been historically high in Wales, by the early 1960s the rise of the council estate had begun to rival the numbers in privately rented accommodation. By 1979, when owner occupation accounted for three-fifths of all housing tenures in Wales, council rents represented a further three-tenths, and private renting was reduced to an eighth. The Conservative government's policy of selling council houses represented another shift of policy at the very end of the period (with 15,000 council houses sold in Wales by 1985) and by the mid 1980s two-thirds of Welsh housing was in owner occupation. Nevertheless, housing in Wales was of relatively old stock, in some cases dating from the early years of industrialization, and two-fifths from before 1914. Although overcrowding had been banished, nearly a fifth of dwellings in Wales were considered substandard in 1981, with 18 per cent of houses in the Rhondda Valleys lacking an inside toilet and 13 per cent a bath or shower.

None of the changes in the nature of Welsh housing made much difference to the uneven distribution of people across Wales. The industrial revolution had created a substantial population imbalance, characterized by a heavy concentration of people in Glamorgan and Monmouthshire. The pattern of demographic growth after the second World War did nothing to alter this. In 1945, 63 per cent of the Welsh lived in the same two counties, and by 1981 this had barely changed. Nearly two-thirds of the Welsh continued to live in an area about one sixth of the size of the country as a whole. However, even within the urbanized south, important changes took place in the second half of the twentieth century. Most of the older mining valleys lost population consistently throughout the period. The Rhondda Valleys saw a fall from 111,389 in 1951 to 81,955 in 1981. In contrast, coastal towns and cities enjoyed continued growth: Cardiff from 243,632 to 273,525, Newport from 106,420 to 133,808, and Swansea from 160,988 to 186,589. Some local authority areas, such as Taff-Ely, the Rhymney Valley and Ogwr, which included mining districts, balanced population outflow from the valleys with the growth of towns such as Pontypridd, Llantrisant, Caerphilly and Bridgend. Elsewhere in Wales the picture was more varied: inward migration was a significant factor in boosting the population totals of Pembrokeshire, Cardiganshire, Powys and the north Wales coast, as well as rural areas in the south, including the Vale of Glamorgan and the northern and eastern parts of Gwent. A considerable amount of this movement was caused by the redistribution of the resident Welsh themselves, with some leaving the still-growing cities to set up home in the nearby countryside, and others, whether of working or retirement age, opting out of urban life in search of a rural idyll. Similar motives attracted English-born people to Merioneth, Anglesey, and the north Wales coast. By the early 1980s, for every hundred people of working age in Gwynedd, there were thirty-seven who had retired. Furthermore, by the 1980s over a sixth of the people of Wales had, in fact, been born in England, and Wales was the most cosmopolitan part of Great Britain, with only four-fifths of its residents having been born there (compared with 90 per cent for both England and Scotland). The Rhondda Valleys were, in terms of birthplace, the most indigenous area, with 93 per cent of its inhabitants having been born in Wales. That said, Wales was not a significant destination for post-war immigration by ethnic minorities. Only in Cardiff did the percentage of the population born in the New Commonwealth and Pakistan approach the British average (2.4 as against 2.8 per cent): across Wales as a whole it was 0.7 per cent. Significant black communities (including many members born in Wales) could be found in Butetown in Cardiff and, to a lesser extent, in other south Wales coastal towns.

For those of the Welsh who left Wales, theirs was not an out-migration born of the levels of poverty and unemployment witnessed in the inter-war decades. The dominant trend was, instead, for movement into England to be linked to upward social mobility, with teaching jobs attracting many Welsh people who benefited from the expansion of higher education and the development of free comprehensive schooling. Already existing centres for Welsh settlement, such as Coventry, Oxford and Slough, were both topped up by new generations of migrants, and supplemented by the more recent growth of Swindon and Reading. Some Welsh people, especially in the 1950s and 1960s, emigrated to Australia, Canada and New Zealand, and others to the U.S.A. Like many of their forebears they remained keen to maintain a sense of national identity, irrespective of whether or not they intended ever to return. And, in similar fashion, the Wales they had known once more slipped through their fingers like a fine sand. In terms of both origins and private lives, the experiences of the people of Wales were more diverse in 1985 than they had been in 1945. Welsh society was even less a homogeneous entity, and more a statistical construct, than it had been. Often, such changes were tied to shifting patterns of work, and reflected in an increasing variety of leisure-time activities.

Work and Play

If the Welsh economy had been on a roller-coaster ride in the first forty years of the twentieth century, the next forty were to be no less turbulent. From the outset, politicians and planners were concerned that industrial diversification should make a repeat of the 1930s, epression impossible. The key to achieving this was to be the attraction of manufacturing industry, to relieve the pressure on the older, staple industries of iron, steel and coal. Yet, such a strategy would take time to become operative and, initially, much energy had to be expended in attempting to rehabilitate Wales's established heavy industries for the new challenges of peacetime.

In the case of coal, any modernization programme had to be linked to the nationalization of the industry, which took place on 1 January 1947. The number of pits taken into public ownership in south Wales (222) was less than half the number that had existed in the 1920s, and total output, at twenty-one million tons, was far below the thirty-five million that had been produced on the eve of the second World War. Output did rise slightly, to a peak of twenty-four million tons in 1952, and was sustained throughout the remainder of that decade, in spite of seventy-four pit closures between 1947 and 1960. There were new investment projects in a number of large pits, but a steady decline in the levels of global and domestic demand imposed their own logic. In the 1960s production dropped first to around nineteen million tons, and then to thirteen million by 1970. At this point there were still over fifty working collieries in the coal-field, but employment, which had stood at 115,500 at nationalization, fell below 100,000 in 1959 and below 50,000 a decade later. In the much smaller coal-field in north-east Wales, production declined from two million tons in 1947 to under a million by 1969, and employment shrunk from 8,808 to 2,513. In macro-economic terms, the coal industry, which had been the largest single employer in Wales in 1948 with 15 per cent of the total workforce, had jobs for only 6 per cent by the end of the 1960s.

Coal's predominance was ended, in part, by a resurgence in the prosperity of the iron and steel industry in Wales, until the 1970s the greatest single success story of the post-war Welsh economy. Growth was largely built around two new works: the Abbey Works at Margam, which opened in 1951 as the largest steelworks in Britain, and the Llanwern Works outside Newport, which began production in 1962. Tin-plate cold reduction works opened at Margam, Trostre and Felindre, new electrolytic tinning plants were opened on existing sites at Ebbw Vale, electrical sheets, tubes, and narrow cold-rolled strip were produced at Newport, and alloy steel at Panteg. South Wales became the leading steel-making district of Britain, with production rising (for Wales as a whole) from four million tonnes in 1950 to a high of 8.6 million tonnes in 1965. Employment in metal manufacture rose from around 82,000 to 95,000 in the same period, with 75,000 of these jobs in iron and steel.

Accompanying the boom in steel was, by the late 1960s, an impressive array of new factories making anything from zip fasteners to optical equipment. Initially assisted by the gradual conversion of the wartime royal ordnance factories to civilian purposes and by government provision of factory space for incoming employers, south and north-east Wales, in particular, found their economic bases transformed by a range of manufacturing industries. Domestic electrical appliances were made by Hoover at Merthyr Tydfil and Hotpoint at Llandudno Junction; Prestcold made refrigerators at Swansea, Rover and Borg-Warner made gearboxes at Cardiff and Margam. The plastics industry developed in Barry, nylon spinning in Pontypool, rubber in Brynmawr, insulating materials at Cwmbrân, rayon in Flintshire, aluminium at Holyhead, tyres at Caernarfon, lager at Wrexham, cornflakes at Marchwiel. Many smaller factories produced toys, batteries, bicycles, paint, optical fibre cable, Christmas decorations, ceramic insulators and furniture. Furthermore, although the shift away from coal in energy consumption undermined the long-term viability of one of Wales's historically most significant industries, it did bring other benefits. The deep waters of Milford

Haven were found to be ideal for accommodating ocean-going oil tankers, and from the early 1960s oil terminals and refineries were built there, transforming the town into a major British port (although doing little for employment opportunities once the initial construction was finished). More controversially, nuclear power stations were built at Trawsfynydd in 1958 and Wylfa in 1964.

In rural areas of Wales, the growth of manufacturing industry was less important than in the existing industrial zones of the south and north-east, and economic progress was less evident. The slate industry was in seemingly terminal decline, with once great quarries at Blaenau Ffestiniog, Llanberis and Dyffryn Nantlle closing. The Welsh fishing industry virtually died out. There were elements of industry, based on wool, leather and textiles but, across the upland expanses of north, mid and west Wales, most regular employment was in agriculture. Much of Welsh farming became more specialized in the post-war era. Wheat production was largely superseded by barley, and dairying remained important in the Vale of Glamorgan, Carmarthenshire and parts of north-east Wales. However, although some farmers prospered, those with poor upland soils struggled along. Over half of land holdings in Wales were classed as only requiring part-time labour by the late 1970s, though many were worked on a full-time basis. Landownership became concentrated in fewer hands, and mechanization hastened the decline in numbers working on the land. The 77,000 of 1951 contracted to around 57,000 thirty years later, only 32,000 of whom were full-time. Agriculture remained a major employer in some areas, accounting for 33 per cent of male employment in Radnorshire, and 29 per cent in Montgomeryshire, but its relative contribution to the Welsh economy fell by about a third between 1960 and 1985.

Overall, economic growth in Wales ran above the United Kingdom average throughout the 1960s, but talk of a 'second industrial revolution' was over-optimistic, and was revealed as such by the serious decline that took place in both the coal and steel industries from the mid 1970s. Diversification had been only a partial success: almost a third of male Welsh workers could be found in the coal and steel industries by the early 1970s, so the loss of nearly 20,000 jobs in coal between 1969 and 1979 was still a serious blow to overall economic health. More strikingly, given its recent expansion, the steel industry contracted so rapidly that at one point it seemed likely that steelmaking in Wales would cease. In 1973 the British Steel Corporation had employed 58,000 workers, but by 1986 it paid the wages of only 15,000. The closures of plants at Ebbw Vale (1978), East Moors in Cardiff (1978) and Shotton (1980) were responsible for 19,000 of these job losses alone, with severe trimming in other plants.

Crisis in the heavy industries was paralleled by a slump in manufacturing across Britain from 1979 onwards. With its branch plants always vulnerable to cost-cutting decisions, this hit Wales particularly hard. Firestone shut its tyre factory at Wrexham in 1980, and there were major cuts in jobs at many plants including BP (Barry), Hoover (Merthyr), Courtaulds (Clwyd), and at Milford Haven's oil refineries. The bright spot on the Welsh economic horizon, as far as manufacturing was concerned, was the emergence of significant levels of foreign investment, with 'sunrise' industries in engineering (especially in electronics and automotive components) from the Far East capturing most attention. Virtually a fifth of all manufacturing jobs in Wales were with foreign firms by 1981, and Wales had the highest concentration of Japanese plants in Europe by the mid 1980s, although in fact most foreign investment in Wales came from the USA (three-fifths by the early 1980s, accounting for over 30,000 jobs).

Nevertheless, the fragility of the 'second industrial revolution' is reinforced by figures showing job losses in manufacturing amounting to 125,000 from a total of 331,000 between 1966 and 1986. In terms of occupational structure and social class, Wales in the early 1980s had a lower than average proportion of its workforce (28 per cent as against a United Kingdom average of 32 per cent) in groups I (professional), II (managerial and technical) and III N (skilled non-manual). The arrival of supposedly 'high-tech' industries from the late 1970s onwards had little impact on historically low levels of skills because, very often, although the products involved were sophisticated, the labour needed and the techniques required were elementary – so-called 'screwdriver technology'.

The most 'revolutionary' developments in the post-war Welsh economy occurred in the service sector, with the rise of white-collar rather than blue-collar jobs. To some extent this was stimulated by government planning policy, with the moving of the Royal Mint to

Llantrisant in 1968, the siting of Companies House in Cardiff, the Passport Office in Newport, and the Driver and Vehicle Licensing Centre (employing over 5,000 by 1977) in Morriston, Swansea. Much was owed also to the expansion of the welfare state and education system, which overshadowed growth in private sector services. Whereas banking, finance and insurance accounted for 55,800 jobs in 1984, other services were responsible for 286,400, representing virtually a third of all employment in Wales. Heavy concentrations of service-sector employment could be found in Cardiff, the Vale of Glamorgan, and Arfon (based on Bangor and Caernarfon). A further 90,000 jobs were linked to the tourist industry, although many of these were part-time or seasonal. Although the 'typical Welsh worker' is a crude concept, it might be said that such a person was more likely to be a clerk, a nurse or a part-time worker in a cafeteria than a miner, steelworker or farmer by the mid 1980s.

Working patterns changed markedly in post-war Wales. Migration patterns, the lure of the countryside, and the revolution in communications helped to boost the numbers who worked from home in rural areas (a fifth of the workforce in Ceredigion, for instance, by 1981), although levels of self-employment remained low, being most in evidence in Radnorshire in the form of agriculture and small-scale retailing. More significant was the slow expansion of economic opportunities for women.

Up to the 1960s only a quarter of all women of working age in Wales were engaged in paid work, the majority of whom were single, and usually young. Most women married relatively early, spending much of their lives raising a family and running a home. However, in the course of two decades, this changed. By the early 1980s, over half of Welsh women of working age were economically active, comprising over two-fifths of the total workforce. Of single, divorced and widowed women, 63 per cent were in work. Although, measured in British terms, Welsh women had not made startling advances, the shift away from the heavy-industrial, heavily-segregated Welsh past was marked. However, the result was not equality. Jobs remained gendered, with men and women rarely working alongside each other in manual occupations, and women usually filling the lowest rungs in any employment hierarchy. Often women's jobs exhibited direct connections with commonly-held expectations of what women's strengths were: caring for the elderly, the physically or mentally ill, and for children; being involved in the preparation and serving of food; cleaning; or using their supposedly naturally 'nimble fingers' on production lines. Much of the increase in female employment was accounted for by part-time jobs (46 per cent of married women's jobs in 1981), particularly in retailing and catering, or even by homeworking, often paid on piece-work rates. Moreover, male earnings remained, on average, well above those of women, despite some narrowing of differentials. Thus, in 1971, female full-time workers in manual occupations earned less than half as much as male workers in the same category, and in non-manual jobs, only 52 per cent of male earnings. By 1985, the gap had narrowed, but only to 62 per cent and 61 per cent respectively. That said, women did find greater opportunities in the service sector, particularly in health and education. By the early 1980s, women were beginning to make an impact of a kind not witnessed before in middle-ranking managerial, administrative and professional posts. In terms of employment opportunities, the Wales of 1985 was not an equal society, but it was dramatically more egalitarian than it had been forty years before.

It is clear that, despite the upsurge of manufacturing industry and the service sector in Wales, historic weaknesses in the structure of the Welsh economy remained. This is evident in per capita figures for gross domestic product (GDP), available from 1966 onwards. In that year, the figure for Wales (£510) was, of all British regions, ahead only of those for Northern Ireland and the North of England, and a long way below the United Kingdom average (£605). The relative position worsened from the early 1970s, and by 1984 Wales was ahead only of Northern Ireland, with a per capita figure of £3850, far behind the United Kingdom average of £4612.

Low levels of GDP per capita can be a reflection of low rates of economic activity amongst the population concerned, and that was certainly the case across much of Wales for most of the period. In the early 1970s, at a time when the Welsh economy was relatively buoyant, only industrial north-east Wales, Newport, the Port Talbot area and Taff-Ely had male economic activity rates in excess of the national average, and no district had above-average rates for females. In 1981, the economically active represented 90 per cent of British men aged between sixteen and sixty-four, with 80 per cent in employment, but in Wales the corresponding figures were 88 per cent and 74 per cent. Similar measurements for women, both married and single, widowed or divorced, reveal matching discrepancies. A combination of already-mentioned factors, including the older age profile of the population, high levels of poor health, and the historical imbalance in patterns of employment and training, were responsible for Wales's relatively poor performance in this respect.

Unemployment was also a spectre that had returned to Wales by the 1970s. Although unemployment rates in Wales were consistently higher than the British average throughout the 1950s and 1960s, they remained at historically low levels (well beneath 5 per cent). By the mid 1970s the 5 per cent barrier had been broken, but this was as nothing compared with the drastic increase in the numbers of jobless at the beginning of the 1980s. Male unemployment virtually doubled between 1979 and 1981, reaching 120,000 by 1985 and representing 16 per cent of the workforce. 127,000 jobs (for men and women) had been lost in just five years, with over 70,000 being lost from manufacturing industry in just three. For Wales as a whole, the overall rate of 14 per cent was well above the United Kingdom average of 11 per cent. In Mid Glamorgan the rate reached 19 per cent, this itself concealing pockets of far greater hardship in the upper reaches of the mining valleys, where unemployment amongst young men aged between sixteen and nineteen could often exceed one third.

The post-war story of Welsh economic growth is thus double-edged. On the one hand, the vast majority of the Welsh population benefited from improved standards of living, reflected in longer lives. On the other, Wales remained a relatively poor region within Britain, with average levels of household income consistently below UK figures. If anything, Welsh people lost ground from the mid 1960s: whereas in the early 1960s average Welsh household income had been 8 per cent below the UK average, by the early 1980s the gap had widened to around 14 per cent. Levels of expenditure on household services, personal goods and services, and on leisure goods and services were low in Wales. Eighteen per cent of household income in Wales was derived from social security, compared with a United Kingdom average of 14 per cent. The level of personal disposable income per capita in Wales was regularly amongst the lowest of United Kingdom regions. By 1985 it was the very lowest, beneath even that of Northern Ireland.

However, for those who benefited from regular employment, standards of living and access to consumer durables rose markedly in the post-war era. Refrigerator and washing-machine ownership spread slowly in the 1950s, and rapidly thereafter. Virtually all households had a fridge by the mid 1980s, and nine-tenths a washing machine. Central heating, hardly in evidence in the 1960s, had reached about two-fifths of homes by the mid 1970s and more than two-thirds by the mid 1980s. Greater prosperity, allied to technology, revolutionized communications in Wales. Televisions could be found in nine-tenths of Welsh homes by the end of the 1960s. By the 1980s three-quarters of Welsh households had a telephone (up from 17 per cent in the mid 1960s), and nearly half, a video recorder. There were computers in a fifth of Welsh homes.

- Outside the home, the motor car was second only to the contraceptive pill in its impact on Welsh society. By the 1970s, half of all Welsh households owned a car; by 1985 two-thirds. In 1950 there were 100,000 cars in Wales, in 1980 there were 250,000. In the 1950s and 1960s their increase in numbers was complemented by a rise in the number of motorcycles, peaking at over 70,000 in 1963 but stabilizing at around 50,000 by the 1980s, whilst cars multiplied across the land. The car revolutionized Welsh life in a way that has yet to be fully appreciated. The opening of the Severn Bridge in 1966, and the completion of the M4 motorway in the early 1980s, generated economic growth along the south Wales coastal plain. The car placed large, often English, towns within reach of Welsh people who wanted to work or shop there. Liverpool and Chester became important shopping centres for most of north Wales, Shrewsbury and the west Midlands for a wide *tranche* of mid Wales, and Hereford and Bristol nibbled at the influence of Cardiff and Newport on the borders in the south. The car also rendered Wales accessible to its own population, and that of its close neighbour. Owning a second or holiday home, for instance, was much easier if one could travel there by car for a weekend and, by the early 1980s, between a fifth and a quarter of households in Dwyfor and Meirionnydd were in this category. Short-break or daily tourism also became more feasible because of the flexibility the car brought to transport.

The car had an enormous impact on travel to work, and thus on residence patterns. Over half the Welsh workforce used a car for workday journeys by 1981, with a sixth walking and a seventh using the bus. The south Wales valleys saw daily journeys to Port Talbot, Merthyr, Cardiff and Newport. Other dormitory areas included the older industrial parts of north-east Wales (where Chester and Merseyside were powerful magnets along with Alyn and Deeside) and Anglesey (from where the service sector in Caernarfon and Bangor attracted many employees, particularly women).

The decline of the railways was as rapid as the rise of road transport. Wales suffered, perhaps more than any other part of Britain, from the impact of Dr Beeching's cuts of the 1960s. In about fifteen years after 1961, total track mileage was halved and the number of stations in use fell from 538 to 184. Large areas of Wales lost all contact with the railways. Gwent, which had fifty-two stations in 1961, had just six twenty years later. In West Glamorgan, the corresponding figures were thirty-eight and five. Lines linking Pwllheli and Bangor, and Aberystwyth and Swansea, to name just two, were closed. Living in much of rural Wales became impossible without access to a car, unless one lived on a bus route.

Outside working hours, the Welsh people came to enjoy a wide range of leisure and recreational activities in the decades after 1945, although these pursuits may have become more individual and family-based rather than community-oriented. The rise of television, for instance, ended the golden age of the cinema, although there was something of a revival in its fortunes from the late 1970s. Both the large and the small screen were influential in the continued spread of transatlantic influences. By the 1950s the development of a distinctive youth culture linked to 'rock'n'roll' was as evident in Wales as anywhere else. Bill Haley and Elvis Presley were, in time, followed by the Beatles, the Rolling Stones, the 'glam rock' of Queen, and the nihilism of punk and new wave. Gang allegiances to mods and rockers, hippies and Hell's Angels reached Blaenau Ffestiniog as much as they did Barry Island. The Welsh-language music scene developed, pioneered by artists including Dafydd Iwan, Caryl Parry-Jones, Geraint Jarman and Maffia Mr Huws. There were, of course, Welsh artists working in English, Tom Jones and Shirley Bassey the most famous, but they had to compete in an international market for the allegiance of their own fellow citizens.

Much leisure-time activity was relatively mundane. Patterns of shopping changed with the rise of supermarkets. Shorter working hours, leading to clearer weekends, helped the growth in popularity of do-it-yourself home improvements and gardening. For many people, going down to the public house or club, to bingo or whist drives, to dance halls or discotheques were regular activities, for some merely occasional indulgences, and for others they remained beyond the pale of respectability. As ever, class, status, age and gender heavily conditioned participation in leisure activities.

The horizons of Welsh people were broadened in the post-war era by the rise of tourism and travel, increasingly abroad. For a while the traditional Welsh seaside resorts – such as Barry Island, Porthcawl and Rhyl – held their own, although the more genteel destinations of Barmouth, Aberystwyth and the spa town of Llandrindod Wells declined. Wales was well provided with a variety of other attractions, all of which contributed to the growth of the tourist industry. The castles at Caernarfon, Conwy and Harlech attracted hundreds of thousands of visitors every year by the 1980s. The National Museum of Wales in Cathays Park and the Welsh Folk Museum, now the Museum of Welsh Life, at St Fagans were capable, together, of attracting at least half a million people annually, giving them a prominence in south Wales challenged only by the Dan-yr-Ogof showcaves, the former Penscynor Wildlife Park and Newport's Tredegar House. In the north, Rhyl Suncentre dominated the recreational landscape, but was complemented by the beauty of the Swallow Falls at Betws-y-Coed, the architectural curiosity of Portmeirion, and the reminder of an industrial past at Llechwedd Slate Caverns. In the south, Big Pit Mining Museum at Blaenafon was just opening as the south Wales miners themselves prepared for what was to be their last major struggle. Much tourism proceeded on a less formal basis – in the national parks of Snowdonia, Pembrokeshire and the Brecon Beacons – and Wales had an estimated half a million regular walkers by the 1980s.

In terms of sport, rugby union enhanced its status as the national game. The great success and attractive play of the teams of the 1960s and 1970s, in particular, consolidated the fifteen-man code's position at the heart of what, for many people, Welshness meant. Wales beat the three home countries and France to win the Grand Slam in 1950, 1952, and then again in 1971, 1976 and 1978. They vanquished England, Scotland and Ireland to win the Triple Crown twice in the

1960s, and five times in the 1970s. Outside-halves – Cliff Morgan, David Watkins, Barry John, Phil Bennett, to name just four – rolled off Max Boyce's proverbial production line, combining with other dazzling talents in the back division, including Ken Jones, Bleddyn Williams, Gerald Davies, J.P.R. Williams, and the incomparable Gareth Edwards. Nor were Welsh teams short of power and courage in the forwards, as a succession of Welsh British Lions, including Bryn Meredith, Alun Pask, Mervyn Davies and the members of the Pontypool front row, demonstrated.

Rugby was, symbolically, Wales's national sport, yet in terms of participation, association football was more than twice as strong and more in evidence than rugby across large areas of the country, with over four times the number of clubs. International success was much harder to come by in soccer than it was in rugby union, and Wales managed to qualify just once for the World Cup, in 1958. Nevertheless, there were great Welsh players, most notably Ivor Allchurch, John Charles, and John Toshack. Welsh clubs struggled hard without enjoying much in the way of sustained success, although Cardiff City enjoyed two spells of Division One football (1952-57, 1960-61) and Swansea City one (1981-83), bringing temporary delight to often long-suffering supporters.

Both rugby and soccer were largely male pursuits. Women's hockey was strongly represented in Wales, as were sports that could be enjoyed by persons of both sexes and of all ages, such as lawn tennis, bowls and golf. Boxing remained strong in the industrial valleys and inner cities, although increasingly challenged by judo. Cricket, snooker, darts and athletics were sports where both participation and spectator interest were enhanced, periodically, by notable Welsh successes, such as the cricket championship-winning Glamorgan XIs of 1948 and 1969, the world champions Ray Reardon, Terry Griffiths and Leighton Rees, and Olympic gold medallist Lynn Davies.

The dramatic economic changes that took place in Wales between 1945 and 1985 left the Welsh economy more varied, more 'modern', but no less fragile. Patterns of recreation and leisure also diversified, becoming more inclusive, democratic and participatory in some areas, and open to a wider range of influences, positive and negative. Sport nevertheless remained very important to the Welsh. Given the steady decline of religious observance, and the erosion of the Welsh language, Welsh endeavour in the sporting arena was one area where a Welsh national identity could be claimed and displayed with a minimum of ambiguity.

Outside Wales, although the stereotypical image of the country as a place of mines, steelworks and sheep, with a million Welsh 'mams' in the background, was less accurate, it remained a difficult one to shake off. All but the most enlightened of English commentators patronized, even insulted, the Welsh if they noticed them at all, notwithstanding the constructive contribution of many Welsh politicians and the international fame won by the verse of Dylan Thomas and the acting talents of Richard Burton. To an extent, the Welsh habit of caricaturing themselves, whether comic (as in the case of the comedian and singer Max Boyce) or ostensibly serious (as with the fiction of Richard Llewellyn), made it easier for Wales to be dismissed as a site of romantic myth-making. More critical was the absence of any consensus, amongst the people of Wales themselves, as to their own political destiny.

BELIEF AND ACTION

By 1985 Wales was no longer a Christian country, if by that was meant a country where even a substantial minority regularly attended a place of worship. All major Christian denominations experienced declining membership in the post-war era, and this was paralleled by a fall in totals attending churches. Numbers of churches and of ministers fell across the country. The Presbyterian Church in Wales, which had counted over a quarter of a million attendees in 1945, could manage little more than half that number by the end of the 1960s. In the early 1950s, around a third of the adult population were church members. By the early 1980s, fewer than a fifth of Welsh people were members of a Christian church, and it was estimated that only an eighth attended regularly. Church was somewhere one was more likely to visit to get married, have a child christened, or bury a relative than to visit for purposes of worship on a regular basis.

Of those who did attend, a survey undertaken in 1982 indicated that 62 per cent were female and only 38 per cent male. Of adult attendees, about a third were over sixty-five years of age, and two thirds over forty-five. Whether measured in terms of the number of attendees, or the number of members, the Church in Wales was the largest single Christian denomination, with a little over a quarter of both, closely followed by the Roman Catholic Church. Adding all Nonconformist denominations together accounted for a further two-fifths of Welsh Christians. Protestant churches, on average, attracted forty adults to a normal Sunday service, Roman Catholic churches (of which there were far fewer, and concentrated in areas of historic Irish settlement) accommodated well over three hundred. Other religions tended to be represented only in certain urban centres, with synagogues, mosques and Sikh temples in the coastal ports of the south.

Attendance at a place of worship was not simply, sometimes not necessarily, a matter of faith and belief. It could also perform an important social function, and in some rural communities in particular, remained a critical focus of leisure activities. The smaller, more static the society, the more likely it was that Nonconformist ministers or deacons would exercise social influence and leadership. Yet even these things waned, as the gradual spread of Sunday opening of cinemas and public houses indicated. Successive local referenda ensured that by the late 1970s only Merioneth, Anglesey and Caernarfonshire (with the exception of the Vale of Conwy), Cardiganshire, and western Carmarthenshire were still enforcing the Sunday closure of public houses. Interestingly, this area roughly coincided with those parliamentary constituencies with a Welsh-speaking population of over 50 per cent.

The second half of the twentieth century was marked by a greater awareness of the problems facing the Welsh language, and by determined efforts to arrest what might still be a terminal decline. Whereas in 1931, 37 per cent of the people of Wales had been registered as able to speak Welsh, that proportion fell dramatically to 29 per cent in 1951, 26 per cent in 1961 and then quickly again to 21 per cent in 1971, before a more gradual decline to 19 per cent by 1981. The total number of speakers fell from over 700,000 in 1951 to little more than half a million by 1981, with monolingualism being extinguished in the process. By 1981, Welsh was spoken by a majority of the inhabitants of only one county, Gwynedd, having slipped into minority status in Dyfed in the course of the 1970s. The numbers speaking Welsh in Mid Glamorgan more than halved between 1961 and 1981.

Studies undertaken of the census at units smaller than that of the county reveal a remarkable variety of patterning, with linguistic divides located within communities, and *Y Fro Gymraeg* (the Welsh-speaking heartland) surrounded and spatially divided by English-speaking majorities. By 1981 Welsh speakers constituted more than 60 per cent of the population in just seven areas – Dinefwr, Carmarthenshire, Ceredigion, Meirionnydd, Dwyfor, Arfon and Anglesey – and there was mounting evidence to suggest that Welsh was not a language to be used automatically in all social situations, but in particular, structured domains. This was certainly the case for the majority of Welsh speakers who lived, not in Welsh-speaking but predominantly English-speaking communities, such as the valleys and towns of the south. Furthermore, the ability to speak Welsh was not a sure guide to full literacy in the language. The 1971 and 1981 censuses indicated that fewer than three-quarters of Welsh speakers could write in the language, and the industrial districts of eastern Carmarthenshire, where Welsh remained strong, was the area with the highest levels of illiteracy.

If there was a turning-point in political attitudes towards the Welsh language, then it came on 13 February 1962, with the radio broadcast by the veteran Welsh nationalist and *littérateur,* Saunders Lewis, *'Tynged yr Iaith'* ('The fate of the language'). This call to arms ('Let Welsh be raised as the chief administrative issue in district and county') inspired some young nationalists to form *Cymdeithas yr Iaith Gymraeg* (The Welsh Language Society). Sensing the cultural and linguistic crisis of Welsh they settled upon a campaign of non-violent direct action, pressing for Welsh-language road signs, the use of Welsh in official documentation, and Welsh-language broadcasting. Some, older nationalists included, found it difficult to accept their methods, but in the long term their campaigns bore fruit. Although the Welsh Language Act of 1967 did not go far enough for many, it signified the beginning of a process of recognition for Welsh in official life, which, by the 1980s, had led to much more obvious public use of the language. As these, largely symbolic, battles were won, *Cymdeithas yr Iaith* turned its attention to the more intractable problems posed to the health of the Welsh language by social and economic change.

Education was another area that witnessed great agitation over, and change in, the status of Welsh. The first state school to operate through the medium of Welsh was opened at Llanelli in 1947 and, slowly, other such primary schools followed. Pressure grew not just for schools in areas where Welsh speakers were in the majority, but for schools in predominantly English-speaking areas, both to accommodate local Welsh speakers, and to offer the alternative of a Welsh-language education to the children of English-speaking parents. The first Welsh language Comprehensive school in Glamorgan was opened at Rhydfelen, near Pontypridd, in 1962, following similar schools in Rhyl and Mold in north Wales. Welsh-language education became increasingly popular in Glamorgan and Gwent, and contributed to a rise in the percentage of young people recorded as Welsh speakers at the census. These developments were not unambiguous, with many schoolchildren reported as making use of Welsh only in the school environment, and leaving it behind both in their leisure time and in adulthood. Nevertheless, growing numbers of adults made attempts to learn Welsh, and even if their efforts did not always result in fluency, they symbolized a positive change in popular views of the status and utility of the language.

The relationship between support for the Welsh language and support for Welsh nationalist politics has been historically close and, although strenuous efforts were made by some nationalists to separate the two objectives, these were only partially successful. Until the mid 1960s Plaid Cymru remained closely associated with the defence of 'traditional' Welsh culture, a stance which, even when it commanded general support across Wales, was the mark of a pressure group rather than of a competitive political party. This was the case in the late 1950s when the party reaped little in the way of electoral reward despite spearheading vigorous and justifiable protests over the destruction of the Welsh-speaking community of Tryweryn, a valley drowned as part of a scheme to build a reservoir for the City of Liverpool.

Yet, less than a year after it ceased publication one magazine had suggested that one of the 'myths of our time' was that 'Plaid Cymru will win a parliamentary constituency' (others were that 'Wales will have a north-south motorway', 'the Welsh language will recover its strength' and 'depopulation can be arrested in mid Wales') the party's fortunes and prospects were revolutionized. In the Carmarthen constituency at the general election of March 1966, Plaid Cymru President Gwynfor Evans had managed only third place (with 16 per cent of the vote) behind the sitting Labour member, Lady Megan Lloyd George, and the Liberal candidate. Nevertheless, following the death of Megan Lloyd George, a by-election was held on 14 July and Evans stormed to a convincing victory, with 39 per cent of the vote and a majority of 2,436 over Labour's Gwilym Prys Davies (himself an ex-Welsh Republican).

For a while after the Carmarthen election, Plaid Cymru believed that any seat might be within its grasp. It may have been possible to dismiss the Carmarthen result as that of an electorate which had given its support not so much to the Labour Party as to Lady Megan Lloyd George, who carried with her the prestige of her father's name, as well as a political career spent, until the mid 1950s, in the Liberal Party. But at two by-elections, in Rhondda West in March 1967 and in Caerphilly in July 1968, Plaid Cymru candidates presented a more serious challenge than ever before to what were thought to be solid Labour seats in the heart of industrial south Wales. In Rhondda West, where Labour majorities had, historically, been enormous, the margin of Labour victory was cut to 2,306. In Caerphilly it was closer still, at 1,874.

In retrospect, Plaid's near misses in the south Wales coal-field were a false dawn. When the Rhondda West contest was repeated in 1970 the sitting Labour MP won three-quarters of the votes, and the result in Caerphilly was scarcely less emphatic. Although Plaid made another determined challenge in a by-election at Merthyr Tydfil in April 1972, in no other seat and at no other time was it again to endanger what was a seventy-year-old Labour hegemony in the coalfield. Instead, Plaid Cymru made gradual advances in the rural, Welsh-speaking constituencies of north and west Wales. Although Gwynfor Evans lost Carmarthen in 1970, after October 1974 Plaid Cymru had three MPs at Westminster (Evans again at Carmarthen, Dafydd Wigley at Caernarfon, and Dafydd Elis Thomas at Merioneth).

However, to view post-war Welsh political history solely in terms of the rise of Welsh nationalism risks inflating the importance that particular political issue had in the lives of most Welsh people. The story of modern Welsh politics falls neatly into two halves, with 14 July 1966 the dividing line, but the reality, both before and after Gwynfor Evans's initial victory, was Labour Party domination. Labour began the post-war era with twenty-five of the thirty-six Welsh seats, having won 58 per cent of the popular vote at the 1945 general election. Throughout the 1950s and into the early 1960s it improved slightly on this position, reaching twenty-eight seats by 1964, and managing a high of 60 per cent of the vote in 1951. Although between 1951 and 1964 the Conservatives ruled Britain, the Tories in Wales could hold, at best, only six seats. The Welsh Liberal Party, despite its long traditions, fell away quite dramatically, reaching a low of just 5 per cent of the vote and two seats in 1959. Plaid Cymru was itself a partial beneficiary of the Liberals' decline, establishing a toe-hold in about half of Welsh constituencies by the late 1950s. At the 1966 general election Labour's domination seemed nearly as total as that of the Liberals sixty years earlier. With 61 per cent of the popular vote, Labour won thirty-two seats. Only the Conservatives in Barry, Denbigh and Flint West, and Emlyn Hooson for the Liberals in Montgomeryshire, held out. Plaid Cymru's 4 per cent of the vote was its worst result since 1955.

After 'Carmarthen 1966', the political climate changed. Labour's share of the vote declined, first to 52 per cent in the 1970 general election, and then below half. It still retained a majority of Welsh seats, but its hegemony, seemingly assured in the 1950s and early 1960s, was seriously threatened. Plaid Cymru presented one threat, fighting all Welsh seats for the first time and polling 12 per cent of the vote in 1970 (though winning no seats) and taking three seats from October 1974. The Liberals found new heart as well, although their larger share of the vote (16 per cent in February 1974 for instance) only found the meagre reward of two seats. Yet, it was the Conservative Party that, in 1970, won its highest total of seats in Wales (seven) since 1924.

Labour faced various problems in maintaining its success in Wales. Historically, it had been the party of the industrial south: its roots in rural and coastal Wales were not deep, and it was often reliant on the personal appeal of its candidates, such as Cledwyn Hughes and Goronwy Roberts. Although the welfare state was the great achievement of the party in office, the Wilson governments of the 1960s had faced numerous problems which had diverted them from a more expansive agenda. The Labour Party in Wales seemed to lack direction: although, belatedly, it had given recognition to the demands for a Welsh voice with the creation of the Welsh Office in 1964 (building on the appointment of a Minister for Welsh Affairs by the Conservatives in 1951), there was no consensus within the party on whether further devolution of powers should follow. Nor was there any greater certainty on how to handle the political and cultural challenge of Welsh nationalism, as evidenced by the inept performance of George Thomas as Secretary of State for Wales (1968-70). Furthermore, Labour's domination of Welsh local government in south Wales had long been associated with stultifying bureaucracy and nepotism: on occasion, justifiably so. Orthodox Welsh politics appeared stagnant, middle-aged and unexciting, at the very time that a mood of rebellion and idealism was sweeping across Europe.

Labour's response in Wales also had the unfortunate characteristic of being largely stimulated not by any internal dynamic, but by even stronger nationalist pressure building up in Scotland. From the beginning, Labour's proposals for a measure of Welsh devolution looked to be the poor cousin of plans for a Scottish legislature. Within Labour's own ranks in Wales there was marked hostility to the project from those opposed to the principle of devolution, while Welsh nationalists had a difficult time persuading themselves that the Assembly was worth the effort.

What was also striking about the devolution debate of the 1970s was that it was carried out amidst widespread apathy and ignorance on the part of the Welsh public. The fact that neither Labour nor Plaid had prepared the ground for public support for devolution became critical when a clause was inserted in the devolution bill to require a referendum on the issue. Opinion polls conducted in the years leading up to the referendum date of 1 March 1979 suggested that public opinion was, at best, lukewarm about the idea and moving gradually against it. When the verdict of the electorate came, it was unambiguous. Those that voted (58 per cent of the electorate), rejected the devolution proposals by a massive four votes to one (956,330 to 242,988). In every Welsh county the vote was 'no': even in Gwynedd the vote was two to one against, and in South Glamorgan and Gwent only around an eighth of the vote was in favour.

The reasons for the failure of the devolution campaign were many. The Labour government itself was relatively unpopular, some prominent Welsh Labour MPs (including Neil Kinnock) campaigned vigorously against the proposals, there was public scepticism as to whether another tier of government would make a positive difference, and the close association in the public mind of Plaid Cymru with the 'yes' campaign was always going to create difficulties for the 90 per cent of the Welsh electorate that had consistently rejected nationalist policies. The divided nature of Welsh society was laid bare, as 'no' campaigners raised, variously, the spectre of socialist domination by south Walians, or the possibility that a Welsh-speaking élite would take over. The ill-informed and unsophisticated level at which the debate was often conducted revealed how under-developed Welsh political culture was, in part a reflection of the weakness of the Welsh media. It was estimated that, of the English-language press circulating in Wales during the referendum campaign, only 37 per cent consisted of papers aimed specifically at a Welsh readership (the strongest being the *South Wales Echo* and *Western Mail* published in Cardiff, and the *Daily Post*'s Welsh edition, published in Liverpool). Most Welsh people, therefore, were reading the London-based dailies, the most popular of which (tabloids such as *The Sun* and the *Daily Mirror*) paid little serious attention to Welsh affairs. Although the Welsh-language weeklies gave extensive coverage to devolution, their combined circulation amounted to only about 30,000 a week (whilst each of *The Sun* and *Daily Mirror* sold nearly a quarter of a million copies every day).

Finally, although there was a more pronounced sense of a Welsh national identity by 1979, in part through the political changes of the preceding decade or more, this has to be counterbalanced by an acknowledgement that most of the people of Wales remained satisfied with Wales's location within the British state, and were uneasy about a policy that suggested a change in that relationship. Many Welsh people were enthusiastic devotees of the Royal Family. Enthusiasm for the coronation of Queen Elizabeth II in 1953, the Silver Jubilee of 1977 and the wedding of the Prince and Princess of Wales in 1981 was no less pronounced in Wales than it was throughout the rest of

Britain. The investiture of the Prince of Wales at Caernarfon Castle in 1969 was more evidently controversial, coming as it did amidst the initial headiness of the nationalist resurgence, but many Welsh nationalists lent at least tacit support to the event, which attracted great public interest and a large television audience. Outside the relatively small circle of nationalist activists there was no greater sense that the Welsh entertained different views of Britain's occasional conflicts – from the Korean War in the 1950s, through to the Falklands War of 1982 – than did the rest of the British people. Most of the Welsh saw no necessary conflict between their identity as Welsh (whatever they meant by that) and their continued allegiance to the British state. Of course, as 'yes' campaigners argued correctly, support for devolution did not imply either republicanism or go-it-alone independence, but the referendum result revealed just how unsuccessful they had been in trying to convince the Welsh electorate.

The devolution débâcle did nothing to improve the beleaguered position of the Labour government, which was voted out of office two months later. Since the landmark general elections of the 1860s Wales had pursued its own trajectory in British politics. It had been a bastion first of the Liberal Party, then, after the first World War, of Labour, largely irrespective of swings to and fro across Britain as a whole. But in 1979, and then again in 1983, there came signs that Wales was moving closer to British norms. In 1979, the Tories took 32 per cent of the vote (against Labour's 47 per cent) and eleven seats, and although in 1983 the Tory vote fell slightly (to 31 per cent), Labour's was eaten into quite significantly by that of the Alliance between the Liberals and the Social Democratic Party, which combined to win 23 per cent of the vote. Although the Alliance did not make their breakthrough in Wales any more than they managed it in Britain, they did turn straight fights between Labour and Tory candidates into three-cornered contests, and when the dust settled the Conservative total of fourteen seats appeared too close to Labour's twenty for the latter's long-term comfort. It was now possible, the Tories claimed, to travel from one end of Wales to the other without leaving Conservative 'territory'.

As for Plaid Cymru, it lost Carmarthen to Labour in 1979, and subsequently underwent its own internal debate over its political strategy and ideological commitment (with some nationalists establishing the ill-fated Welsh Socialist Republican Movement).

Gwynfor Evans's last significant act as a politician was to threaten a hunger strike in order to force the new Conservative government to carry out its election pledge to establish a Welsh television channel (*Sianel Pedwar Cymru*, which began broadcasting in 1982). That Wales should have lost an opportunity to establish its own democratic voice but gained a television channel (even if it was in Welsh) speaks volumes about the paradoxical nature of Welsh politics and modern Welsh identity. Plaid Cymru's subsequent performance at the 1983 general election was its worst (in terms of percentage vote won), since that of 1966. Whatever its rhetoric, and the undoubted sincerity of many of those on its left wing, who continued to struggle to develop a strategy and appeal that went beyond an exclusive ethnic and cultural nationalism to address the social and economic problems of all the people of Wales, Plaid showed fewer and fewer signs of being able to win public support in the industrial, urban, and English-speaking parts of the country. Again it appeared to be not so much the 'Party of Wales' as the party of *Y Fro Gymraeg*, the Welsh-speaking north and west. Some on the fringes of the nationalist movement turned to more aggressive strategies in frustration, although the activities of both *Meibion Glyndŵr* and the Workers' Army of the Welsh Republic were deserving of as much pity as condemnation, as had been those of *Mudiad Amddiffyn Cymru* and the farcical Free Wales Army in the 1960s.

If the nationalist dream seemed to be, at least temporarily, dead in the water, then the Welsh Labour movement could be no more optimistic about its future. The British Labour Party's crushing defeat at the general election of 1983, together with the lurch of the party to the left and the rise of the Social Democrats, raised the prospect that Labour might never regain office, and that, henceforth, the loyalties of the bulk of the Welsh people to Labour (despite the erosion evident in 1979 and 1983) might prove to be out of step with those of the rest of Britain. With its ostensibly pitiless monetarism, its assault on the welfare state and the rights of trade unionists, allied to a pandering to an individualism that seemed indistinguishable from greed, 'Thatcherism' represented a significant break with the post-war consensus. In what was an increasingly polarized, embittered atmosphere, the miners' strike of 1984-5 assumed a political and cultural importance reminiscent of that of 1926.

Industrial relations problems were latent in the mines, particularly in south Wales. Most miners had welcomed with high hopes the nationalization of the coal industry, but the lack of any real industrial democracy and the increasing remoteness of the National Coal Board (NCB) bureaucracy from the day-to-day concerns of the mining work-force bred alienation. By 1951, many of the old frustrations were returning, and levels of (small-scale) strike activity were high. In 1966 the south Wales coal-field, which produced less than a tenth of total British output, was responsible for over half of the total output lost through industrial disputes.

On 21 October 1966 a colliery waste-tip high above the village of Aberfan, in Glamorgan, slid down the mountain and engulfed Pantglas Junior School and a score of houses. One-hundred-and-sixteen children (mostly between the ages of seven and ten) and twenty-eight adults (five of them teachers) were killed. This was, arguably, the most horrifying mining disaster in the history of a coal-field that had seen more than its fair share of brutality and death. Although this terrible tragedy, unique in its scale and suffering, cannot simply be assimilated to any wider social or political trend, it did reinforce public disillusionment with the NCB, and evoke world-wide sympathy for the people of the mining communities of south Wales.

Popular support for the miners' wage demands in 1972, and, to a lesser extent, in 1974, did provide the National Union of Mineworkers with a certain moral authority in its clashes with the Conservative government of Edward Heath. Yet, despite their success, these strikes represented the last gasp of an aggressive mining militancy, and did nothing to address the very real problem of deindustrialization in the coal-field, and the economic marginalization of former colliery settlements. Coal remained, in some areas, an important employer of men: in 1981, it accounted for 28 per cent of male employment in the Cynon Valley, and 27 per cent in Islwyn. Any threat to the future of the industry, particularly at a time of growing unemployment and widespread economic depression, was bound to provoke strong reactions: a 'demonstration for existence' in the words of south Wales NUM President, Emlyn Williams. After an inconclusive squaring-up between the NUM and the new Conservative government in 1981, the latter, with the connivance of the NCB, sought a head-on confrontation with the miners in 1984.

To many in the Tory Party, the NUM were, in Thatcher's own words, 'the enemy within', a remarkable phrase evoking a clear parallel with Britain's war against Argentina over the Falklands in 1982. To some in the Labour movement, including NUM President Arthur Scargill, the miners were the vanguard of the working class, historically charged with the specific role of humiliating Conservative governments. Over-confident, the union leadership accepted battle on the worst-possible terrain. After more than a year of struggle, in which the resourcefulness, courage and doggedness of union members and their families shamed both the foolhardiness of their leaders and the naked malevolence of the state, the miners were defeated. The consequences for many British coal-fields were disastrous, but for none more so than south Wales. On the eve of the strike, 20,000 miners had been employed in the twenty-eight mines of south Wales, producing seven million tons of coal. A decade later the last deep mine was to be considered for closure. For those on the left, embracing many outside the Labour Party who had backed the miners and developed new, inclusive forms of politics in the process, the crushing of the NUM represented a historical closure no less final than that of the mines themselves.

Paradoxically, it was the near-total nature of the defeat of both Welsh nationalism and Welsh socialism in the late 1970s and early 1980s that, eventually, generated a renaissance of both. Although there was no Welsh Assembly, there was an increasingly strong Welsh 'proto-state'. The Welsh Office had, since the early 1970s, acquired greater responsibility in matters of the economy, health and education, at the same time as the independence of local government had been undermined. Wales might lose mines, steelworks and factories, but in 'quangos' it had found a growth industry. Bodies such as the Welsh Arts Council, the Wales Tourist Board, the Sports Council for Wales, the Land Authority for Wales, the Welsh Development Agency, the Development Board for Rural Wales and the Welsh Consumer Council were paralleled in civil society by the Welsh TUC and the Welsh CBI. BBC Wales joined the cultural ranks of the Welsh Rugby Union, the Welsh Football Association, the Welsh National Opera, and the Royal Welsh Show. The University of Wales survived threats to its integrity and expanded, as did the National Museum and the National Library. From 1955, the recognition of Cardiff as the capital city of Wales was symbolic of a greater sense of nationhood. By the late 1970s, a panoply of public institutions operated within a distinctive, all-Wales environment.

This, of course, had been part of the case for the Assembly. However, although the Welsh electorate had rejected that vision (perhaps because, almost despite itself, it was heavily tainted with nationalism), fewer than a third had voted for Thatcherism. The case for a measure of democratic control over Welsh life by the people of Wales was energized, not retarded, by the political, industrial, and economic traumas of the Thatcherite years. It may be one of the great ironies of Welsh history in the 1980s that it was Peter Walker, Secretary of State for Energy during the miners' strike, who, as Secretary of State for Wales (1987-90), gave the clearest example of what could be achieved by an administration more attuned to the needs of the Wales it governed.

* * * * * * * * * *

The Welsh are in the process of being defined, not in terms of shared occupational experience or common religious inheritance or the survival of an ancient European language or for contributing to the Welsh radical tradition, but rather by reference to the institutions that they inhabit, influence, and react to. This new identity may lack the ethical and political imperatives that characterized Welsh life for two centuries, but it increasingly appears to be the only identity available. (R. Merfyn Jones)

The Wales that the Welsh of 1985 bequeathed to those who were to follow was a very different Wales to that inherited in 1945. Although the past is never irrelevant, the Wales that had existed before the second World War became progressively less pertinent to an understanding of the experiences, beliefs and attitudes of the people of Wales as the post-war era unfolded. As Merfyn Jones recognized, many of the characteristics that had previously marked out the people of Wales, competing and conflictive though they often were, had been gradually unmasked as anachronistic and misleading. If a new identity was to be generated that could accommodate all those who had made Wales their home, all those who, whatever their birthplace, ethnic background, linguistic ability or even self-definition, constituted the

'Welsh people', it would, and will, have to be pluralist, inclusive, and constructed on a basis of citizenship rather than on the possession of certain 'essential' attributes, attitudes or beliefs.

In 1985, it was difficult to be enthusiastic about this ideal, any more than about the future of the Labour movement, of Welsh nationalism, or the long-term survival of the Welsh language. Writing on the eve of the millennium, it is too early to make bold predictions about any or all of these projects, and history has a habit of making prophets appear foolish. Yet, the twin polls of 1997 and the first Assembly elections of 1999 have given the people of Wales, for the first time, something akin to a democratic voice. The storms of which Raymond Williams wrote, so evident in 1985, will no doubt rage again, although it is to be hoped that they continue to come largely from outside rather than from within. The Welsh people have an opportunity to make their own future, but for that future to stand any chance of success they must acknowledge the complexities of their turbulent past, and seek to define the nation on the basis of characteristics that unite and not divide. In 1985 Gwyn A. Williams ended his *When Was Wales? A History of the Welsh* by commenting, despairingly, that the Welsh were now 'nothing but a naked people under an acid rain'. Walking together into the next millennium is the best chance we have of finding new clothes.

CONCLUSION

THE NATION'S PEOPLE

DAI SMITH

For centuries patriots and administrators have striven to shape the intractable, various Welsh people and for centuries that protean people, buffeted as they were by all manner of material circumstance, have been themselves shaping and re-shaping their identity in the territorial and cultural spaces they were told was Wales. The Welsh have always been a problem for Wales for, if a nation is a box, a people are not to be boxed. They overflow the constraints of the imperious container. Yet, at the very end of this millennium almost all of the living touchstones of identity – material and cultural, antique and modern – which have given the Welsh whatever distinctive singularity they have possessed are also now in doubt. If they choose to reaffirm them or, better still, make them afresh in the next century, as Welsh people they will need to make choices first and foremost as citizens. Or, to put it another way, Wales itself is now a 'Question for History'.

Knowledge of history is the citizen's only trusted guide through the minefield of any tyrannical Present. History itself is the ideologues' nightmare from which they wake screaming into the midst of a world they would wish to fastfreeze and call the Future because they so resent the Past that is actually carrying them into it. The proponents of historical knowledge are never the traditionalists or the builders of monuments or the purveyors of kitsch and nostalgia. They are, indeed, the 'People's Remembrancers', for mere memory, even if public, is not history. The inducers of popular amnesia, substituting symbols for explanation and analysis, are both those who consider themselves to have been dispossessed of their patriotic desires for a True Past by an actually unfolded history and those whose bustling country would be easier to administer as a pasteurised unit rid of the live culture of history. You could call such an homogenized place, Wales, but you would not find the Welsh living in it any longer.

These, then, are critical times. Their most paradoxical feature is that it is precisely now that Wales, as an entity, offers, for the first time in any modern consciousness, the flexibility to accommodate a diverse, unified Welsh people. The means, of course, is institutional; the creation, however shakily, and the support, however hesitantly, of the National Assembly for Wales. This is the apex of the haphazard growth of devolved, or rather localized, powers since the 1960s. More, it requires the involvement in it, and responsibility towards it, of all citizens because it is both democratic in form and pan-Wales in nature. It is a people's cultural space and not just a managerial function of government. The 'Question of Wales' will be posed, as never before, within its domain. To answer it the existing Welsh will require a sense of themselves through their history so that they can choose exactly how to be a different, yet still Welsh, people in that unknown future.

It was to this end that BBC Radio Wales conceived a double-edged millennium history of the People of Wales. In book form this is most definitely a real contribution to the historiography of Wales: essays written with the weight of expert scholarship but directly addressed, in clear and elegant style, to the general readership of their fellow citizens. This is no simplistic narrative but it is, adamantly and rightly so, an analysis that is chronologically grounded. As we celebrate the nature of Welsh life at the century's close, the chapters of this cogently argued volume establish, over and over, how the most revolutionary changes in our history – of invasion, war, migration, technological shifts, exploitation, immigration, in beliefs and in language, urbanization and globalization and post-industrialization – have been met, on the ground, by people who – as individuals, groups or communities – have secured themselves in this place over such times as the people of Wales. That is no mean achievement for any species of human settlement, and luck has played no small part in such survival. It is not as if, in other times and different places, people of self-worth but radically different cultures have not known what was at stake: even to the point of extinction.

The Plains Indians, confronted by the expansion of post-Civil War America were, to all intents and purposes, wiped out in the years to

1890. Memorials now haunt their hunting grounds and visitor sites keen their varnished story in river valleys and on bald hills. It is a form of Heritage not to be despised. There was certainly an ardent Welsh equivalent, a mishmash of tourism and angst in the know-nothing decade that dribbled out of the carcass of 1984. But inheritance does not have to linger in a mausoleum. It can be caught on the wind: in the early 1930s, Black Elk, one of the very last survivors of the warrior Oglala Sioux who had fought on with the intransigent Crazy Horse until that fierce, indomitable spirit was murdered in 1877, told two visiting historians that there was no point in searching on the Plains to look for the spot where his friends had taken Crazy Horse's body from the white man's jail for burial since: 'It does not matter where his body lies, for it is grass but where his spirit is, it will be good to be.'

The second string to Radio Wales's millennium history is a soundscape of that history, eighteen half-hour programmes intent, by illustration and by comment but, above all, by imaginative use of the medium, on taking us to where the meaning of the body has fled. And that is, of course, to what the contemporary people of Wales will make of their history. Always the historical impulse is for kinetic movement not resigned stasis. It was one reason why going 'on air', broadcasting, has been seen such a vital element in transfiguring the shared knowledge of themselves the Welsh have needed to overcome the often divisive aspects of geography and language. Those specifics can be seen in a different way when transformed by generic images of landscape and concepts of the past. So, one necessary strand of broadcasting was to reach out beyond locality, to hover almost over the mind's map of Wales, so that as John Davies, BBC Wales's official historian, surmised, the 'artefact' which was modern Wales was, in many ways, the creation of the BBC. Insofar as this century is concerned, John Davies was pointing up a central truth. Tendencies had been increasingly fissiparous: what else could hold the seams together? Wyn Griffith, veteran of one world war and survivor of the other, had earned, along with his country's long-suffering people, the right to question. He wrote, in his sparkling little book *The Welsh*, in 1950, that: 'There is not much enthusiasm about anything in Wales, nor indeed in Europe: this is not the age of delight, except in the minor joys and beliefs. It is enough, perhaps, to have survived two wars and to be able to express an opinion without prior consent.' Of course. And yet, also, perhaps. Wyn Griffiths continued:

> But Welsh people are quick-spirited and capable of response: they need to be enthusiastic about something if they are to be themselves . . . [Not flattened] . . . into uniformity, into a two dimensional world. If it were not for the Welsh staff of the BBC, the voice of Wales would be little heard. As things are now, the radio programmes are the only available means of reminding Welsh people that they are Welsh. These programmes ought to be extended, and they ought to be better heard than they are now, but Wales owes more to broadcasting than it is willing to admit.

That was half a century ago and, undeniably, broadcasting has swelled to fill that role in the interim. Yet, Wyn Griffiths' addendum, fifty years on, remains true, too:

> These are days in which it is not easy to visualise the future of a small country and the probable course of life of its people . . . But there is something in mankind which persists in a belief in some kind of continuity, in some prolongation into the future of what has made the present. And to a Welshman, too honest to gain comfort from the repetition of eloquent phrases about national achievement and the virtues of sentimentality – disguised as patriotism – there still remains the conviction that at any time, anywhere, there would be found in him something which would distinguish him from, say, an Englishman. To say this is not to imply that he would be better, or worse, but merely that he would be different, and that although that difference can vary greatly in extent it can never totally disappear. What, exactly, is this difference, and how does it manifest itself, at its extreme or at its minimum? These are questions which neither an Englishman nor a Welshman can answer, for they demand an objectivity of which neither is capable. A Welshman can do no more than search into the past and glance at the present of his country, with as little prejudice as possible, in the hope that what he has chosen to describe reveals, even in the mere choice, something of what seems to him to be relevant to the issue . . . [for] . . . the pattern can, and indeed must change with the years, but the strands persist.

The authors of this present book have chosen wisely and relevantly, so that the changing pattern is made clear to the reader. It has changed consistently since 1950 but with such dramatic irreversibility, from the 1980s, that we may now need to peer hard to discern the persisting strands in our economic and social life, in our politics and our daily environment. Nor is it enough, as Griffiths discerned decades ago, to take refuge in sentiment or self-promotion, whether rhetorical or statistical. The strands are in the culture if they are anywhere. The base metal of the culture is historically mined and materially configured but its alchemists are those, in the arts, who transmute it to give meaning to the changing pattern. The meaning, of course, can be radical or disturbing rather than comforting and settled. Meaning, at many levels, is clearly what the voices and witnesses we hear on the radio programmes yearn for or derive from their lives. The constant for an evolving Wales will have to be a culture intent on connecting with those meanings, past and present.

It may be that the written and spoken word, traditionally both key elements for Welsh sensitivity in both our languages, will not be the principal conduits for an expression of Welsh culture, Raymond Williams's 'whole way of life', in the next century. The uncovering of our native visual tradition, notably by Peter Lord, has been a vital piece of missing social history which BBC Wales has brought to the screen in *The Big Picture* (1999); it will be complemented by Anthony Jones's television essays, *The Painted Dragon* (2000), on a millennium of fine arts, and their wider aesthetic inter-connections in Wales. What is unarguable is that we have been living through five decades, and more, of exceptional work by the painters of Wales: work of deep perception and cunning artefact in which form and colour and passion and intellect exist to tell of the Welsh vision beyond language or clichéd imagery. Here is a legacy, still largely undiscovered and certainly publicly unavailable, that we must disseminate urgently and widely as an inheritance beyond price. Nor should the uniqueness of its purchase on Welsh lives and landscapes by tactile pigment and hand-craft obscure the revelatory nature of images of ourselves and our country made by more mechanical means of representation. In a sense it is exciting that we are, as yet and with a few lone climbers out of sight, on the nursery slopes of Film and Animation but what we do have, including the heartstop of photographic archives, is the means to tie all this together to touch the past in different ways: in the ways, by sight and sound, that echo ordinary lives. We should build a National Gallery for our eyes and our hearts as ardently as we construct a National Assembly for our ears and minds. That is one real and new connection that can give meaning to our continuing endeavour as a people.

And another, more familiar perhaps yet threatened in other ways, will be the connection between Music and the Nation, one to be posed acerbically for BBC Wales Television by Lyn Davies in the millennium year. When does a tradition become a travail? When the work is just assumed to have forever bubbling wellsprings in the natural order of things in Wales. Not so, of course. Even the bold sounds of the late 1990s' bands emanate from support structures and cultural formations at risk or already gone, even as the music reverberates. Here especially, as with the magical unity of crowds through Sport, we have an articulation of our separate selves through the greater unity of the moment, and of the shared memory. This is not sentimental pap; it is modern poise.

Modernity in cultural terms may become, for a people knocked roughly into this century's shape by industrialization and urbanization, a combination of technology and urbanity, in town and countryside, one expressive of style: in vernacular building, in the planned environment of work and leisure, in fashion, in architecture of some moment and an evanescence of available delights in food, views, travel and conversation. If these are 'the good things of life', their only moral downside is their relative scarcity for the Welsh in both the private and public spheres of their lives. The former is intractable though not unconquerable; the latter is a compound of taste and will power whose properties for good should place it on the top of our public agenda. What is best practice elsewhere should be common practice at home. What is uncommon about our best practice is what will help make us responsive citizens. 'For myself,' wrote one such Welsh citizen, Aneurin Bevan, 'I should judge that the sight of the civic centre should be almost a daily experience of its citizens. Only in a community of such a size can the individual hope to identify himself with the corporate life . . . and take an intelligent interest in public affairs. There is no conflict between a wide cosmopolitanism and a rich local life. The one gives meaning and particularity to the other.'

For that reason alone Bevan would have shuddered at the low turn-out of voters in the first elections to the National Assembly for Wales. Those intriguing results may herald a sea-change in the political culture of Wales, one to match the underlying social and economic transformation that has already occurred; or they may be a psephological blip on the voting chart, one amenable to massage and treatment. Either way, and for all concerned, electors even more than elected in truth, the absence of a fully participatory democracy must be unacceptable. It will be facile, as well as unproductive, to berate those deliberat stayed-at-homes as apathetic. Dissident apathy is a positive force. And the genuinely unconcerned, perhaps heavily weighted amongst the young, will not trace the lineaments of a future in the faces of a generation that appears, too readily, to spurn the wisdom of youth and the bravado of old age. Once more, the shackles of the present need to be thrown off to allow us to roam imaginatively, forward and back.

That happened, often with bitter and divisive consequences, in the last decade of the last century when the people in Wales (some becoming the people of Wales, some already Welsh) teetered on the brink of so many novel features of life. The invention of moving pictures, of the combustion engine that would shrink the world as the steam train had shrunk nations, of air travel and cheap newspapers, of seaside holiday destinations and front-room pianos, of new kinds of democratic politics and demands for the rights of others, especially of women, to be accorded, of available education for working-class children, and indeed of adults, and circulating libraries and gas or electric light by which to read the books that opened the world up; that generation, Bevan's generation in effect, were young in their young country. History had released them; because they knew where they had come from they had a self-directed future to find. They withered, albeit valiantly, as the future they walked into, of wars and poverty, checked their realizable dreams and restricted their possible actions.

A century later, if we choose to know where we have come from, we can also choose a new, common route to put flesh on dreams again. Communication, the sight on a daily basis of a totemic civic life, does not now need to be confined to the physical. The global is now the local. We teeter, again, on the edge of yawning possibilities for human societies to enhance their material and their soulful welfare. Minor constitutional issues, even deeper symbolic ones concerning nations and states, are not as central to our destiny as is the fundamental focus on citizenship, on education, on participation and on being informed in order to decide. Nor does an involved society have to be the bland outcome of a worthy lesson in civics. We should encourage conflict, of mind and of imagination, within the restraints of a society's acknowledged consensus of behaviour, customs and laws.

For the new Welsh now emerging, as they surely and clearly are, a common inclusiveness in their history will not smother them; it will afford them the right and the ability to debate the change of direction. Effective political life is instituted by people; political institutions do not, ever, form a people. History alone does that. Whatever institutions, political and otherwise, which we now have in Wales all require the imaginative power of that people to be committed if the elected and the appointed who service them are to be representative for a purpose beyond power. 'I do not need to remember a Dream. The reality is there. The fine, live people, the spirit of Wales itself,' wrote Dylan Thomas.

This book is the story of that people's life through this millennium and is so offered to all the lives in Wales that are yet to come, and become one with us.

FURTHER READING

General histories

John Davies, *A History of Wales* (London, Allen Lane, 1993)

Philip Jenkins, *Modern Wales 1536-1990* (London, Longman, 1992)

Gareth Elwyn Jones, *Modern Wales* (Cambridge, Cambridge University Press, 2nd. edn., 1994)

Dai Smith, *Wales: A Question for History* (Bridgend, Seren Books, 1999)

Prys Morgan and David Thomas, *Wales: the Shaping of a Nation* (Newton Abbot, David and Charles, 1984)

David Walker, *Medieval Wales* (Cambridge, Cambridge University Press, 1990)

Gwyn A. Williams, *When was Wales?* (Harmondsworth, Penguin, 1985)

Histories and sources for specific periods

1000-1415

A. D. Carr, *Medieval Anglesey* (Llangefni, Anglesey Antiquarian Society, 1982)

R. R. Davies, *Conquest, Coexistence, and Change: Wales 1063–1415* (Oxford, Oxford University Press, 1987); reprinted in paperback under the title, *The Age of Conquest* (Oxford, Oxford University Press 1991)

R. R. Davies, *The Revolt of Owain Glyn Dŵr* (Oxford, Oxford University Press, 1995).

Wendy Davies, *Wales in the Early Middle Ages* (Leicester, Leicester University Press, 1982)

Nancy Edwards (ed.), *Landscape and Settlement in Medieval Wales,* (Oxford, Oxbow Books, 1997)

Gerald of Wales, *The Journey through Wales and the Description of Wales*, translated by Lewis Thorpe (Harmondsworth, Penguin Books, 1978)

Ralph A. Griffiths (ed.), *The Boroughs of Mediaeval Wales* (Cardiff, University of Wales Press 1978)

Dafydd Jenkins and Morfydd E. Owen (eds.), *The Welsh Law of Women* (Cardiff, University of Wales Press, 1980)

Keith Williams-Jones (ed.), *The Merioneth Lay Subsidy Roll 1292-3* (Cardiff, University of Wales Press, 1976)

Glanmor Williams, *The Welsh Church from Conquest to Reformation* (2nd edition, Cardiff, University of Wales Press, 1976)

1415-1642

Eamon Duffy, *The stripping of the altars* (Yale, Yale University Press, 1995)

Trevor Herbert and Gareth Elwyn Jones (eds.) *Tudor Wales* (Cardiff, University of Wales Press, 1988)

A.O.H. Jarman and Gwilym Rees Hughes (revised Dafydd Johnson), *A Guide to Welsh Literature*, vols II and III. (Cardiff, University of Wales Press, 1997)

J. Gwynfor Jones, *Wales and the Tudor state* (Cardiff, University of Wales Press, 1989)

J. Gwynfor Jones (ed), *Class, community and culture in Tudor Wales* (Cardiff, University of Wales Press, 1989)

J. Gwynfor Jones, *Concepts of order and gentility in Wales, 1540-1640* (Llandysul, Gomer Press, 1992)

J. Gwynfor Jones, *Early modern Wales c.1535-1640* (London, Macmillan, 1994)

D. Huw Owen (ed), *Settlement and society in Wales* (Cardiff, University of Wales Press, 1989)

Glanmor Williams, *Renewal and Reformation in Wales c.1415-1642* (Oxford, Oxford University Press, 1987)

Glanmor Williams, *Wales and the Reformation* (Cardiff, University of Wales Press, 1997)

Peter Smith, *Houses of the Welsh Countryside* (London, HMSO, 1975)

Frances A. Yates, *The Occult Philosophy in the Elizabethan Age* (London, Routledge and Kegan Paul, 1979)

1642-1780

A.H. Dodd, *Studies in Stuart Wales* (Cardiff, University of Wales Press, 2nd. edn., 1971)

Trevor Herbert and Gareth Elwyn Jones (eds.), *The remaking of Wales in the eighteenth century* (Cardiff, University of Wales Press,1988)

David W. Howell, *Patriarchs and Parasites* (Cardiff, University of Wales Press,1986)

Geraint H. Jenkins, *The Foundations of Modern Wales: Wales 1642-1780* (Oxford, Oxford University Press, 1987)

Geraint H. Jenkins, *Literature, Religion and Society in Wales 1660-1730* (Cardiff, University of Wales Press, 1978)

Philip Jenkins, *The Making of a Ruling Class. The Glamorgan Gentry 1640-1790* (Cambridge, Cambridge University Press, 1983)

Donald Moore (ed.), *Wales in the Eighteenth Century* (Swansea, Christopher Davies, 1976)

Prys Morgan, *The Eighteenth Century Renaissance* (Swansea, Christopher Davies, 1981)

William Rees, *Industry before the Industrial Revolution* (2 vols. Cardiff, University of Wales Press, 1968),

Peter D.G.Thomas, *Politics in Eighteenth Century Wales* (Cardiff, University of Wales Press, 1998)

W.S.K. Thomas, *Georgian and Victorian Brecon: Portrait of a Welsh County Town* (Llandysul, Gomer Press, 1993)

1780-1870

Chris Evans, *Labyrinth of Flames: Work and Social Conflict in Early Merthyr* (Cardiff, University of Wales Press, 1993)

Neil Evans, 'Two Paths to Economic Development: Wales and the North East of England' in Pat Hudson (ed.), *Regions and Industries: A Perspective on the Industrial Revolution in Britain* (Cambridge, Cambridge University Press, 1989)

Neil Evans, 'Regional Dynamics: North Wales, 1750-1914' in Edward Royle (ed.), *Issues of Regional Identity: Essays in Honour of John Marshall* (Manchester, Manchester University Press, 1998)

Melvin Humphreys, *The Crisis of Community: Montgomeryshire, 1680-1815* (Cardiff, University of Wales Press, 1996)

Angela John (ed.), *Our Mothers' Land: Chapters in Welsh Women's History, 1800-1939* (Cardiff, University of Wales Press, 1991)

David Jones, *Before Rebecca: Popular Protest in Wales, 1790-1835* (London, Allen Lane, 1973)

David Jones, *The Last Rising: The Newport Insurrection of 1839* (Oxford, Oxford University Press, 1985)

David Jones, *Rebecca's Children: A Study of Rural Society, Crime and Protest* (Oxford, Oxford University Press, 1989)

Ieuan Gwynedd Jones, *Explorations and Explanations: Essays in the Social History of Victorian Wales*, (Llandysul, Gomer Press, 1981)

Ieuan Gwynedd Jones, *Communities: Essays in the Social History of Victorian Wales* (Llandysul, Gomer Press, 1987)

Ieuan Gwynedd Jones, *Mid-Victorian Wales: The Observers and the Observed* (Cardiff, University of Wales Press, 1992)

David Williams, *The Rebecca Riots: A Study in Agrarian Discontent*, (Cardiff, University of Wales Press, 1955)

Gwyn A. Williams, *The Merthyr Rising* (London, Croom Helm, 1978)

1870-1914

Russell Davies, *Secret Sins: Sex, Violence and Society in Carmarthenshire 1870 – 1920* (Cardiff, University of Wales Press, 1996)

Trevor Herbert and Gareth Elwyn Jones (eds.), *Wales 1880-1914* (Cardiff, University of Wales Press, 1988)

David W. Howell, *Land and People in Nineteenth-century Wales* (London, Routledge, 1978)

Geraint H. Jenkins (ed.), *Language and Community in the Nineteenth Century* (Cardiff, University of Wales Press, 1998)

Angela John (ed.), *Our Mother's Land: Chapters in Welsh Women's History 1830-1939* (Cardiff University of Wales Press, 1991)

Merfyn Jones, *The North Wales Quarrymen 1874 – 1922* (Cardiff, University of Wales Press, 1982)

Michael Lieven, *Senghennydd: the Universal Pit Village 1890-1930* (Llandysul, Gomer Press, 1994)

Kenneth O. Morgan, *Rebirth of a Nation: Wales 1880-1980* (Oxford, Oxford University Press, 1981)

Dai Smith, *Aneurin Bevan and the World of South Wales* (Cardiff, University of Wales Press, 1993)

David Smith and Gareth Williams, *Fields of Praise: The Official History of the Welsh Rugby Union* (Cardiff, University of Wales Press, 1980)

Chris Williams, *Democratic Rhondda: Politics and society 1885 – 1951* (Cardiff, University of Wales Press, 1996)

John Williams, *Was Wales Industrialized?* (Llandysul, Gomer Press, 1995)

1914-1945

Angus Calder, *The People's War. Britain 1939-1945* (London, Pimlico, 1992 edn.)

Tony Curtis (ed.), *Wales: The Imagined Nation. Essays in Cultural and National Identity* (Bridgend, Poetry Wales Press, 1986)

John Davies, *Broadcasting and the BBC in Wales* (Cardiff, University of Wales Press, 1994)

Hywel Francis and Dai Smith, *The Fed. A History of the South Wales Miners* (London, Lawrence and Wishart, 1980. New centenary edition, Cardiff, University of Wales Press, 1998)

Angela Gaffney, *Aftermath: Remembering the Great War in Wales* (Cardiff, University of Wales Press, 1998)

Trevor Herbert and Gareth Elwyn Jones (eds.), *Wales Between the Wars* (Cardiff, University of Wales Press 1988)

Kenneth O. Morgan, *Rebirth of a Nation: Wales 1880-1980* (Oxford, Oxford University Press, 1981)

Kenneth O. Morgan, *Modern Wales: Politics, Places and People* (Cardiff, University of Wales Press, 1995)

G. D. Roberts, *Witness These Letters: Letters from the Western Front, 1915-18* (Denbigh, Gee, 1983)

Margery Spring-Rice, *Working-Class Wives* (London, Virago, 1981 edn.)

Leigh Verrill-Rhys and Deirdre Beddoe (eds.), *Parachutes and Petticoats. Welsh Women Writing on the Second World War* (Dinas Powys, Honno, 1992)

Carol White and Siân Rhiannon Williams (eds.), *Struggle or Starve. Women's Lives in the South Wales Valleys between the Two World Wars* (Dinas Powys, Honno, 1998)

J M Winter, *The Great War and the British People* (London, Macmillan, 1987)

1945-1985

Jane Aaron, Teresa Rees, Sandra Betts, and Moira Vincentelli (eds), *Our Sisters' Land: The Changing Identities of Women in Wales* (Cardiff, University of Wales Press, 1994)

Martin Adeney and John Lloyd, *The Miners' Strike 1984-5. Loss Without Limit* (London, Routledge and Kegan Paul, 1986)

David Foulkes, J. Barry Jones and R. A. Wilford (eds.), *The Welsh Veto: The Wales Act 1978 and the Referendum* (Cardiff, University of Wales Press, 1983)

K. D. George and Lynn Mainwaring (eds.), *The Welsh Economy* (Cardiff, University of Wales Press, 1988)

Trevor Herbert and Gareth Elwyn Jones (eds), *Post-War Wales* (Cardiff, University of Wales Press, 1995)

Christopher Meredith, *Shifts* (Bridgend, Poetry Wales Press, 1997)

Alun Richards, *Selected Stories* (Bridgend, Poetry Wales Press, 1995)

Huw Richards, Peter Stead and Gareth Williams (eds.), *The Character of Welsh Rugby* (Cardiff, University of Wales Press, 1998)

Dennis Thomas and Dot Jones, *Welsh Economy and Society Post-1945: A Database of Statistical and Documentary Material* (Cardiff, University of Wales Press, 1996)

Ned Thomas, *The Welsh Extremist* (Talybont, Y Lolfa, 1991)

Raymond Williams, *The Fight for Manod* (London, Hogarth, 1988)

THE CONTRIBUTORS

NEIL EVANS is Tutor in History and Co-ordinator of the Centre for Welsh Studies at Coleg Harlech, and honorary Lecturer in the School of History and Welsh History, University of Wales, Bangor.

MATTHEW GRIFFITHS is an associate Lecturer with the Open University in Wales and Director of the Civic Trust in Wales.

PHILIP JENKINS is Distinguished Professor of History and Religious Studies at the Pennsylvania State University in University Park, Pennsylvania.

BILL JONES is Lecturer in the School of History and Archaeology, University of Wales, Cardiff.

GARETH ELWYN JONES is Research Professor of Education, University of Wales, Swansea.

HUW PRYCE is Senior Lecturer in the School of History and Welsh History, University of Wales, Bangor.

DAI SMITH is Head of Broadcast (English Language) at BBC Wales.

CHRIS WILLIAMS is Lecturer in the School of History and Archaeology, University of Wales, Cardiff.

MARI A. WILLIAMS is Research Fellow at the University of Wales Centre for Advanced Welsh and Celtic Studies, Aberystwyth.

INDEX